Opportunity Knocked

How an Idaho farm boy
became a successful businessman and advocate of
West Yellowstone, Montana

Clyde Seely

 FriesenPress

Suite 300 - 990 Fort St
Victoria, BC, V8V 3K2
Canada

www.friesenpress.com

Copyright © 2016 by Clyde G. Seely
First Edition — 2016

ISBN
978-1-4602-8214-4 (Hardcover)
978-1-4602-8215-1 (Paperback)
978-1-4602-8216-8 (eBook)

1. BIOGRAPHY & AUTOBIOGRAPHY

Distributed to the trade by The Ingram Book Company

Table of Contents

Note to Reader

When I was 19 years old, I thought I had my life all planned out—I would serve my mission, return home and marry, get my teaching degree and settle down to a happy life as a teacher in the winter and a farmer in the summer near St. Anthony, Idaho.

But that's not how it turned out.

Instead, I ended up developing businesses in West Yellowstone, Montana. Over the past five decades, I have witnessed, and even played an important role, in transforming this small summer town into a major winter vacation area using snowmobiles and snowcoaches.

The purpose for writing this autobiography is twofold: first, to record for my family, posterity, and friends the events of my early farm and family life that helped to shape my destiny; and second, to tell of my experiences and involvement in West Yellowstone that have become historically significant. Although at the time some of these events seemed insignificant, now looking back they appear quite pivotal.

I recount these events as they were seen through my eyes. Others will be able to relate other versions of these experiences and help complete the picture. Documents, memorabilia, and personal notes were dug out of their hiding places in order to be included in this book. It's a personal story written in first person, but I would never wish to suggest that I am solely responsible for whatever successes I have enjoyed. I gladly acknowledge that I stand on the shoulders of giants, or many others who walked before and with me. I also stand with a partner, teammate and companion who never hesitated to help in every way and get her hands dirty.

Although this book can be read like a novel, from start to finish, I have tried to identify sections so you can also turn to chapters that interest you, if preferred. It is written in various sections, or pebbles, that deal with the following:

1. The events and people who have influenced me in my childhood, youth, and young married life

2. My recollections and involvement in the growth of the Yellowstone area

It is peppered with motivational and inspirational quotes that have had a great influence on my life. I have enjoyed dredging up the many memories necessary to fill in the sections of this book. I hope you enjoy reading it.

Introduction

*I would much rather have men ask why I
have no statue than why I have one.*

~Marcus Porcius Cato

When I was a young farm boy, I used to throw pebbles out into
the middle of our pond and watch them hit the smooth water. From
the energy and splash of the pebbles, ripples extended outward in a
circular pattern until they finally faded away. A larger rock would
cause the ripples to reach farther, sometimes covering the whole
surface of the water. Many times over the next sixty-plus years, I
have thought about those innocent and carefree rock-throwing days
of my childhood.

The pebble in the pond and its ripple effect has become an
important metaphor for me. My life has been shaped by others who
have dropped pebbles into my little pool. Of course, every metaphor has its limits—while the pond on the farm quickly returned
to its original state as I went off to attend to my chores, the pebbles
cast in my life's pond have forever left a change. First my life's
character was shaped by others' pebbles dropped into my little pool.
As I grew older, I found it was my turn to drop pebbles in other
people's pools, and thus leave an impact on their lives too. As I
have tried to share my blessings, I think that most of the "pebbles"
I've dropped have caused positive ripples for good.

As I began reflecting on my life's experiences, I started to record the figurative pebbles thrown along with their ripple effects in my personal journal. Soon, however, these entries began to morph into something more. Many of my personal experiences over the last fifty-plus years are tied to the growth and development of West Yellowstone, Montana. My story in many ways is also a community story.

Because of this, I found that I wished to go beyond a recounting of personal and family incidents and include observations and insights of West Yellowstone that have, over the decades, become historically significant. Such events include both joyful and painful experiences that convey the values and passions of my life.

While writing this book, I began to appreciate even more those who have been a good influence in my life. As I pondered these experiences, I could also see that I too have made a difference. As we brush shoulders with those around us, these encounters continually help to mold and change our lives. I would be pleased if those who read this memoir would become more cognizant of the effect their actions, knowingly or unknowingly, have on others' lives. Perhaps readers may even be inspired to ask themselves how they are doing along their own lives' journeys.

While much of this book will focus on the development of West Yellowstone and the opportunities found there, it begins with my childhood on the farm where the first ripples in the pool of my life began. The values I learned as I was growing up have been a driving force in my life. The memories are vivid, and yet it amazes me to realize that they occurred nearly seven decades ago. The little farm community of Twin Groves, Idaho, and its way of life have changed dramatically since that time. But never to be forgotten are the roots that were established there.

Part One: My Early Life

Pebble 1: First Recollections of West Yellowstone

I am only one, but I am one. I cannot do everything, but I can do something. And I will not let what I cannot do interfere with what I can do.

~Edward Everett Hale

Every summer morning around 5:30 from my childhood farmhouse, I heard a short whistle followed by a steady long whistle. Over a mile away, the Yellowstone Special was loudly announcing its presence while zipping past a railroad crossing on its way 70 miles north to West Yellowstone, Montana. Several hundred passengers were always onboard, eager to visit Yellowstone National Park.

Then close to 8:00 every evening, that same whistle marked the return of the train loaded with hundreds of other people who had just spent a few days or a week in Yellowstone.

It was such a consistent passenger train, and we could almost set our clocks by it.

And with each whistle, I could envision the excitement these travelers felt coming from all over the country to experience for the first time the unbelievable sights, sounds and smells of Yellowstone.

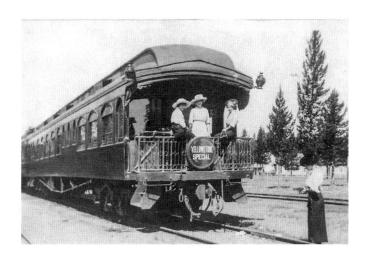

Yellowstone Special passenger car in West Yellowstone

For us, every spring after the crops were planted, Dad and Mother would load us kids and sometimes my Aunt Eva and Cousin Connie into our little pickup truck to go see Aunt Mary Ann. She lived at Burlington, a little farming community across the Park, about an hour east of Cody, Wyoming. It was a long trip with the three adults sitting in the one seat bench, with maybe one of us little ones on a lap. For the rest of us, Dad built a cover out of canvas so four or five of us could ride in the back. I suppose this setup was a forerunner to the first pickup campers.

But the trip was always worth it. Along the way, our travels were often interrupted by bears and other animals. Then add the geysers, canyons, and waterfalls, and this very special place easily etched itself in my heart. From very early on, I fell in love with Yellowstone, and the whistle of the Yellowstone Special always beckoned me to return.

I first became aware of the Three Bear Lodge and its owners Mike and Frances Wilson when my sisters worked there. Since our little family farm could not produce enough revenue to make ends meet, my sisters, Norma and Donna, spent their summers working in West Yellowstone. They saved their money and sent it home to be used by our family for other expenses. Getting by financially on the farm was a family affair, and when it came time for college or Church missions, the sale of potatoes, grain, and wool provided the money for such things.

Donna first worked at Three Bear as a maid when she was 15 years old, and in Frances Wilson's eyes she could do no wrong. The next summer, Norma, who was two years older, joined Donna.

The farm work ethic was impressive to Frances, and my sisters quickly became trusted employees.

One summer when I was about fourteen, Norma and Donna came driving up to the little farmhouse in a brand new light green Lincoln convertible with a white top. We had never seen such a beautiful car.

Frances had said to the girls, "Why don't you just take the car and go home for the night?"

The next morning the turkeys had roosted on the car and of course, they deposited their markings on the white convertible top.

In order to take the car back unsoiled, Norma and Donna scrubbed and cleaned the white top meticulously. And Frances never knew her new car had been used as a turkey roost.

Another summer my brother Sylvan worked at Three Bear Lodge as a night watchman and all-around helper. They asked him to come back the next summer, but during the course of the winter, Sylvan got engaged. He wanted to be with his fiancée, Gail, and he used the time to get ready for their wedding in the fall. This is when I first got involved with Three Bear.

Sylvan needed the money he could earn in West Yellowstone but also needed to stay home to prepare for his wedding. I worked on the family farm with no thought of getting paid anyway, so, like my sisters had done, I volunteered to go work in Sylvan's place at the Three Bear Lodge and send him the money I made. Besides, I thought it might be sort of fun to get away for the summer. I went to

West Yellowstone and told Mike and Frances that I was substituting for Sylvan for the summer.

Small as she was, Frances was a real taskmaster. She could verbally dress down anybody that crossed her path or did not do her bidding. Everyone was afraid of her, but for some reason our family got on her good side and escaped most of her wrath.

In fact, one day during my first year of work, I was helping Frances work some soil and plant a lawn (where the current lawn still grows). She offhandedly said, "One day, Clyde, when you own this place," and went on with something else. I was a farm boy from Twin Groves, Idaho, who knew nothing about the business world.

At first those words just bounced off, and I couldn't believe she had really meant them, but I knew I had heard her say them to me. Then I thought, oh well, that was just idle chatter. However, over the course of the next few years those words stuck in my mind.

Though I was not aware of it at the time, these people and Three Bear Lodge (sometimes referred to as just Three Bear) dropped a pebble in my pool that affected me and my family for the rest of our lives. Much of what I have been able to accomplish has been leveraged from the base that was provided for us by Three Bear Lodge. It has been the anchor and focal point of our family's daily activity in West Yellowstone.

Three Bear Lodge provided an opportunity to teach our kids the value of a good work ethic. They may not have had to lamb out the sheep (See Pebble 5), dig potatoes, or do the nightly farm chores, but they learned to sweep under the doormats, bus tables, gas snowmobiles, and wait tables in the restaurant. The lodge gave us a built-in way of providing work for our kids, without worrying about child labor laws. Experiencing this work ethic has blessed our children's lives.

We live in a great land of opportunity. Throughout my life, I have marveled at how a simple farm boy ended up living the life I have lived. Perhaps it's because of the influences of others, which like pebbles in a pond, have left ripples deep inside of me. Such influential examples have stirred me to try harder in my own life to succeed.

In fact, by looking at the life of my ancestors I see the genetic makeup, signs, and examples of great homesteaders, pioneers, and trailblazers.

My story would not be complete without a reference to some big decisions made by my Seely ancestors several hundred years ago. Their lives and stories have inspired me in countless ways, especially as I see that I wouldn't be who I am without the important decisions made by my ancestors generations earlier. Two key ancestors who changed the course of my life are Robert Seely and Justus Azel Seely.

Robert Seely

On July 4, 1602, Robert Seely, one of my progenitors, was christened in the Church of England at Huntingdonshire, England. He was the ancestor who made the courageous decision to cross the Atlantic Ocean to the New World, a land of opportunity.

Robert and his wife Mary were members of the Winthrop Society—Puritans who were seekers of religious freedom with the desire to purify the Church of England from within. This group differed from the more radical Mayflower Pilgrims who set sail from England in September of 1620. Those on the Mayflower were a Separatist group and wanted to separate from the Anglican Church. But the Winthrop group also decided to immigrate to the New World to build their city on a hill free from the corrupting influences of the Church of England.

The Winthrop Fleet consisted of eleven ships—nine for the 700 emigrants and two for cows and horses. The sixty-eight-day voyage took its toll. Two hundred of the seven hundred emigrants (and seventy cows) didn't make it. But Robert, Mary, and their two sons survived the crossing and landed in Salem, Massachusetts on June 10, 1630.

Our Seely history relates that Robert was a poor apprentice cordwainer (a worker in leather) in England and owned no property. When he came to America, he became a freeman, landowner, and founder of a city. He became a soldier, a lieutenant, and a then captain. He became a trusted and prominent citizen and marshal of the colony of New Haven, Connecticut.

Robert progressed from an apprentice leather worker in England to a prominent landowner and trusted gentleman in the colony in the New World. All of this came from his adventurous spirit and his willingness to work hard for himself and the community he helped to build.

Justus Azel Seely

The next ancestor who made a big decision affecting my life was Justus Azel Seely, my great-great-grandfather. He was born in Litchfield Connecticut, November 17, 1779. When he was about 3 years old, his family moved to New Brunswick. While living in Canada, on February 15, 1838, he and his wife Mehittibil joined the fledgling Church of Jesus Church of Latter-day Saints, the Mormons. This decision has had profound ripple effects on his posterity.

Justus and Mehittibil later moved their family to Nauvoo, Illinois, where they had a home and acreage. However, at this time, persecution faced by the Church was increasing. Although the Nauvoo Temple was not quite completed, on February 3, 1846, Brigham Young announced that everyone should begin to load up their wagons and evacuate the city. Records indicate that Justus Azel Seely and his wife Mehittabil had their names recorded in the temple on February 3, 1846. On that same day, because of threatening mobs, the first wagons ferried across the Mississippi River, and the greatest exodus in the history of the United States of America, eventually involving over 70,000 Mormon pioneers, began.

The Seelys arrived in the Salt Lake Valley on September 29, 1847, one of the first pioneer parties to make the arduous trek. They settled in Mount Pleasant in Sanpete County and became well known for their sheep and cattle. In 1911, my grandfather Stuart Randolph Seely moved to Chester, Idaho. Looking for new opportunities, my grandfather on my mother's side, Soren J. Hansen, moved his family to Twin Groves, Idaho, where they homesteaded the farm that I would eventually grow up on. My dad, Ferry Randolph Seely, and my mother, Oneta Hansen, knew each other when they were children in Mount Pleasant, Utah, but it was not until they were in their thirties and had moved to Idaho that they married.

Pebble 2: My Parents

*Parents can tell but never teach, unless
they practice what they preach.*

~Arnold H. Glasow

The people who unquestionably had the biggest influence on my early life were my parents, so it would be appropriate to introduce them at the beginning of my story. I was blessed with a mother and dad who taught by example about love and loyalty and who showed me the rewards of hard work, ingenuity, and determination.

Ferry Randolph Seely

My dad, Ferry Randolph Seely, was born February 14, 1898, to Stuart Randolph Seely and Millie Nielsen, and was the oldest of nine children. Dad was born in Mount Pleasant, Utah. In 1911 when Dad was 13 years old, his family moved to homestead in Chester, Idaho. Being the oldest child, Dad worked side by side with his father to clear the land and build a house. The Seelys had been known in Utah for their well-bred sheep and cattle herds. Raising sheep seemed to be in their blood, so it wasn't long before they carried that reputation for top-grade sheep to Idaho.

My mother's family, the Hansens, had been neighbors of the Seelys in Mt. Pleasant, and in 1898 purchased a small farm in Twin

Groves, 3 miles east of St. Anthony, Idaho. In connection with this they homesteaded eighty acres one mile away.

The friendship between Ferry and Oneta continued when the Seelys homesteaded in Chester a neighboring farming community. In 1930, when both were age 32, the long friendship was capped by marriage. In 1933, during the Great Depression, Dad and Mother were given the Hansen homestead and moved their little family there. There was no house on it, so Grandpa Seely gave them a granary, which they moved to the farm, and it became their first home, the home that I grew up in. At first the inside was covered with cardboard, and Dad later remodeled and added to the house.

Dad was a hard worker, working from 5 a.m. until the chores were done around 7 p.m. Sundays were set aside for the necessities, such as milking cows, (the hardest thing about milking cows is that they don't stay milked), changing the irrigation water, feeding the livestock, and attending church. I spent a lot of time in the field with Dad and as a kid, I always had daily chores that had to be done. Farm life was a seven-day-a-week affair, from sunrise until sunset. Even though I knew it was okay with Dad if we just played when we were little, I do remember when I was about 6 or 7 years old, playing in the dirt with a caterpillar tractor that he had made for me. I heard him coming home on the tractor and I hurried and put away my toy tractor so Dad would not see me just playing around.

In the evenings, Dad sat next to the radio, which sat on Mother's sewing machine, and listened to his favorite programs, such as *The Shadow* or *The Lone Ranger*. Sometimes he took the family to a "show," a movie in town. Mother agreed to come too, even though she couldn't hear much.

I never heard Dad say, "I love you," but there was no doubt in our minds that he did. He expressed it in many ways, as he worked hard to provide for our family. We worked together side by side, day after day, doing what farmers do. He was always kind and thoughtful, and what he had, we knew was ours when we needed it.

Dad's life was remarkable and what made it even more amazing was that throughout his life, he suffered from epilepsy. His frequent spells were never used as an excuse for him to slacken his efforts. He would just pick himself up afterwards and go on with his day. But, of course, the family had to be vigilant to try to prevent injuries as much as possible. If he had a seizure, he would lose consciousness. If he were standing, we helped break his fall and let him down in a prone position until his body and facial features returned to normal. Sometimes the spells lasted a couple of minutes before he regained consciousness. After a severe spell, his body would be stiff and sore for several days. He had a difficult time understanding that he could not get up and continue moving immediately after coming out of a seizure. He insisted that he was okay, but we had to restrain him from doing anything until we were sure that he was completely back to normal. These spells would happen a couple of times a month on average, but there was no way of predicting when he would have the next one.

Whenever Dad drove a vehicle, someone would always sit next to him. I don't know why he was allowed to have a driver's license, but in those days, it was a necessity. If he began to have a spell while driving, Mother, my siblings, or I would turn the key off, take it from the ignition, and hold onto the steering wheel until the pickup stopped. As soon as the main spell was over, Dad would reach for the key so he could start the motor again. However, we would keep the key until it was obvious that his "coming to" phase was past and he was fully recovered. Later, when my siblings and I were old enough, we always drove. One time, Dad and Mother were taking a load of sheep to a sale in Rexburg when Dad had a spell. The truck ran off the road and drove through a fence before Mother could get it stopped. Another time, while in St. Anthony, Dad went over a four-foot embankment. Mother broke a couple of ribs and was pretty bruised up from the event.

Each spring, after the crops were planted and it began to rain, Dad and Mother would put a canvas over the back of the pickup, load us kids into the back, and we would go see Aunt Mary Ann in Greybull, Wyoming. We always held our breath while Dad drove over Sylvan Pass, the Buffalo Bill Dam, and the canyon near Cody, Wyoming. It was a very narrow, winding, downhill road, and it would have been difficult for Mother to turn the key off and stop the pickup if Dad had a spell. I remember when my sister Norma was big enough to drive through these dangerous areas. Though she was barely old enough to drive, I was relieved that she took the wheel.

There were many close calls in Dad's life. Many of his spells came at inconvenient times, some when he was alone. He might be driving horses or tractors, milking cows, or crossing a footbridge over the canal when a spell occurred. Sometimes, he came back bruised from falling while milking the cows and being stepped on or wet from falling off the flume into the canal. Other times, he had spells at church. For a time, Dad was in the Sunday School presidency, which required him to sit on the stand. We were always a little nervous while he was up in front of the congregation. It was a little awkward for him to hold church positions that required him to be up in front of the people; however, when sitting on the stand, he was always so proud when one of us kids would give a little talk.

Dad's word was his bond. Because of this, if Dad borrowed money in the spring, the banker never wondered if he would get paid off in the fall. I don't remember Dad having to fill out or submit financial statements. All I knew was he just signed a piece of paper and paid the loan back with the sale of the wool from the sheep or the crops. Dad set an example for us by always paying off his debts and bank loans, just as he said he would. He believed that, "One thing you can give and still keep is your word."

Dad kept a three-compartment coin purse on the middle shelf of a cupboard—one compartment held coins, and the other held bills. There was never much money in it, but if we needed some, we knew where it was located. We didn't abuse Dad's trust, for he knew how much was in that purse, and we never went to the purse unless we really needed to. Sometimes, we asked Dad or Mother for money and they might tell us to take what we needed. When we were little, it may have been a quarter for school lunch or for a movie. But when we were older, and our school or college needs exceeded what was in that purse, then the "crop" money or the banker was brought in.

I have always tried to follow Dad's example. In later years after I was married, the credit card "plastic" became a frequently used form of borrowing. My wife and I have used them for years to avoid the necessity of carrying extra cash and to have a monthly record of our purchases. However, the ease of using credit cards can encourage people to live beyond their means. It is very easy to get into debt, but interest never sleeps. The exorbitantly high interest rates may cause a person to pay double for a purchase. Sometimes a person can never get out from under the debt incurred. However, our strict rule has always been to avoid putting more on the card than can be paid off in the same month. Because we have always been able to follow this rule, we have been able to avoid being buried in personal debt.

In her journal, Mother wrote about my older brother, Dean, and Dad.

Dean was not 4 years old when he would run to meet his dad. One time he said, "I walked in your tracks all the way, Daddy."

Then she quoted the following poem entitled "A Little Fellow Follows Me" by Reverend Claude Wisdom White, Sr.

A careful man I want to be,
A little fellow follows me.
I do not dare to go astray,
For fear he'll go the self-same way.

I cannot once escape his eyes;
What'er he sees me do, he tries;

Like me he says he's going to be,
The little chap who follows me.

I must remember as I go
Through summer's heat and winter's snow;
I am building for the years to be,
That little chap who follows me.

I have tried to follow in Dad's footsteps as well.

***

My dad died on December 8, 1976, when he was 80 years old, in the Madison County Hospital in Rexburg, Idaho. Although somewhat unusual for a traditional funeral, I was asked to give a few graveside remarks following his funeral.

Those at the graveside were all gathered around Dad's casket; his younger brothers and sisters, nieces and nephews, children and grandchildren, and close friends were all there. I was asked to thank everyone for being there that day. Then in my impromptu remarks, I expressed the family's appreciation, and from there felt impressed to say more.

I remember saying that it was not difficult for me to imagine this same little group of people, those who had gathered here to honor Dad and say their goodbyes, also in a similar setting 80 years ago. We were yet unborn and in a spiritual state then, but we said goodbye to this same man, who we also loved there. He left our presence to lead the way to this earth life. Eighty years later, we were again gathered to say goodbye. It was a sad time, but also, as we look at the bigger plan, it will only be but a short time before he welcomes each of us back home, one by one, and we will all rejoice once again.

Dad was one of those who dropped a large pebble in my pool. The ripples from that impact have influenced my life and will consequently influence the lives of my kids and grandkids.

My dad lived a good life. He was not a flamboyant sort of a guy, but was quiet and unassuming with a dry, sort of off-the-wall sense of humor. He believed in being honest and doing whatever he said he would, working tirelessly, and always finishing what was needed. He rarely talked about his feelings, but rather expressed them with his actions.

Near the end of Dad's life, when we had just finished our new home, I took him down to show him the family room. There was the mantle made from the farm footbridge and on it some memorabilia from the old farm. The walls of the room had wainscoting made from barn wood that I had salvaged from the old granary he had built many years before. Dad couldn't get the words to come out, but tears filled his eyes and his lower lip quivered a telltale sign that he was feeling what he could not say.

Oneta Hansen Seely

My mother, Mary Oneta Hansen, was born June 26, 1896, in Mount Pleasant, Utah. In 1898, her parents purchased a little farm and moved all their belongings by horse and wagon to where she would grow up, 3 miles east of St. Anthony, Idaho, in an area known as Twin Groves. In conjunction with the farm they purchased, they homesteaded eighty acres about a mile away. In 1898, my Grandpa Hansen built a little three-roomed log house on this property. It was there that Mother's sister, Eva, was born in 1899. They lived in this little house until Mother was about 13 years old.

Little house built on the homestead; photo taken when
it was 100 years old, before demolition

Mother tells of her carefree childhood days while living there in her book of remembrance:

> Eva and I would have a lot of fun when Mother would clean house. Mother would take out the carpet, shake it good, take the straw out from under the carpet and put in new straw. Then we would empty all the old straw out of the straw ticks and put new straw in. The straw ticks would be so full and high Mother would have to lift Eva and myself up into the bed.

This little house was used as a granary and coal storage during the time I was growing up. By then it had a wooden floor. It was a focal point of our outbuildings and was also used for tool storage and other uses.

Of the homesteading, Mother writes:

> The first year in Idaho was hard, clearing away the sagebrush and planting their first crop of grain,

which froze in the early fall or late summer. Father hauled what was left to Market Lake, which is near Roberts, Idaho in a wagon. He got ten cents a bushel. I had long, curly hair that would get tangled in the sagebrush, so Mother braided it. Dad was a good manager; slow at work, he never got excited, but he was a very good farmer and he always did things right. Father was always referred to as having good judgment. Mother was very industrious and a good manager, and always looked ahead.

My grandparents were another good example for me to follow. They didn't know that the pebbles they were dropping in their children's pools were also going to be dropped in their future grandchildren's pool too. When they got older, they gave the home-steaded farm to my parents. The little cabin my grandparents built had been vacant for 24 years and was used as granary and storage building. Mother writes:

April, 1933 we moved to the old homestead. Dad couldn't farm anymore. There was no house on it but Grandpa gave us a granary he had on his farm at Canyon Creek. Grandpa Seely and Ferry moved it down and set it on the homesteaded farm. It was only one room. We lined it with paste board boxes. We carried water in from the ditch and had a coal oil lamp. How happy we were. A house to call our own.

Then as the family grew, Dad expanded the house from time to time. I will always remember the farm and that house with fondness as this is where I grew up; it's where my roots were planted.

Like Dad, Mother had to deal with a severe physical challenge from the time she was a small child. From her book of remembrance we read,

When I was 5 years old I got diphtheria and we were quarantined in. No one could come closer than the gate. I was so sick and the Doctor said, "I don't think she will get well. If anyone wants to see her they can look through the window." The Doctor said to put warm salt bags on my ears. But the warm salt packs had dried up my ear drums and I couldn't hear. When I saw my little friends I wanted to hide from them. My folks felt so bad. . . . I started school in Twin Groves but it was hard. I learned to read lips but if the teacher would talk with his back turned, I couldn't understand.

Later, in Chester, Idaho, Mother was given a blessing that one day she would be able to hear common talk. As she recounts in her journal,

When Clyde was about a year and a half old, Mother and I went to Salt Lake to see if I could get fitted for a hearing aid. Mother paid all expenses. When I tried an aid on, I said, 'what is that noise'? They said airplanes flying. Oh, how happy I was. How happy Mother was. However, she died in six months. What an interesting world. I could hear the children talk, I felt like I could enjoy talking to people. And then I wanted to go places. I was living in a new world. If only Mother was here to see how happy I was. The blessing I had received at Chester had come true.

While her hearing aids allowed her to hear "common talk," the sound was still somewhat distorted. Between the hearing aid and her ability to read lips, she got along pretty well as long as she could see the lips of the person speaking. When I was little, she always tucked her large hearing aid battery under her blouse. New technology eventually made the battery smaller, but she still attached it under her blouse with the cord leading up to the earpiece in her ear.

Mother always told me if I had to give a talk in church that I should speak loud and slow, so she could hear. She became very good at reading lips to help augment her understanding of what was being said. We tried to repeat things to her that she didn't hear, especially if someone asked her a question. The only time I was aware of her complaining about her hearing loss was when I was called to be president of the West Yellowstone branch of the Church.

She wrote about it in her journal:

> September 22, 1968. Most of our family went to West Yellowstone when Clyde was made Branch President. It's only September and the pines are just laden with snow. It's just beautiful. It's just like Christmas. The meeting was so nice and Clyde, how proud we are of you. That was [the] one time I wanted to hear all [of] what was said, but I couldn't. How much I have missed hearing all through the years. But I must not complain.

Just as with Dad, Mother never allowed her physical handicap to slow her down. She was an excellent cook, seamstress, and family manager. Her energy and output were remarkable. She was normally around the stove tending to her cooking. She used the stove summer and winter. If it was hot outside it was hotter inside, but the hot homemade bread, fried chicken, mutton chops, and fried eggs were the product of this little inconvenience. Mother could open the oven door and put her hand in a little way and know when the temperature was just right to bake whatever she needed. She knew when to add another piece of wood or turn the damper down. The smell of the plump, golden-brown loaves of bread beckoned us to devour a big slice with her homemade butter, apricot jam, or honey. The pies, roasted chicken, Christmas fruitcake, or whatever else was cooked on top of the stove or in the oven never burned and was always just right. In later years, we bought Mother a new electric stove. She wouldn't use it.

That kitchen stove processed hundreds of pints and one-quart bottles full of items harvested from the farm to keep the family nourished through the long winter. Mother canned corn, string beans, apples, raspberries, and applesauce, most of which we kids helped to pick or prepare. She bottled chicken to go along with her mashed potatoes and her homemade chicken noodles. In the fall she bought peaches, pears, apricots, plums, and we picked our locally grown wild chokecherries and made them into jelly. There were always too many bottles to store in the house, so the bottles were loaded onto the hay wagon and then put in the potato cellar, where they kept without freezing.

In her journal, Mother also described carrying water in from the ditch, then heating it up so she could wash a thousand bottles for canning, as well as provide bath water for our round galvanized tub. She also wrote about how we dug the potatoes, shocked the grain, and pitched and hauled the hay.

Mother's world was totally wrapped up in us kids. She would do anything for us, and she was supremely proud of our accomplishments. The last thing I ever wanted to do was disappoint her. I remember sometimes when I did something wrong, Mother said "I'd be ashamed if I were you." And often I was.

One time I said to my mother, "Other kids are beginning to swear. Why shouldn't I?" She responded, "Well Clyde, it's up to you. You decide, but keep in mind that when you go on your mission that would be one less bad habit to break." To this day, my own kids, my wife, and others have never heard me swear. It is amazing to me how many times other people, even not of my faith, will apologize to me after they let a swear word slip out.

I also found this poem written in my mother's hand in her journal that aptly describes the mother she was and the mother she wanted to be.

I'm shy and quiet as a mouse,
always busy "keep'n house."
There's meals to get and bread to bake.
There's floors to sweep and beds to make.
For in the summer when it's hot,
or in the winter when it's not,
Empty stomachs must be fed,
and tired bodies tucked in to bed.
My face is strange, my name unknown;
Fame or fortune I've not known.
But when I leave this world for another,
I hope 'tis said,
"She was a good Mother."
~Unknown

Mother was a kind and caring person. When we hurt, she hurt. When we were sick, she seemed to know exactly how we were feeling and what to do for us. When I was little, if I would get sick to my stomach and need to throw up, Mother got the slop jar, which was the canister we had prior to having running water and a toilet in the house. She held my forehead in her hand as I let it all come out, I don't know why that helped, but her hand was always there to steady us and let us know she cared.

If I was constipated, Mother would pour milk of magnesia, a thick, white, chalky gunk, into a tablespoon, and I would swallow, or rather gag, it down. Castor oil, a thick, yellowish substance, was equally disgusting. Sometimes she would follow it with a chaser spoonful of honey to make it go down more easily. Other times, I felt like I was eating chocolate when Mother gave me Ex-lax. If none of these remedies worked, out came the pinkish-colored rubber water bottle with a long tube screwed onto one end. The other end was inserted in me up to what felt like my tonsils, and warm water came out, gravity-fed from the water bottle hanging above my head. This was one of my most embarrassing treatments. What goes in must come out. The enema was normally quite effective; as generally, much more came out than ever went in. This same water bottle could also perform more pleasant tasks. During cold winter nights, we would fill it with hot water and use it along with hot rocks stuffed into socks to help warm our cold beds.

Mother was short and a little rotund. She had a soft lap and would tell us stories or quote poems to me when I was small. She had five children later in life. Some of my friends had grandmothers her age. As a teenager, I became a little self-conscious about that. I remember as a boy of about fifteen, going with my mother to the grocery store to sell eggs. In return for the eggs, she bought the groceries that we could not raise on the farm. I remember looking down the aisle of the little grocery store and seeing a school friend of mine. I quickly steered him down another aisle so he wouldn't know she was my mother. I remember a fleeting moment of feeling just a little embarrassed. It was only for a short time. I was ashamed of my feelings at the time and have never forgotten how short-sighted and ungrateful I was. Just as Peter from the Bible repented after denying the Savior three times, I repented as well.

Years later I was asked to give a talk on Mother's Day. Memories came back about the embarrassment I felt that day. I have included here a portion of that Mother's Day talk I gave in May 2002, in which I paid tribute to my mother:

> After a funeral held here the other day, my wife, Linda, said to me, "You know the thought kept running through my mind, 'You can't judge a book by its cover.'"

> Last night as I was preparing my talk for Mother's Day, that statement kept running through my mind in regards to mothers.

> Too often we judge someone from their outward appearance, and when we get to know more about them, we find a great appreciation for their life and what they have gone through. In other words, some

may tend to judge a person by what they look like on the outside without knowing what is really on the inside.

As part of my talk I told about the incident with my friend and then said,

I knew and loved what was beneath the cover of my mother's book. But, how could he? How could he see beneath her cover? How could he know that when she was a little girl of five she contracted diphtheria and almost died and was left deaf as a result? There was so much pain in her head that a doctor put hot salt packs on her ears thinking it would ease the pain. When she recovered, her hearing was gone.

How could he see my mother as she raised five kids without being able to hear our voices when we cried in the night? How could he have known that my mother put her hand through the slats of my homemade crib that was right next to her bed, so she could feel when I went to sleep? One of the first things I can remember was waking up in the night and feeling that my mother's hand was not there. I had thought it was there all night long. I climbed up over the side onto her bed and found her hand. She put it back through the crib, and I went back to sleep. How could my friend know that all that really mattered to my mother was the love she had for us kids?

My friend wouldn't know that on a moonlit night our mother would turn the lights out and sit in a chair in front of the living room window to be with us kids. In our homemade pajamas, we would all sit on her lap or next to her and watch the jackrabbits from the front window. And she would say, "Watch them dance in the moonlight."

My friend wouldn't be able to listen to my mother pray. You see, when it was too cold in the bedroom, my mother would take out her hearing aids. She called them her "ears." Then she knelt by the Heatrola, a stove in the living room, and pray before she went to bed. Of course, when she took out her hearing aids, she thought she was whispering, but her prayers became audible enough for us to hear. Without knowing it, she taught us all how to pray, as we listened to her pray for us and for the missionaries and for the soldier boys.

My friend wouldn't know how she cared for me when I was sick. Or that she would do anything for us without asking for anything in return. You see I was afraid my friend would only look at the cover of the "book of my mother" and not see what was written within. My mother taught me things that gave me insight into life and a love for the gospel that she loved so much."

My mother wrote her last journal entry the year she passed away.

I went to West Yellowstone and enjoyed it. I got in the car, the cool, fall wind from the pines was blowing. My son, Dean came to the car, hair turning grey; I couldn't help but let out a few tears when I realized that the years had gone by so fast and me eighty-seven years old.

The pages in her journal are blank after that entry. It was fitting that the last thing referred to was West Yellowstone. She loved to come up to West Yellowstone amid the pines where all five of her kids had worked and where both Dean and I were still living.

Near the end of her journal, mother recorded a poem she addressed to her grandkids who were graduating high school.

You are the fellow who has to decide,
Whether you'll do it or toss it aside.
You are the fellow who makes up your mind.
Whether you'll lead or linger behind.
Whether you'll try for the goal that's afar,
Or just be content to stay where you are.
Take it or leave it it's all up to you.

~Author Edgar A. Guest

She then signed her name as "Grandma"

I remember working alone at the reception desk of the Three Bear Lodge one time with a lobby full of people. I was checking them into their rooms and checking out snowmobile clothing when I received a call telling me that Mother had just passed away. I wanted to leave and go through the appropriate feelings, but there was nothing I could do but go on and pretend nothing was the matter. When the people started to leave, the hollow feeling in my stomach became more acute, and I had to choke back what I was feeling. Like my Dad before her, I knew we would miss her so much. It was Abraham Lincoln who said "All that I am and ever hope to be I owe to my angel mother."

At 87 years of age, Mother's earthly life ended on March 2, 1984. It is hard to express my feelings and those of my siblings for her in just a few words. We loved her, respected her, and tried our best to please her. She was a mother that lived a humble life spent in the service of her children. She had a heart that was kind, tender, and loving. She was slow to anger, but when pressed to the limit, she threatened us kids with the yardstick on our behind. Her world focused primarily on her family, neighbors, and the small community in which we lived.

It would be trite to say that she dropped a little pebble in my pool. Her's was a very large pebble, the ripples of which have reached far beyond me and my generation.

Division of Mothers' Things

I believe I can best pay tribute to my mother by using her own words and relating the things she did for us. I will mention some of the things she recorded in the handwritten books that she left for us.

After her death, we children all gathered at her house to decide where her belongings would go. We all agreed there was not much of worldly value, but the memories attached to her possessions were priceless. So we gathered one evening in March 1984 to divide between us the last worldly possessions of our mother and father, who had preceded her in death by seven years.

Of all the possessions she left us, her book of remembrance, written in her own hand, is without question the most precious. This special book chronicled her life from the time her family moved from Mount Pleasant, Utah, as a little girl to the homesteaded farm in Twin Groves, Idaho. Her book also recounts her marriage, includes mementos of her children as they grew up, and pictures from the past. The book was several inches thick and handwritten with a steady hand. It contained poems, songs, pictures, and all sorts of mementos that only had value to those for whom they were written. Mother's sensitive feelings and love for her children and husband were written on page after page. Remembrance, impressions, and lines of inspiration were almost flawlessly written. These pearls of wisdom were recited to us many times. She kept the book up to date until the year of her death.

She also assembled five other little booklets called our baby books. In these she included pictures from the time we were babies until the time we were married. She wrote in these personalized booklets things we had said and her feelings about each of us. It is hard to read through these without tearing up. I remember sometimes when I came in from work or on a Sunday afternoon, I would find her writing in these little books or pasting in our pictures. Much of the information that follows throughout this memoir comes from these books that are treasured by each of us kids.

After the book remembrance, the rest of the items didn't fall under any order or priority. There was an old bowl from a cream separator that was deep and rounded on the inside. Somehow, it made do as a mixing bowl from which the hot, homemade bread we grew up on was made. I remember the sifted flour went in first, then the potatoes, water, and yeast. Plump hands mixed it all together and finally separated the dough into large, white loaves that were left to rise. Soon, the smell from the old, wood, cook stove would permeate the house and we were rewarded with a slice of hot bread with butter and honey.

There was an old gray steamer. When I thought back, I could almost taste the flavor of the dressing that would come out of the steamer on Thanksgiving Day. I also remembered the carrot puddings that she always steamed just right.

The old Singer treadle sewing machine stood next to the window. It wasn't even electric. Who would even know how to use one, let alone want to buy one? But then, if it could talk, what a story it could tell. How many dresses had it made? How many pairs of Levi mittens? How many pairs of boy's shorts were made from bleached flower sacks? How many white shirt collars had been turned? I could still hear the rhythm of the treadle and the wholesome, homey singing of the little lady that meticulously guided the cloth.

The machine's drawers were still full of buttons and nose rags. I suddenly remembered when I would take the nose rags to the kitchen stove and toss them in so they could fuel the fire. A tatting needle, spools of thread, and other things were conveniently located in the remaining drawers. When not in use, a towel or other such covering was placed on the machine. When it was put away, a Christmas cactus plant or a radio was placed on it for decoration. No, not much value, not to anyone but we kids who grew up with that machine as an integral part of our childhood memories.

In the bathroom was a little wooden box covered with vinyl. Anyone else might have just thrown it away. But for us, tears came when we remembered reaching under its lid in the old farmhouse for a fresh towel and washcloth. This towel box was handmade and as old as most of us. It had outlasted many different coverings that Mother had changed periodically to keep it looking nice.

Throughout the kitchen, living room, and bedroom was a wide assortment of knickknacks. They were just little things that children and grandchildren gave to help convey their love to my mother and father. My mother treasured these, whether they were made by little hands or brought to her from foreign lands. These gifts would be returned to the givers, that they might become mementos and keepsakes for a younger generation.

There were other items, some still present and others recently removed, which were earlier bequeathed by Mother. These were items of great significance to her, and she had wanted to make sure that each went to the person who would find it most meaningful. Her wedding rings were given to my sister Norma, and her precious book of remembrance was given to my other sister Donna. Mother referred to her girls as her best friends. Indeed, they were. They were always there for her. Somehow, even during her months of weakness and discouragement, they could laugh and joke with her and had a magical way of lifting her spirits. Why, you would have thought that they had just returned from New York's Saks Fifth Avenue when they would come in toting two dresses they had picked up at the D. I. for 25 cents each. Mother would model as they tucked and pinned and oohed and awed. These three were always close, and although difficult, it was fitting that my sisters were with my mother when she passed away.

The chipped, white, porcelain quart cup went to my brother Dean. That cup, along with the silver spoon holder, always had a special place in the kitchen cupboard. They weren't of much value to anyone else, but they were prized by their recipients, Dean and Norma.

My brother Sylvan had spent the last several months of Mother's life cooking breakfast for her. He would come in to check on her, and then get out the old cast iron frying pans to cook Mother an old-fashioned breakfast like she used to cook for us. He fried eggs and bacon, mutton chops and hamburgers, fried potatoes, and spud omelets. Mother had told me how nice it was of Sylvan and how she looked forward to him coming in and whistling away as he prepared breakfast. Darkened with age as they are, these old frying pans could be purchased at the D. I. for only 25 cents each, but you couldn't buy them from us for even 25 dollars. Of course, it was fitting that the frying pans went to Sylvan.

The sewing machine went to me. I was both surprised and pleased that Mother would earmark that for me. Donna said there really should be five sewing machines so that each of us could have one. We all agreed. The old gray steamer also went to me which was fitting since my family already was hosting the annual Seely Thanksgiving weekend at our house in West Yellowstone, and part of this yearly tradition was Mother's old steamer and her special dressing recipe.

All these things, which weren't of much monetary value, were taken in five different directions for keepsakes and remembrances of our folks. The five of us will prize and cherish them and pass them on. They are physical reminders, and a way for future generations to value our mother and father and the legacy they left us.

Growing up with two parents who needed our help could be seen by some as a burden. Sure, we sometimes wished that Mother could hear and that Dad did not have epilepsy. However, looking back, all I can see are the blessings we kids received for being watchful, protective, and compassionate to parents who would do anything they could for us.

Pebble 3: My Childhood: A Close Call

*All the water in the world, however hard it tried, can
never sink the smallest ship unless it gets inside.*

~Author unknown

I was born on January 9, 1939 in a converted schoolhouse in St. Anthony, Idaho. My dad had moved it from Island Park and made it into a livable house. Previously he had moved a granary onto the homesteaded farm 3 miles east as the makings of a home for his family. Because the winters were very harsh, the family had only lived there in the summer. The winter I was born, the dogs got into the sheep and killed some of them so the family was moved back to the farm into the makeshift house that became home to me.

We had no electricity in that house until June 1939, when Fall River Electric came to install electricity on the farm. At six-months old, I was taking my midday nap on the bed in the living room when Mother was prompted to move me to another place. I suppose it was one of those moments of mother's intuition. Only a few minutes later, a large rock fell through the roof, smashed through the ceiling, through the bed, right where I had been sleeping, and crashed to the floor.

The power company had been blasting rock not far from the house in order to install a power pole. Apparently they used a little too much dynamite and a 175-pound rock ended up in a new location: my bed. If it were not for my mother's prompting, I would not have lived to tell the tale.

My earliest childhood memories are on my family's small farm. It was located 3 miles east of St. Anthony in Twin Groves, Idaho, on the eastern edge of the state. The pond and canal where I threw pebbles were less than a hundred yards from the farmhouse. There was a large yard and typical outbuildings including a granary, chicken coop, shop, sheep shed, and what appeared to me to be the biggest barn I had ever seen (built by my dad with a handsaw and hammer when I was about 6 years old).

The outhouse was located out of sight behind the granary, complete with a thick Montgomery Ward's sales catalogue. Pages from this catalogue could be torn out, softened by crumpling them up and then they worked quite nicely as a substitute for toilet paper.

I spent many fun-filled hours in these simple surroundings. We had no well and used water from the ditch just outside our back door for cooking, bathing, and drinking. In the winter, Dad would chop a hole in the ice of the canal to get water, and when that was not possible, he would haul water in a ten-gallon milk can from our little county schoolhouse a mile away.

The home where Clyde grew up

We would have our weekly bath in a round number 3 galvanized tub. This was a metal tub that was about thirty inches in diameter and sixteen inches deep. With a handle on each side, it could hang in its normal place of residence, on a nail on the back porch. The bath water would be heated on the wood-burning cook stove in a big double boiler. Since I was the youngest, my siblings, Dean, Norma, Donna, and Sylvan each took their baths first. I was last to use the water before it was dumped out the back door. The tub would sit next to the kitchen stove and when the water started to get cold, Dad would dump in another pan of hot water. I could sit cross-legged in the tub and fit pretty well, but I don't know how my teenage sisters or Mother got into that tub. For a little privacy, chairs were set around the tub with towels draped over the back, although, because I was so young, modesty didn't matter much to me.

We often visited my Aunt Eva and Uncle Glen in St. Anthony. They lived in a house across from the one in which I was born. Their house, which I later bought and owned until 2013, had a full-sized, regular bathtub. As kids, we bathed there sometimes and my first memory of that tub was when my cousin Connie turned a handle and water miraculously came out of the wall and filled the tub with hot water. When I got into the tub there was a thick layer of bubbles on top from the bubble bath. She was going to wash my hair and told me to take a washcloth and "cover up down there." I couldn't understand why I needed to, since she couldn't see anything because of all the bubbles. But she insisted and had me close my eyes while she washed my hair and poured water over my head to wash out the shampoo. When she was finished and I opened my eyes, the bubbles were all gone, and there was my washcloth covering up my private parts. I would have really been embarrassed without it there. It's strange how such trivial memories can stay vivid in my mind after almost 70 years.

Dean was my older brother by nine years. One afternoon, when I was about 4 years old, my parents went to town in the pickup. Of course I wanted to go with them, but for some reason they would not let me. I remember standing in the yard and really crying hard. I could not stop. This went on for a time, and then Dean grabbed his bike and said, "Come on and we'll go catch them." He put me in front of the seat of his bike and we were off. By now I could see the dust of the pickup on the dirt road about a mile away. Dean peddled so hard I thought for sure we would catch up. However, soon it became obvious we would not be able to catch my parents in the pickup. It wasn't long before I felt better, was enjoying the ride and forgot all about crying. I also enjoyed riding behind Dean on our horse Fritz. I always knew when we were about to gallop or "lope" as we called it, because Dean would put his hand on my leg so I wouldn't fall off. He was always so kind and protective. After all, he was my brother.

Just younger than Dean were my sisters, Norma and Donna, who were separated by about two years. They were always together and were the best of friends. We very seldom said one name without the other. It was always Norma and Donna did this or that. They were also very kind to me and kept me in fashion with clothes during my school years.

Sylvan was four years older than I. I looked up to him and tried to follow, but sometimes I felt like I was in the way. We were just close enough in age and yet far enough apart so we didn't have the Norma-and-Donna relationship. We spent many hours in the fields together and, in our later years, we have enjoyed traveling together.

We all worked together on the farm. The girls would help Mother cook. They would help cut potatoes for planting in the spring and pick the clods out of them when they were being harvested. We boys always had our morning and evening chores to do in addition to the entire daily farming responsibilities. We worked well together, except when Sylvan and I would get into it, as brothers often do, because of the common argument, "I'm doing more than you are." I suppose I was often a pain in the neck to him as only a little brother can be.

Pebble 4: Fun and Games on the Farm

A bit of nonsense now and then is relished
even among the wisest men.

~Roald Dahl

While I was born well into the twentieth century, in many respects our lifestyle in Twin Groves had little change from the century before. In some ways, I feel like I have lived in three centuries: the ninetieth, twentieth, and twenty first.

When I was a boy, the Twin Groves Ward meetinghouse, often just referred to as the "church house," was the center of activity for our community. It was a one-room hall with a stage and a curtain that could be rolled up and down for plays and programs. There was a large stove in the back corner surrounded by rows of benches made out of 1" x 4" boards. A series of tight, horizontal wires with sliding curtains attached could transform the large room, used for various meetings and activities, into divided sections for various classrooms. Of course these curtains didn't remove the neighboring sound, but at least we couldn't see those in the next class.

Parties and dancing were something all of us looked forward to. At the church house, the seventeenth of March party was the biggest of the year. Mormons and non-Mormons alike came from miles around for a huge dinner and celebration. The long benches, normally used for church meetings, were set up around the tables, which were laid out with an unbelievable array of food. Normally there was a reading, a very funny story told in a whimsical way by my Aunt Eva or Pearl Rigby, which left most of us laughing uncontrollably.

Years later, at my dad's family reunion in 1997, we were asked to come prepared to reminisce about things that used to happen. I remembered the gist of one of those readings that I thought would be fun to read but could not find a copy. We were also going to play the childhood game of "Button, Button" so I adapted from what I remembered to make up my own version and entitled it "Button, Button." This silly little poem was read in a light-hearted way and everyone laughed at the reunion as they had at the ward party.

"BUTTON, BUTTON": AN EXPERIENCE LONG PAST

At the "Seely Reunion" I have heard we're
going to play "Button, Button."
Well, let me tell you of an experience that was really somethin'.
I once heard a cowboy poet who sent me a laughin'
But to recall all the details—my memory is lackin'.
So please forgive me as I make up my own recollection,
About a lady in church and a little boy's reflection.

The lady was rather portly, as I recall,
As she stood up to speak from the podium to all.
Now she was all nicely dressed, as she stood to speak in church,
I could see that from behind, as I sat on my perch.
Her dress was stuck up between one of those embarrassing places,
I had to act quickly before someone
else noticed and got flushed faces.
She looked awfully uncomfortable just standin' there
And was probably too embarrassed to reach
down and just pull it out of there.
Now, I had always been taught by King Benjamin about service,
I knew this was my chance, so she wouldn't get too nervous.
So, feeling certain this lady would have great appreciation,
I squatted down behind and crawled up to relieve the situation.
My hand reached up and pulled her dress
right out from where it was stuck.
I turned to my seat, when I felt like I was hit
from behind by a great big truck.
For she kicked me so hard, I slid across the floor,
Right back over to where I was sittin' before.
Now she continued right on with her talk,
O how I wished I could just go for a walk.
I sat there with my head in my hands totally confused,
For I thought I had done a good deed, but instead felt all abused.
I guess my good intention had been mistook,
She must have wanted her dress hangin' there like it was on a hook.
With all my church learnin', somethin' had gone awry.
For I remembered when doing a wrong you must also make it right.
Now realizin' she must have wanted her
dress there, I made a resolution
And began to plan out how I could make restitution.
Remember as kids, "Button, Button," we would play?
Maybe with this technique I could again get her dress to stay.
I figured this would accomplish my mission,
If I merely reversed the position.

So without giving it another thought, again I squatted,
And crawled up behind her to do what I thought she wanted.
With my hands cupped tightly together, I see-sawed
her dress in an upward motion.
Oh! If it was bad before, well another truck
would have caused much less commotion.
For I had just started to return to my seat, feeling right proud,
When from behind without making sound,
She hit me with her purse on the side of my head with such a blow,
I slid back across the floor, it must have been quite a show.
Someone told me later, I had laid there for an hour,
Until someone, on my face, cold water they did shower.
Well, when all is said and done, I still believe in my religion,
Even though the blessings of service and
restitution were not very Legion.
There is only one thing I regret, after all these many long years.
For I am sure I would have laughed until it brought many tears.
I never got to see the expression on her face,
When I first withdrew, and then replaced her dress
in that very special place.

Clyde Seely, 1997

After the readings, the tables were moved out, the benches lined up around the walls, and the local band began to play for the dance. It was a lively time. The little ones joined in with their two steps forward and one step back, while the other couples and older singles grabbed a partner and filled the dance floor.

Then someone would call out *"Virginia Reel."* Quickly, small groups were formed and there was whooping and hollering as the familiar line dance took place.

Eventually, the old church house became inadequate and needed to be enlarged. That entire building from my childhood days was remodeled to serve as a large multipurpose room, or the cultural hall, of our new church building. Much of the labor was provided by the members. Even I, at age 13, helped. Then in 1952, the project, which cost the considerable sum of $45,000, was complete and the building dedicated.

Still, I carry with me such vivid memories that are tied in with the one-room church house.

I recall at one of these winter parties, probably at Christmastime, a blizzard pouring down lots of snow. The roads were seldom plowed, so Dad hooked up our horses to a bobsled and added some hay onto the back. He drove the team knee-deep, pulling us through the deep snow. We dressed as warmly as we could. I had on my long stockings, which came to my hips and were held up by panty-waist fasteners, and lots of heavy clothes.

Mother brought a bunch of blankets, and we had a big cowhide or buffalo hide blanket that we all huddled under. We lived a mile or so from the church house, but it was worth the long cold ride to get there. The nighttime sky was clear with the moon big and the stars shining. It was an indelible memory.

It was at another one of these parties, on the 4th of July, when one of my friends and I went outside and pretended to smoke with some dud firecrackers that hadn't gone off. My friend put the one end between his lips, lit a match to the other end, and puffed on it. Unfortunately, it turned out after all not to be such a dud and "bam!" I had the dubious honor of going back into the party and telling his folks so they could come and patch up his swollen and bloody lips.

***

During my childhood, because of the lack of technology, children's games were simple. Nintendo, Wii, or other video games, and even televisions and cell phones, were not even dreamed of. In contrast, I think of my 2 year old granddaughter Ila who, upon finding my iPhone, unlocked it, found the app for Angry Birds and started playing.

Six months ago, I had never even heard of Angry Birds. In contrast, the childhood games that I played are seldom even heard of today. Since we did not have a TV until I was in high school, we played a lot of games that equipment requirements were only human energy and a sense of fun. I will list some of these games in order to preserve and remember the simple ways we entertained ourselves in those days. I think it would be sad if knowledge of these games faded into oblivion.

In contrast to the indoor, electronic games played today, most were outside games:

- **Button, Button**—This game I remember playing often in Primary, a church meeting for boys and girls between the ages of three and twelve.

  The game begins with all the children sitting in a circle except one child who stands in the middle of the circle. He has a button trapped between his closed hands and begins as he moves from one child to another, "see sawing" his closed hands between the others' closed hands, until he has gone around the entire circle. But while he moved around the circle, he dropped the button secretly into a person's cupped hand, and then kept going, pretending to drop the button into each child's hands.

  When he finishes, the kids chant, "Button, button, who's got the button?"

  Each child tries to guess who has the button. The one who guesses correctly is the winner and gets to be the next button dropper.

  Sometimes kids dropped the button in the hand of their little boyfriend or girlfriend. But when I played, I remembered my mom's repeated lessons about including everyone in our play, and I often chose one of the kids that seldom got the button.

- **Red Rover**—My friends and I played many games during my childhood, but this one was a long-lasting favorite.

  Red Rover, Red Rover is a group game consisting of two lines of children facing each other. In each line, the children interlock arms, making two human chains that face each other.

  Then one side, through a quick huddle of whispers, selects one person from the other side, and then calls out, "Red Rover, Red Rover, send Sally (the person they chose) right over."

  Sally, starting at a dead run, tries to break through the human chain which faces her. If Sally is unsuccessful in breaking through the line she must join the opposing team's line. But if Sally is successful, and breaks through the chain, she gets to take a child from the broken link.

  When a team only has one child left, that child has one last chance to break the other team's chain and get another player back on his team. If he can't, the other team wins.

- **Marbles**—I played marbles with my friends a lot during school recess. Each of us had our favorite taw, a marble a little larger than the rest.

  First, someone draws a circle in the dirt, about one foot in diameter, and the group places a few marbles in the center. Then players take turns shooting taws with their thumbs and try to knock the other marbles out of the ring. If a player shoots a marble out of the ring, they get to keep that marble and take another turn. Of course the object of the game is to end up with the most marbles.

  I had a little girlfriend in the third grade who slipped me a little bag of marbles every once in a while. At our 50th high school class reunion, she reminded me of this.

- **Pots**—This was a less popular marble game we played. To play, someone digs out shallow holes in the dirt and places a few marbles in the holes. Then everyone takes turns rolling big marbles known as boulders, or shiny metal ball bearings known as steelies and tries to bowl out the other marbles in the pots.

  The girls sometimes joined in Pots, but, for some reason they mostly played jacks, hopscotch, and jump rope.

- **Eenie Aye Over**—In this game, one or more kids stand on each side of a building. The team with the ball calls out "Eenie Aye Over" and throws the ball over the roof to the opposite team. If someone catches it, that person runs around to the other side and throws the ball at a member of the opposing team like dodge ball. If the person was hit, he joins the team on the opposite side of the building.

- **Kick the Can**—This was another one of my favorite outdoor games. It is best played at night. Ideally, a can is placed under a yard light out in the middle of the yard. One person guards the can and walks around the perimeter of the light, while others attempt to run into the light and kick the can while the guard's back is turned.

- **Knock Up and Lay Down**—One kid bats a softball while others try to catch it. If someone catches the ball, the batter lays the bat down on the ground. Whoever catches the ball rolls it back in an attempt to hit the bat. If they hit it, they get to be the next batter to bat the ball.

***

I developed a heart murmur in my youth, so I could never participate in regular school sports. Yet one time I received a basketball for a present, and my brother Sylvan and I cut out the bottom of a wire potato basket and nailed it up on the wall inside the barn at the appropriate 10-foot height. Since it was quite a bit smaller than a regular basket, we thought we were pretty good when our shots went in. The barn had a dirt floor and was just a little deeper than where the foul line would normally be. However, I always enjoyed what little basketball I could play with my friends in that barn.

As I grew older I learned to dance. In junior high, we would occasionally have a dance on a Friday afternoon. This consisted of holding a partner in the traditional ballroom dance position, which is very different from today's more independent style. The 12 year-old dancers would slide two steps forward and one back. From above, it must have resembled a big, slow-moving whirlpool as everyone progressed around the room until they returned back to where they had started.

There wasn't a lot to do at night on the farm. Having no modern entertainment devices made for long evenings and normally we did not stay up past 9:00 p.m. But sometimes my brother Sylvan and I took the car and drove the 3 miles to the nearby town of St. Anthony. In fact, the only time I remember taking advantage of mother's deafness was one night when Sylvan and I asked our parents if we could take the car to town for no special reason.

Mother said, "No, it's too late," but Dad, on the other hand, didn't really seem to care. So when Mother had taken out her ears and we had all gone to bed, Sylvan and I got to talking, a bit loud. Since our bedroom was separated from that of our parents by only by a thin wall with no door on the opening, Dad could hear everything. We discussed how Dad didn't seem to care if we went to town, and we both bet that he wouldn't tell Mother if we went. We said, "Let's get dressed and go get the car. Mother won't hear us, and we won't turn on the lights until we are out of the yard."

And that was exactly what we did. We were gone a little over an hour and when we drove back into the yard, we turned off the lights and parked the car in its usual place. Then we returned inside, undressed, and got back into bed. The next morning, there was a little twinkle in Dad's eye, but he didn't say a word.

However, another time, my adventures did not end so well. My friend Randall's folks had an old 1936 Chevy coupe. It was a neat old car and even had a rumble seat in the back. A rumble seat is like the trunk of an old sedan car, except the handle is on the top next to the back windshield. You could turn the handle, lift up the cover and it became an outdoor seat where two people could sit, like they were in a convertible. One night, Randall said he was going to come pick me up so we could go to town. He had a driver's license by then, so the only problem was that Randall's folks were gone and he took the car without permission. We went to town and dragged Main (five or six blocks long), which was the popular thing to do at the time. Then it got late, so we headed back home.

Near our farm, our narrow little country road made a bend that went between a canal on the one side and a hill of big rocks on the other. As fate would have it, just as we were coming around the bend, the lights on the little coupe went out. It was in the fall and pitch black. Randall knew he couldn't just go straight. If he did, we would run into the canal. And if he bore left, he'd run into the rocks.

He chose the latter. The car jumped, jerked, and finally stopped high-center on a big rock. I can still remember as if it were in slow motion, the car teetered back and forth and finally tipped over on the side where I was sitting. Randall stood up started jumping up and down, and said something like, "Spade! (my high school nick-name) I'm really going to be in a lot of trouble, what am I going to do now?"

I said, "I don't know, but stop jumping up and down on my stomach!"

We opened the door, which was now facing skyward, and climbed out. I think this was the last drive that neat little car ever took. I'm glad I wasn't around when he had to tell his folks. I *was* there one time when his mother caught us in her chicken coup, and that was bad enough.

***

In the early 1940s, we had electric lights in our farmhouse but no well or running water. We had a simple lifestyle. Mother wrote, "We were such a very happy family, rich in love, unity, and humility, and rich in spirituality, but not rich in the material things of life."

The house was simple with what seemed to me as a little boy a fairly large kitchen and a living room where we basically lived. There was a wood-fired cook stove in the kitchen that was used for both heating the kitchen and cooking. (The other heat source in the house was another stove, a "Heatrola" that could burn either wood or coal, in the living room.)

My family lived mostly off the land, just as my grandparents did. We raised sheep, cows, pigs, chickens, geese, and sometimes a turkey or two for the appropriate occasions. We had a large garden on our 120-acre farm where we grew potatoes, grain, hay, and some-times peas. What we could not raise or grow, Mother bought with money she made from the eggs she sold to the grocery store. She used her hundreds of jars to bottle everything from peas and corn to applesauce and plums. We seldom had a meal without opening a jar of something that was kept in the back room where, between there and the potato pit, there were always hundreds of bottles sitting in neat rows on the shelves.

From the time I was a little boy, I would often see Mother sitting at the old Singer treadle sewing machine in front of the kitchen window. She made almost everything for us, including quilts, feather ticks, pillows, and the flannel sheets that were used in the wintertime. The most versatile, free pieces of material were the big flour sacks from which she made our boxer-type shorts, among other things. The colored labels bleached and washed out leaving the material reasonably white. Finally when Dean started high school, Mother decided to splurge on store-bought shorts because it became a little embarrassing to undress for P.E. in our homemade shorts.

However, because the flour sack was used for so many things in our youth, Mother later copied, by hand, "The Versatile Flour Sack" by Colleen B. Hubert. Years later, the reading of this poem became a part of our annual Seely Thanksgiving dinner and was always a hit among my grown-up siblings and me. Of course, it often took some explaining to our young children, who could not imagine such a thing as having clothing made out of flour sacks.

I quote just two stanzas here that were so applicable:

Pillsbury's best, Mother's and Gold Medal too,
stamped their names proudly in purple and blue.
The string sewed on top was pulled and kept.
the flower emptied and spills were swept.
The bag was washed and dried on a rack,
that durable, practical flour sack.

Bleached and sewn, it was dutifully worn
As bibs, diapers, or kerchief unadorned,
It was made into slips, blouses and shirts,
Little girl's pinafores and little boys shirts.
Ruffled curtains were made for houses or shack,
from that humble, but treasured flour sack.

The poem aptly described the frugality of my mother, the flour-sack shorts, and other things she made for us kids. Several years went by, and then my sister Norma wrote a follow-up poem. My mother's name was Oneta, and PeeWee was the nickname for my older brother Dean.

Oneta's Versatile Flower Sack (Part II)

When I was a maiden fair,
Mother made our underwear.
With five tots and Dad's poor pay,
How could she buy lingerie?

With treadle and sewing box she stitched,
Flour sack garbs, seemed to be her niche.
Panty waists that always stood the test,
With "Gold Medal" written on the chest.

'Twas at the gym PeeWee made his debut,
His "Fruit of the Looms" were now in full view.
Like a model on the runway, struttin' his stuff,
'Till finally the coach cried, "We've had enough!"

Tougher than a Grizzly bear
'Twas his flour sack underwear.
Plain and fancy, three feet wide,
Stronger than a Hippo's hide.

But through the years every child did wear,
Mother's labor of love showed that she cared.
Waste not, want not, we soon learned,
a penny saved is a penny earned.

Bedspreads, quilts, dish-towels, too,
table cloths to name a few.
But the best beyond compare,
Was our flour sack underwear.

~Written by my sister Norma, her daughter
Lynn, and her son-in-law Dave Martin.
November 28, 1996

Mother also made work mittens out of Dad's overalls or old
worn-out Levis. She reused buttons, patched holes in clothes, and
unstitched and turned over the collar on Dad's white shirts. She
basically used and reused everything she could. She cut up our old

white shirts or any white material that had been used for other purposes, so we could use them as nose rags. She put them in the top, left drawer of the old Singer treadle sewing machine so later we could get them out to blow our noses. Mother never wasted anything and used things up before she threw them out. The late Boyd K. Packer often quoted a common saying: "Use it up, wear it out, make it do, or do without." Our simple life on the farm seemed to mirror this statement.

Pebble 5: Feed the Lambs

If a job is worth doing, it's worth doing well.

~Proverb

If there was a farm animal that was a pebble in my pool, it was the sheep.

As a boy, the animals seemed to be the focus of most of my daily efforts, and I loved to work with them. I spent the most time, however, with the sheep. My job was to herd them and to keep them in the right fields. I would whistle and tell my dog, Beep, to "git around 'em," and he would circle wide out in front and then bring them back to where they were supposed to be. I felt like a boy shepherd with the sheep under my care and keeping.

Sheep, like our other farm animals, were totally dependent upon us to take care of them. When lambing time came, there were always little lambs whose mother lacked enough milk. These we called "bum lambs," and because of them, Dad would often remind us kids to "feed the lambs."

This was done by pouring fresh cow's milk into pop bottles, pulling nipples over them, and holding the bottle so the lambs could suck out the milk. When they were little we would have to open their mouths and put the nipple in, but it didn't take long before they learned how to suck by themselves. Later, as the lambs got bigger, I would have to hold my ground as they would swarm me and almost push me over with their enthusiasm to eat.

At the time, when Dad would remind me to "feed the lambs," I wasn't really aware of the biblical significance of lambs and sheep. I only knew that I felt good when I took care of their needs. In later years, when reading the New Testament in the Bible, I could relate in some small way when I read the scripture John 21:16–17, in which Jesus counsels the apostles to feed His sheep. I can still remember my Dad's reminder to "feed the lambs."

In the fall during the breeding season, we would turn the bucks into the herd so we could start lambing in March. Then to prepare for the lambing season, we would put a huge canvas over the rafters of the sheep shed so it was protected from the wind and cold. We would partition the shed off with panels to make 4' x 4' pens with clean straw for where the newborn lamb would be placed by its mother.

The lambing process normally took about a month. Since Dad worked all day long, my brother Sylvan and I would split the lambing night shift. Those nights were long and cold and sometimes with blizzards that lasted through the night. When it was my shift, I would get dressed and go out every hour to check for newborn lambs.

I know I set the alarm for one hour, but it always seemed that I would just get to sleep when that alarm would go off again. Then if I didn't get out from under the warm covers quickly, it would be easy to slip back into a sleep, and a new little lamb might not make it. So I would get dressed, grab the flashlight, and go out to check for newborn lambs. If there was one, I would drag it along by its hind legs so the mother could smell her new lamb and follow us into a little pen in the sheep shed. Then I would grab two of the ewe's legs, tip her over on her side, and help the lamb suck the first milk. If the lambs did not get the mother's new milk, or had been outside in the cold for too long, they could die.

About 2:00 a.m. the shifts would change, and Sylvan would take over so I could catch some more sleep. These were short nights for Sylvan and me because a few hours later we would have to catch the school bus.

I recall first starting to help with the lambing process when I was about 12 years old. At the time this was hard, and I usually ended up being sleepy in school, but I knew I couldn't leave it all up to Dad. He simply couldn't work that many hours, and Sylvan couldn't do it all alone. Still, I remember being envious that none of my other friends had sheep to lamb out. But it just had to be done. And now in later years, I remember these experiences with fondness.

Often, a ewe could not have her lamb on her own. If the lamb's nose and front feet did not come out first, there was a real problem. If it started to come out breach, or backwards, the mother wouldn't be able to have the lamb and it could mean the death of the mother. We could not afford to call a vet each time this happened, so sometimes we had to help the mother give birth ourselves.

Because I had small hands, Dad would have me push my hand up inside the mother so I could feel the position of the lamb. Then, Dad would explain how it needed to be turned so it could come out correctly. After that, I would push the lamb back in and turn it so I could get the two front feet between my fingers and pull the lamb out slowly. This was obviously very painful for the mother.

Once, I hesitated several times and said, "It hurts her too bad."

In response, Dad said something I will never forget. He said, "Clyde, sometimes you just have to put your heart in your pocket and do what has to be done."

In most cases this all worked out well, and I was able to help complete the birthing process. After I had pulled out the lamb, I would bring it around, open its mouth, and help it get its first milk. And then, all would be well.

Clyde, sometimes you just have to put your heart in your pocket and do what has to be done.

This has been a reminder to me over the years that sometimes hard decisions have to be made. These decisions can be painful to others or me in the short term, but these decisions will bring great rewards in the end.

I suppose we now refer to it as tough love. Personally, I have realized that sometimes the hardest road to take brings the greatest rewards in the end. Farm life was hard, and we kids soon learned that a job didn't get finished unless we did it. The more we stayed on task, the sooner we would finish, so before quitting for the night, we always made sure that all the chores were done, even the unpleasant ones.

Unlike most other kinds of crops, sheep provided two harvests. One harvest was in the fall when we sold the lambs that weighed between 90 and 100 pounds. The other was in the early summer when we sheared the sheep. That was always a big day.

Several times a year we had to separate some of the sheep from the others to be sold or sheared, or sometimes to weed out barren sheep from the herd. The cutting chute came in handy for this. It was long and narrow and just wide enough for a single sheep to pass through.

Near the end of the chute, we would have a panel, or a little gate that we could swing back and forth. If we were going to sell the lambs, we would swing the gate one way to allow the lamb to go through the gate and eventually into a truck. By swinging the gate the other way, at just the right time, the sheep we wanted to keep would go into a different pen. These would eventually be turned out to pasture and kept to have another lamb and another fleece of wool.

We hired sheep shearers to come in and shear the wool off our sheep. This was hard, back- breaking work, so the shearers used a sling on a spring, just under their ribcage, to help support their own weight as they bent over all day long, often almost wrestling the sheep. They ran their huge, hair clipper-like shears next to the sheep's skin and peeled the fleece off almost like an orange peel. When finished, the shearer kicked the bundle of wool off to the side, and we kids would lay a piece of string across our feet, tuck the wool between our legs, and tie the fleece together. Then, we would throw the bundle way up into the nearby ten-foot tall wool sack that was suspended from a frame.

It often fell to my lot, as a young boy, and then as a teenager, to climb up on top of the frame, holding the 10' x 3' burlap wool sack. Next, I would throw five or six bundles of wool to the bottom of the sack, and then jump in and tromp the wool down so more could be put in.

Once down in the sack, there was no way out, until more wool was thrown in on top of me. I would reach up and catch each fleece, pull it underneath me, and tromp it down. Eventually, I worked myself up to the top of the large wool sack. It would then be sewn at the top and replaced with another sack. "Tromping wool" was a sweaty, sticky, and dirty job, but somebody had to do it. Since it didn't require much skill except being young and agile, the job was often mine.

After the sheep were sheared, they looked rather naked and white. We knew many of them by sight, but after shearing we could no longer recognize them. In order to distinguish our sheep from others, we branded them with our registered brand. Instead of using a hot iron, which is generally used on horses and cattle, we used red paint while our neighbors used green. While we dipped the branding iron in paint, the sheep would come down a long narrow chute. Then we pressed the iron onto the back of each sheep as they went by. This included the new lambs that were, by now, about three months old. With new brands on their back, they could easily be identified as ours.

I spent a lot of time herding sheep, keeping them in the appropriate pasture and away from the hay or grain fields, and sometimes stopping them from finding a hole in the fence, which would have led into the neighbor's field.

Sheep are herd animals and normally stay together as a group. But one season there was a little group of ten or fifteen sheep that would frequently break away from the herd and get into trouble. One time I came home late from chasing this little group.

My dad asked where I had been and I told him, "I have been chasing those bloomin' individualists."

He got a real chuckle out of that. I suppose it struck him as rather funny because of my early age.

Over the years we began to increase the size of our herd of sheep. We could no longer pasture them on the farm because most of it was used for crops. Instead for the summer, we combined them with Cy Young's herd, and they spent the summer in Island Park, Idaho, near Mount Sawtelle.

Then one summer, Dad had an opportunity to lease a sheep range for one summer in Island Park. We were grateful for that opportunity, but of course needed a herder for our sheep. So Dad decided that he and I would take the sheep to the new range while the farm responsibilities were left to my two brothers and the rest of the family.

The sheep range was located on the Ashton Hill, about 10 miles north of Ashton, and about 30 miles from our farm. We had 300 head of ewes plus lambs. It must have been quite a site as we started driving our sheep herd from our farm to the range.

On the first night, we made it to Chester, but Dad had to return to get something from the farm and left me, the horse, and the dog, to keep the sheep in a sagebrush field. It soon got dark, and I began to imagine things. I thought there was a porcupine just in front of me, which turned out to be tumbleweed, and a bear that turned out to be a bush. Minutes seemed like hours. Finally I prayed that Dad would come back quickly. Then pretty soon, I heard the familiar rattle of the truck—Dad was back, and everything was alright.

That summer I was 13 years old and grew especially close to my dad. We were seldom apart, and I never remember a cross word spoken by either one of us. It was a special time for both of us.

Dad bought a camp wagon for $40, and we spent the summer sleeping in the same bed in our little sheep camp. While we were there, a survey crew came and surveyed the route for a new highway that would eventually bypass Warm River and make the road much shorter from Idaho to West Yellowstone, Montana.

We ate well that summer. My uncle, who was also a sheep man, taught us how to make "spud omelet." I often made this on our little camp stove. Whenever we ran short of something, spud omelet was the answer as it was easy to make. I would slice up some potatoes, a few sliced onions, and a little ham if we had it, into a big frying pan with melted butter. Leftover baked potatoes could also be used, which took less time. I would let it cook for a while until the potatoes were just about done, add salt and pepper, and then crack two or three eggs over that. I would turn everything frequently so the eggs got mixed in and cooked with the potatoes, and then top it with sliced cheese, salt, and pepper. I would then cover the spud omelet with a lid for a minute or so to melt the cheese, and it was done. Serve this with some Catsup, Tabasco or picante sauce, a slice of bread and butter, and a glass of milk and we had our favorite meal. I still cook this for my kids and grandkids. It's a yummy meal in a minute or five.

Also we never passed up the opportunity to shoot a grouse. I would skin it out and fry it in butter with a little seasoning and, you guessed it, it tasted like chicken.

Mother wrote about our sheep range experience.

> Dean and I would take food up every few weeks and spend a few hours. The first time we went up to see them, the gnats were so thick you could hardly see, and Dad's face was all swollen where he had been bit. Dad would always cry a little when we came and I am sure Clyde would have liked to cry when we left.

I remember after Mother saw our swollen faces, she made us some netting for the brim of our hats, which hung down to our neck so the gnats couldn't get to us. That was a great blessing for us.

Each morning, the sheep awoke before I did, and Dad would slip out of bed at daylight and stay with the sheep as they went about their early feeding. He would return in time for breakfast, and by then, I would be up with some cooked breakfast on the little camp stove. When the sheep bedded down in the heat of the day, we would both mount on Fritz, our horse, and ride to check out new grass areas, or to haul water for the sheep. In the evening, the sheep would start moving again, and we had to stay with them to keep them from straying away.

One evening at dusk, we watched the herd of sheep as they drank from a pond of water. All of a sudden, from the other side of the water, a big grizzly came into the herd, swapping his claws at our sheep. We only had a .22 caliber bolt-action rifle, but Dad got so excited, he got what we called "buck fever." But fortunately, instead of pumping one shell into the chamber and shooting the bear, he began to pump the shells out of the chamber and onto the ground.

"Dad, don't shoot it," I said, "You will only wound it, and it will come after us." Instead, we yelled and whistled. The bear stood up on its hind legs, looked at us, and then turned and walked away.

"The Making of a Tall Tale" by Gary Carter N.W.R., from Clyde's memory

However, we were not always as lucky. Early one morning, Dad came back to the camp, telling me the upsetting news that a bear had gotten into the sheep and killed a couple of them.

While at the sheep range, Fritz, the horse, and Beep, the sheep dog, were my best buddies. To pass the time, I trained them both to do a few tricks.

The summer passed quickly, and it was eventually time to load up the sheep and haul them back to the farm. This time, we took many trips in our little truck making it an all-night process.

I often think about this summer, especially as I drive up the "new highway" over the Ashton Hill and pass through our old sheep range. There is a big forest service sign now on the right, part way up the hill, which stands and marks the spot where we loaded and hauled our sheep home. This was a summer that very few boys experience. I spent it with my dad, nature, Beep, Fritz, and of course the sheep. I don't remember the details of many summers but I will never forget that one.

***

Today, the small family farm represents a vanishing culture. It is being replaced with mega-farms and automatic tractors. Small ma-and-pa shops and neighborhood groceries are being replaced with Walmarts and other big-box stores. The farm life was very rewarding though. It really felt good to finish plowing a field, baling up hay, finishing a new fence, or bringing in a herd of sheep. Every day we could look back and see what had been accomplished. Then each harvest season, we paid off the bank, and hopefully had enough left over to pay for schooling, or sometimes even to purchase a newer car or pick-up.

But with all the hard work, there were also lazy, carefree days; days when I entertained myself doing non-productive things. I became an expert at hypnotizing chickens. At night, the chickens would roost in the chicken coop. But in the daytime, we would open the door to the chicken coop and the chickens would roam freely around the yard. I would catch a chicken, hold it on its side, stretch its head and beak out on the ground, and slowly draw a line in the dirt from its beak straight out a couple times. It would become hypnotized and just lay there like it was dead.

One time I had eight or ten chickens laid out all over the yard when my folks came home in the pickup. They wondered what had killed all the chickens, but when they drove up, the chickens came out of their trance and we all had a good laugh.

We were responsible for everything on the farm, every crop, every animal, and every piece of machinery, so it seemed we were on call 24/7. We always had six or eight sheep wearing bells around their neck to alert us if sheep were being molested. Sometimes the bells rang during the night, letting us know that the sheep were running from something. Dad would grab his .22 rifle and leave to confront the problem. Sometimes the coyotes got into the sheep, maliciously taking them down. Sometimes a group of local dogs, owned by the neighbors, ran together at night and chased them. Generally, the dogs wouldn't try and kill the sheep but would mangle their hind legs, mostly for sport. In some cases, the results of these attacks were so bad we had to put down the wounded sheep.

One early morning, just at dawn, the ringing of the sheep bells woke Dad. A pack of dogs was attacking the herd. Dad shot at them and wounded one of the culprit dogs. A few hours later our neighbor Virgil brought his wounded dog back to us and told Dad "You wounded it, now you finish it." I guess he thought he could teach Dad a lesson, but I didn't think Dad had done wrong. In my mind, he was right to defend the sheep, so I told Dad I would take care of it. I took the wounded dog to the barn and pulled the trigger. *Clyde, sometimes you just have to put your heart in your pocket and do what has to be done.*

My family was always vigilant about the safety of the animals. We were always quick to respond to any warnings, whether it was the sound of sheep bells ringing, dogs barking, or noises coming from the chicken coop. Our chicken coop had about 100 chickens. Once, in the middle of a warm summer night, Dad called from his bed through the wall, "Clyde, wake up, something is bothering the chickens."

The most common threat to the chickens was usually a skunk. That night the chickens were squawking loudly. No time to get dressed, I just slipped on my shoes and joined dad outside.

Visible in the yard light, clad only in my white homemade flour sack boxers, Dad carrying his .22, in his white long johns (which he wore year around), shoes, and, out of habit, his hat! Dad never went outside without his hat. I still remember thinking how funny we both looked in our 'undies'... and Dad in his hat. We must have scared whatever it was away, because as we went into the chicken coop, in our white regalia, the chickens quieted right down.

Pebble 6: Youth

*The chains of habit are too weak to be felt
until they are too strong to be broken.*

~Samuel Johnson

Living on a farm required knowing how to operate equipment. My first experience driving a tractor was at my uncle's when I was 6 years old. While I was playing and watching them dig potatoes, the main tractor wasn't quite powerful enough to pull the potato digger by itself. So my uncle put me behind the steering wheel of "Little Eva," a small international tractor. First, he started me driving down the row and said; "If someone hollers 'Stop,' push on the clutch." I was so small that I needed to stand up to push the clutch all the way down. At the end of the row, my uncle jumped back on the tractor just in time to turn the tractor around and start me back down the next row. Even at an early age, I became pretty proficient in driving tractors and operating equipment.

Tractors were not Dad's long suit because he grew up driving a team of horses. Whenever Dad got in a tight spot, he climbed down off the tractor and said, "You do it." Of course this made me proud because he trusted me, young as I was.

Farm equipment can be hazardous to operate, especially when you are alone. Due to his seizures, Dad escaped some very danger-ous situations when he was alone on equipment. I also had a like experience. Once in the fall, I was alone and greasing the potato digger when I nearly had a fatal accident. I had left both the tractor and power take-off running. The power take-off receives its power from the tractor's motor and turns the equipment, in this case the potato digger. My shirttail was hanging out and my Levi jacket was opened down the front. I reached over the power take-off to grease a bearing when a bolt, protruding from the power take-off, caught my loose shirt and started to pull me down into the equipment. As it pulled me down, I yanked up as hard as I could and ripped part of my shirt off. It continued to pull me down, and I resisted, yanking against it again. By doing this, I finally tore the entire shirt off my back from under my Levi jacket, causing rope burn like abrasions around the back of my neck and shoulders. The bolt also took a bite out of my right bicep. I still have the scar from it.

Thankfully, my much tougher Levi jacket did not get caught. If that had caught and wound around the power take-off I would not have lived to tell the tale because it would have chewed my body into pieces. Instead, when the folks came home, I showed them my bloody arm.

Now years later, as I look at the scar on my right arm, I also see another on my left arm. I received it while at my best friend's house. Some of the boys wanted to play softball, but my best friend didn't. He wanted to shoot birds instead. While we were playing, I heard a shot and felt pain in my left arm. I looked down and saw a hole in my shirtsleeve with blood running down my arm. My friend came running over, laughing, but when he saw the blood, he turned pale. He said that he did not mean to hit me. He just wanted to scare me. It grazed my arm, and although in my mind all was well, our parents were a little concerned and we got a good talking to.

While helping on the farm, my siblings and I still attended school just a mile away. I spent school grades one and two in our little two-room Twin Groves schoolhouse. Mrs. Cazier taught the first four grades in one room while another teacher taught grades five through eight in the next room. Each row represented a separate grade.

I'm not sure how our teacher taught all four grades at once, but I look back with fondness on those two years. The school had a big potbellied wood stove for heating the building and a water-well from which we filled a ten-gallon milk can for drinking. There was a big bell at the top that rang when it was time to start school in the morning and after lunch. In the schoolyard was a giant set of swings, a slide, and a horse barn to keep our horses in. To travel the mile to school, my brother and I rode our horse, old Fritz. In the winter, some kids skied behind the horse or walked cross-country on the crusted snow.

The next year the bus came. The school bus marked the end of our little Twin Groves country school, as we knew it. The school, where so many memories were made, was torn down around 1950.

Twin Groves country school built in late 1890s. Clyde's mother attended here, and it was torn down after Clyde finished second grade.

All my brothers and sisters had gone to Twin Groves. Mother had also graduated from the eighth grade there on May 24, 1913. Beulah, my future mother-in-law, was taught there by my Aunt Eva. Twin Groves School and the people who were educated there have played an important part in my life.

Pebble 7: Called as a Missionary to England and Ireland

When I was a child, I spake as a child, I understood
as a child, I thought as a child: but when I
became a man, I put away childish things.

~1 Corinthians 13:11

My parents shared the goal of having all five kids graduate from college. Everyone pitched in to help. Part of our wool, potatoes, and grain sales went wherever it was needed for college tuition and expenses. My folks were so proud when each one of us graduated. Ironically, we all became teachers.

For me, after graduating from South Fremont High, I attended Ricks College in Rexburg, Idaho, for one year. At this point, I was the only one living at home to help with the farm, so I went to classes during the day and drove home each afternoon to combine (harvest) the grain, dig potatoes, or do whatever was needed. After the crops were all in, I moved to Rexburg to finish my first year.

At the age of 20, I was called to England on a two-year mission for The Church of Jesus Christ of Latter-days Saints, sometimes known as the Mormons.

It may be of interest to explain a little about LDS missions. Many wonder what this strange practice is all about. Quite simply, the Church encourages single young men between the ages of 18 and 25 to devote two years of their lives, at their own expense, to telling people about the principles of the Church. Young women may also be called at the age of 19, but only for 18 months.

Missionaries receive their assignment from Church headquarters and are sent only to countries where governments allow the Church to operate. Missionaries do not request their area of assignment and do not know beforehand whether they will be required to learn a language. Upon arrival to their assigned area, which could be in any of more than 160 countries, missionaries are assigned a companion of similar age who has been out serving for a while. The rules of the church are that companions are always together. They study together, teach together and are basically with each other 24 hours a day, 7 days a week until they are transferred to another area and companion.

I will not go into great detail about my mission because way too much could be written. Suffice it to say that my two years spent in England were some of the most influential years of my life.

I have often said I would not trade my two years on a mission for anything else, like two years of college. But for young men to give up two years of the prime of their life out of love for people they don't even know, and especially when many are not even interested in listening, is understandably strange.

However, there are also those who have been waiting for this message and whose lives have been changed as a result.

I will relate just one of these life-changing experiences. One afternoon in late 1959, my companion and I knocked on a door. I still remember the address, 179 Caernarvon Road, in Cheltenham, England. After a brief discussion, we asked the lady of the house,

Beryl Sutton, if we could come back in the evening when her husband was at home. She agreed. What we didn't know was that her husband, Cecil, had a dislike for Americans as he had some feelings stemming from the war. She gathered her strength and told him a couple American missionaries would be calling back.

To make a long story short, Cecil agreed to meet, and it wasn't long before they joined the Church and became stalwarts in the ward. Since that time, my wife Linda and I have become lifelong friends with them. They have visited us in West Yellowstone and we have visited them many times in England. Cecil has long since passed away, but we still visit Beryl. We most recently visited her in 2012. I dropped a pebble in their pool all those years ago and they and their family have continued reciprocating.

Missionaries live selfless lives for two years, setting aside girls, schooling, athletic aspirations and any otherworldly activities. They are often given leadership opportunities. I will tell of only two of my experiences.

After I had been in England about 16 months, I was called to reopen a branch. A branch is the smallest congregational unit within the Church, and this particular branch had been closed for almost 20 years. It covered the area known as the Potteries, where Royal Dalton, the famous English china, is made. In the early 1840s, missionaries had much success in this area and at that time period England became a stronghold of the Church. Then the call came to come to Zion, and many members took up the call and migrated to America. Later, World War II took its toll, and eventually there were not enough members to keep the branch going.

Then, 20 years later, I was called to go back and reopen this branch of the Church. My mission companion and I, with another pair of missionaries, rented a little public hall, repainted it, and contacted the newspapers to set up an appointment to meet with the Lord Mayor. Two newspapers came to interview us and took our picture with the Lord Mayor, Gordon Dale. The paper announced that four young men from America were here to open a branch of The Church of Jesus Christ of Latter-day Saints. We found six members that were still there and officially reopened the Church in the Potteries. Twenty years later, Linda and I returned to find there had been great growth. When there are enough members in the area, the congregation is called a ward. And where there is additional growth, several wards make up a larger organization unit called a Stake. During my mission days, we started with six members in that little hall on Percy Street. Now there is a large stake building with seven different Ward buildings in the area. This growth, over a span of 20 years was indeed humbling to see.

Presenting Lord Mayor Gordon Dale with Book of Mormon

Before coming home from my mission, my last assignment was similar to the Potteries branch assignment, but this time my companion and I were to reopen Dublin, Ireland to missionaries. We were asked to tour the whole of Southern Ireland and recommend where missionaries should be sent. What an opportunity for a 21-year-old boy to see Ireland and help to set the stage for future missionary work. Again, 20 years later, when Linda and I returned, we found not only branches, but also wards and stakes in the areas where we recommended that branches of the Church be reopened.

Looking back, it seems I had served as a pioneer on my mission and paved the way for others. When Linda and I visited these sites in England and Ireland, we met strong members who had known nothing about thc church at the time I had served there. But upon their conversion, their lives had changed, and they in turn shared the Church with their friends, who then also found spiritual meaning in their lives. Like the ripples from a pebble in the pool, the good work continued to expand even after I was gone. As a result of the work done 20 years before, there were hundreds of members of the Church and many chapels. Having these experiences as a missionary made me feel extremely blessed, both then and now.

Those two years, when I put the rest of my life on hold, have proven to me to be among the most important years of my life. My missionary experience was a pebble in my pool, and it was an opportunity for me to drop little pebbles along the way that have had far reaching ripple effects on other people's lives, many of whom I have never even met. I believe that happens with all of us.

Well, you know, two years is a long time. I had a girlfriend when I left. We wrote letters for a while, but they became fewer and farther between. I must say that statistically speaking, a large percentage of those good intentions change. While the missionary is out devoting one hundred percent to serving the Lord, other guys are actively trying to find the girl of their dreams. And, while absence is supposed to make the heart grow fonder, many girls write their missionary with that dreaded break-up letter that missionaries call a "Dear John."

Absence makes the heart grow fonder,
fools say as departure nears.
But the same have cause to ponder, if
the absence lasts two years.
Though you started by declaring- She's the only girl for me.

Chances are it's not meant to be.
Oh, beware of the lips that promise, "I'll
be faithful while you're gone."
Though your name be Floyd or Thomas, you
will soon be called - "Dear John."

Though I never received a "Dear John," the girl I left behind was married before I returned.

Pebble 8: The Girl That I Married

Definition of a Kiss:
It is a noun because it is common, proper, and possessive.
It is a verb because it shows action.
It is a conjunction because it connects two things together.
It is plural because one follows another.
It is a pronoun because she stands for it.
It is an adverb because it tells how much he loves her.

~Author Unknown

The girl that I married has been and remains one of the main pebbles in my life. Linda was just a little girl when I first met her. She was a cousin to Sally Young, who started school with me in the first grade. Whenever Linda visited Sally, I saw her, with her long brown ringlets or braids, and I got to know her a bit then. She was a cute little girl. Later, we knew each other casually in high school.

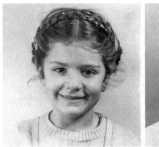

Linda Fischer and Clyde Seely as childhood acquaintances

After I had returned from my mission, my sister-in-law said to me, "Linda Fischer is back from school. Why don't you call her up and take her on a date?"

I did. But when I called her on the phone, I was pretty nervous. I said, "This is Clyde Seely."

She said, "Who?" Still I persevered and asked her out on a first date. But when the designated evening arrived, as I walked up and knocked on the door, I felt a little intimidated. Especially when the door opened, and there she was, all grown up and beautiful.

Linda at college graduation; Clyde at the time of his mission

Since she had grown up in Ashton, which was 14 miles away from my family's farm, and had attended a different high school, I didn't know her family well. I never knew her father, as he died when she was just 16 years old. Norman, her brother, had moved on to become a fashion designer and no longer lived at home. Linda had already graduated with a teaching degree from Utah State University but was living at home with her mother that summer.

On the evening of our first date, we went to a movie called *The Absent-minded Professor* with Fred McMurray. Although we began the date reserved, we soon gave up on that act and just about died laughing thanks to the movie. I quickly discovered that she was easy to be around, and even though I often felt tongue-tied around girls, I talked easily with Linda.

We continued to date, and before we kissed for the first time, I knew I wanted to marry her. However, she had signed her first contract to teach in California for the next school year, so our courtship continued as we corresponded by letter.

During Christmas break, I went down to see her at Balboa Island where she lived. I convinced her to teach in St. Anthony for the following school year, and she agreed. The next summer she lived with her Aunt Vera and Uncle Cy, Sally's parents and friends of our family, to be closer to me.

During that summer, while we were sitting in the car, I was toying with the ring she was wearing. I slid it off her finger and slipped on a diamond ring. Eventually she noticed. To my great joy, she was ecstatic and accepted my silent proposal for marriage. The biggest decision we would ever make had just been made!

Our marriage in the Idaho Falls LDS Temple was November 16, 1962. While we were kneeling across the altar, before she was asked if she would take me to be her husband, tears began running down her cheeks. I wondered if she was having second thoughts, or if those tears were due to a spiritual experience that we both were having.

I was relieved to know it was the latter. Over time, I've later learned that she becomes emotional easily, especially when she is having one of those special experiences that touches her deeply. Our wedding ceremony was all of that and more, as we committed to take each other as husband and wife for time and all eternity.

After the marriage ceremony, we went to Scotty's Drive Inn, got 35-cent hamburgers, and started on our honeymoon. (We had our reception when we returned a week later.) We drove to Dillon, Montana, where we spent our first night together.

The bride and groom, Linda and Clyde

Now this may sound really strange to many, but we had previously discussed what would happen on our wedding day. We knew that day would be the first day of the rest of our lives and that we would be setting a pattern. We considered our relationship to be not only physical, but also spiritual and sacred. We had decided to kneel by our bed each night in prayer, a practice that I had become accustomed to on my mission. We thanked the Lord for each other, for our marriage that day, and asked that it be sanctified, and prayed for continued guidance. We have continued that practice to this day.

Since our marriage we have always slept close together. One night before drifting off to sleep we were having our pillow talk about our kids, our relationship, etc. While I was just drifting off, I noticed that tears started to fall down Linda's cheek onto mine.

I asked, "What's wrong?"

She said, "Nothing, I was just thinking how much I love you."

That is the kind of love we have for each other. Like our folks before us, we have always been a little reserved about how we express our love in front of others. I suppose many people think of us as all business. But many times, even in public, we slip each other our little secret, subtle signs: a brief touch, or a whisper that reminds us of our love for each other.

The summer after our marriage, Linda and I began to work for Mike and Frances Wilson in West Yellowstone at Three Bear Lodge for the season. But what began as temporary shifted into a more permanent plan, and over the course of a couple years we transitioned from farm life and teaching school to this new frontier of making a livelihood for ourselves in West Yellowstone. Little did we know all that was ahead for us.

All of our children, with the exception of Rochelle, were born while living in West Yellowstone.

Our oldest, Rochelle, was born May 12, 1965, at the hospital in Pocatello, Idaho, while I was attending Idaho State University.

After Rochelle's birth, we thought it would be nice to have another child fairly soon so that she would have a playmate. However, several months into the next pregnancy, complications set in and Linda began to miscarry. Beulah, my mother-in-law, was working for us in the laundry at Three Bear Lodge and did not know yet that Linda was expecting. (We didn't use the word pregnant much then, it was kind of embarrassing to say.) I ran out and told her first, that Linda was expecting and second, that she was having a miscarriage. She took over the lodge so we could go quickly to the hospital.

I grabbed some towels and rushed Linda to St. Anthony, to the hospital that was 70 miles away. She had lost a lot of blood, so the staff rushed someone to Rexburg to get her blood for a transfusion. It was rather frightening, and I was pretty worried, wondering if everything would be okay. I remember watching her while she was sedated and thinking how beautiful she was and how much I loved her. There she was, looking almost lifeless having lost the baby and a lot of blood.

Gradually, she opened her eyes and not yet seeing me asked, "Is Clyde all right?"

That was typical of her.

It was for her they had rushed to Rexburg to get blood. It was she who had just had a jolting miscarriage and whose life I was concerned about.

Yet, the first words out of her mouth were, "Is Clyde all right?"

My love and appreciation for her increased that day and has continued to increase since that time so many years ago. How blessed I am to have a companion like that.

Our next daughter, Stephanie, was born March 8, 1969, in the St. Anthony, Idaho Hospital. When Linda was close to delivery, I took her down to her mother's house in St. Anthony with the plan of getting up early the next morning, driving back to West Yellowstone, and opening Three Bear Lodge for the March Snowmobile Races. The motel was not winterized, and I needed to get the heat and the water turned on and ready for our incoming reservations. I got up and was ready to walk out the door about 8:00 a.m. when Linda started to have pains. Within an hour, I stood at my place at the head of the delivery bed and watched another miracle happen. Everything went normal. Within a few hours our cute little dark-haired, brown-eyed daughter arrived. I hoped for a little girl who would be as beautiful as her mother and I was not disappointed.

In the years that followed our sons Michael Clyde, Steven Brook, and Douglas Norman joined our family. Like my angel mother, Linda was an angel mother to our children.

In the years that followed, our home became a gathering place for our kids and their friends. With the forest as our backyard and the vacant railroad property as our front yard, there was plenty of space for the kids to play. They always had things to do. Plus, inside the house the family room was a natural hangout for the kids with Linda always making these little friends feel welcome. As they grew older, she always kept track of our kids' friends and expressed an interest in what they were doing.

Years later, when the kids' college friends came to visit, Linda always made these new friends feel at home. She would visit with them and had a knack of establishing a relationship that seemed to impact their lives. In later years, when she would see them, instead of just saying, "Hello," she would always ask how they were doing and was genuinely interested in their lives. There are many instances when those friends have told our kids how much they admired Linda and what a great person she is. In 2013, our sons' friend passed away. As Doug and Brook scrolled through their friend's Facebook page, they found a post where this friend had shared the most inspirational people in his life. There were just five listed: his parents, his grandparents on his mother's side and Linda Seely.

Linda is very caring and loving. She is kind and thoughtful and affectionately pushes me to be the same. I feel alone and intimidated when she is not there. We fit together as a team; she handles the social affairs while I normally handle the issues at hand and feel more comfortable in those settings. There are certain things that my kids want to talk with me about, but other times, they specifically want to talk to their mother.

We have now been married over 50 years. She has been the mainstay of my life. She has been the mother of our five children and my love. She has been my encouragement, my confidant, and the rudder that holds my boat steady. She is the litmus test that helps me decide whether I should embark on some wild endeavor. When it comes to social events and visiting in casual situations, I am the one that is in her shadow. Like my dad, I am not very comfortable in social situations. But like her mother, Linda is always outgoing and friendly. It was said of Robert Kennedy that he was not good at small talk, and I can relate to that. I am often more comfortable when she is with me in public. She visits with people openly and freely and can always find things to talk about and nice things to say.

She truly is "the wind beneath my wings."

Pebble 9: Our Family and Balancing Priorities

*Things which matter most must never be at the
mercy of things which matter least.*

~Johann Wolfgang von Goethe

After our marriage in 1962, our early life together was really quite
simple. I had just graduated with a provisional teaching certificate
from Ricks College (now known as Brigham Young University–
Idaho), and during the evening of our wedding reception, I was
offered the chance to finish out the second half of the school year
teaching in Ashton, Idaho.

The following year, I taught in Parker, Idaho, under my
brother Dean who was the principal. To put the timing in perspective, I was in Parker, standing at the blackboard in front of my class
when we heard that President Kennedy had been shot.

After teaching at Parker on a provisional teaching degree
for $3,300 per year, we decided it was time for me to finish my
four-year teaching degree at Idaho State University. It was here, in
Pocatello, Idaho, that we started our family. With the birth of our
first daughter, one special pebble was dropped into our pool. Four
other special pebbles would soon follow, with each one bringing
enormous amounts of joy and life-changing experiences.

As evidence of how fast life has slipped by since our marriage, let me quote from what is now, an old Christmas card that I just recently found. It was a card from me to Linda.

> Dear Mum:
>
> This is our twenty-sixth Christmas together. These have been exciting years as we first spent them selfishly all alone. Later we shared them with our #1 daughter, then #2. Perhaps there should have been #3 but that was not meant to be.
>
> We burst into the boy business 15 years ago this very morning as we plowed through the deep snow for 70 miles. Santa's sleigh would have been more appropriate for our #3. Then we shared these special days together with #4 and then #5. Though we sometimes don't act like we appreciate you for all you do for us, we really do love you for it.
>
> There is no one in the world I would rather spend eternity with. I don't believe it is possible for one to love another more than I love you.
>
> Dad

Let me fill in the names of numbers 1–5, those to whom we have been privileged to become their parents. The names corresponding to the numbers on that card are as follows: Rochelle was born on May 12, 1965, Stephanie was born on March 8, 1969, Michael Clyde on Dec 25, 1973, Steven Brook on March 21, 1975, and Douglas Norman on May 16, 1977.

Little family in front of Grandma Beulah's house in St. Anthony

As noted, Rochelle was born in Pocatello where we lived close to a hospital.
All the rest or our children were born in the hospital in St. Anthony, Idaho. But we lived in West Yellowstone, Montana.
With the adrenaline flowing, when it was time for Linda to deliver, it was a very fast 74 mile ride south from our home to the hospital.

Each time we learned Linda was expecting, our hearts were full of joy and anticipation as we waited nine months to find out the gender. (Back then there was no such thing as knowing ahead with an ultrasound.) This was only the first of many questions. Through the years, we asked "How will they do in their schooling" followed by "Will they be happy, and ultimately, be successful in building a life of their own?" We shared joys in their accomplishments and empathized with them when their little tears flowed. Overall, the experiences and emotions of raising five children are legion.

I suppose parents never quite feel up to the challenge and responsibility of raising kids of their own. Sometimes we try to spare them the tough things we went through as kids, when many of those tough things are what made us who we are. We think we should have the wisdom of Solomon, when in reality we are just learning too, sometimes with one mistake at a time as we go along. Perhaps a smidgeon of what I mean can be summed up in a few experiences I had with my kids; that of being a doting father over my two girls, and as you will see some unusual rescues and good times with my boys.

Our first daughter, Rochelle, gave us a scare when she was born. The doctor had a hard time getting her to take her first breath. She was later diagnosed with asthma and plagued with it for the rest of her life. Her entire life, we tried to get it under control. Still Rochelle was a vivacious girl with long blonde hair and had a giggle and personality that made others feel good just by being around her. All during high school, she was a cheerleader and a magnet to the boys, which meant I guarded over her like a leery father. We had many daddy-daughter talks, and I kept an eye on the clock when she was out at night.

Stephanie was the only brown-haired kid in the family. Often Rochelle would tease Stephanie and say she was adopted because she stood out among the kids. However, her hair color matched Linda's, and like her mother, she was a real knock out, although Stephanie was quite oblivious to that fact. She had a number of close girlfriends that she palled around with much of the time. I was glad for that. We were glad when after hanging out with a want-to-be boyfriend, she would come up and plop down on our bed and tell us all about where they had been, what they had been up to, etc. For some reason, I never felt the urgency for those daddy-daughter talks with Stephanie. Though in retrospect, I wish I would have had them anyway just for bonding purposes. Still, the urgency wasn't there because she was a very good kid, as were all of our kids.

Next in line was Mike, who taught me a valuable lesson. One Sunday morning when I was branch president in our little church, Mike, then about 8 years old said, "Dad I need to talk to you." I told him we would get together right after church, and meanwhile I wondered what was on his mind that he needed to talk to me about.

So after dinner we went back into my office, sat down, and I asked him what he wanted to talk about. He shocked me by saying, "I don't know Dad, you hold the priesthood; you decide." Well, turns out, he wanted to talk to me all right, not about any great problem; he just wanted to talk to me. He wanted to have a meeting with me like I did with other people, so we talked about what he had learned in church that day, and how he was doing in school, and a handful of other things.

My second son, Brook, also taught me a lesson about my time and meetings, of which I certainly held more than a few. When Brook was seven, Linda was bringing the kids back from skiing at Big Sky, and Brook said, "It would be neat to have a dad that could do things with art, like make an elephant like the one Aunt Donna has."

Linda asked, "Do you think that kind of dad would be neater than your dad?"

He looked at her with a cute smile and said, "No. The only thing I don't like about my dad is all those meetings. I hate those meetings he has to go to." Then he added, "Like when he pushes us on the swing, he only pushes us about twice and then he has to go to a meeting." Sometimes we learn great lessons from our kids. Brook's words taught me a lesson and helped me examine my role as a father and, I might add, also as a husband.

Doug was the only one to be born when we were living in our new home. He was our fifth and biggest child, weighing in at 8 lb. 3 oz. He was an unexpected surprise, as we hadn't really planned on another baby. As a result, everybody made a fuss over him, and of course, accused us of spoiling him. Rochelle dubbed the soft little baby roll around his middle "pizza dough." He was always easy to take care of and good natured.

In school, Doug was quiet and unassuming, yet his teachers said that even though he didn't raise his hand at every question, he always knew the answer. We enjoyed him so much, especially as he was the last one to leave the nest. This was a similarity I shared with him, as I too was the baby of my family. During those formative years, I always felt I had a little advantage over my siblings because after they left home, it was just me with my parents. And, since I was the last one to live with my folks when they were getting older, I felt a deep responsibility for them.

As I mentioned, Brook's spontaneous, naïve, yet candid, comment about my meetings, hit a nerve inside me and caused me pause. The continual tug of war on my time between business, family, church, and community meetings, has always been a challenge. To this day, I am not sure I have always sufficiently balanced my one-on-one time with my kids and other 'just' things. But in the end, even though these meetings and other responsibilities took a toll, they also offered a downpour of rewards too.

For instance, I am reminded of one memorable example when I was in the Stake Presidency, a leadership position that covered a large region within my Church. This particular Sunday, I got up at 5:00 a.m., left at 6:00 a.m. to drive the sixty-mile drive to Ashton, and attended my first meeting at 7:00 a.m. After this, I visited two separate congregations and spoke in their meetings. Then I drove the 57 miles home. It was a long and draining day, spiritually and emotionally, and I felt tired and physically exhausted. On top of everything, I had been fasting on this particular Sunday and returned home tired and hungry.

I can still remember and, in fact, feel what happened as I came home to Linda and the kids. Linda was standing in the kitchen. I didn't say anything, just went over to her and gave her a big hug. As

I squeezed her tightly, I could feel her strength come into my body. Finally I started to let go and she kept holding on and said, "Wait a minute, I'm not through with you yet." Soon, our three little boys arrived at the scene and aimed to separate our hug. They pushed between our legs and said, "Break it up. Break it up."

I chased them all up to our bed, threw them on it, and began to wrestle them. They were all laughing and I was saying, "I'll teach you guys to try and break us up."

Mike started calling out "dog pile, dog pile," and sure enough our little schnauzer dog jumped in the middle of us all, barking like crazy. For some reason, I was no longer tired. And I felt like I could do it all again. There were many rewarding experiences like that.

***

In the moment of our trials, life can seem a little overwhelming, but sometimes in retrospect those trials turn into some of our fondest memories.

For us, whether it was having to get up in the middle of the night and drive my loader to pull out multiple 4 X 4s driven by my boys and their friends from being stuck in mud bogs, or helping rescue my stranded jeep from nearly tipping over on the side of a mountain, we survived it all.

At such times, rather than lose my cool, I remember when Dad and Mother were gone and my friends and I sloughed school and took the truck to go goose hunting in Island Park. Well, that was the plan anyway.

As I was driving around a bend on the highway, I took my eyes off the road. In that split second, the truck left the highway, crashed through a farmer's fence, and stopped only after the front wheels were torn of and left in a ditch. I remember how nervous I was when I tried to explain to my dad why I skipped school and wrecked the truck. I made a meager attempt, and I will never forget

Dad thoughtfully saying, "Well Clyde, if it bent the frame, we will have to buy a new truck." Even though we couldn't afford, it that is what we did.

I don't remember that Dad and I ever laughed about my blunder. But my boys, their friends, and I, have had some good laughs due to their teenage escapades that went awry.

***

With all that I have had to balance, between my family, business, and community responsibilities, perhaps I asked my kids to be mature beyond their years and understanding. Maybe there is a parallel between Dad and me, as a boy, and me, as a dad, with my kids. I never really learned to fish, because the cows needed to be milked, the water had to be turned, the hay had to be baled and hauled, and so much more.

Our kids quite often comment on how hard they worked when they were little. We started them off by sweeping under the mats in front of each of the motel doors. Then they stripped and replaced linens in the rooms. Eventually, they graduated to bussing tables in the restaurant and from there to waiting tables. The boys also became snowmobile gassers (and would ride them around enough to make sure they could do some cool tricks on the way to the pumps).

But with all this hard work, there also came some rewards.

In 1979, when Stephanie was just 10 years old, we took her and Rochelle to Spain to see Linda's cousin Russell, and to Switzerland and Germany to see my cousin Connie. My daughters didn't handle the European food very well, but once they saw a McDonalds in Zurich all was well. To this day, Stephanie still remembers that trip and the fun she had bonding with her 2nd cousins in Europe.

Many people from Utah and Idaho buy second homes on Hebgen Lake for their summer retreats. We were fortunate to have this lake in our backyard. I remember with fondness the years we took our boat out, during that magical time in the evening when the water was like glass. The boat cut through the water like a knife, leaving a ripple wake behind. Then we added fifty-foot ropes and pulled a couple of our boys or their friends on a variety of water toys. Their favorites were the body boards they brought from Maui. The boys would lay flat on their stomachs, and while going 30 miles per hour with just 2 inches of foam between them and the water, they would laugh and jump over the boat's wake.

But long before our Hebgen Lake memories, we became hooked on what would become our real annual vacation in Maui, Hawaii. It all began when we took our five little stair-step children and bought a timeshare at Maui Hills. We left our long cold winters in the snow to go for two weeks and enjoy the ocean in this tropical paradise by snorkeling, body boarding, and whale watching.

But first, the main course of the morning was to build sand-castles. These started out small with little plastic tools but grew as our kids and grandkids grew until we resorted to an irrigation shovel and really got into it, big time. Our prize was a replica of my memory of Chichen Itza. Such creations have grown in size to be about chest high.

When Linda and I were first married and trying to get a start in life, I asked her Uncle Clarence if he would help fund the purchase of some cattle. He consented and then said. "Clyde, you are sitting in the golden chair of opportunity." Now, many years later, our children and grandchildren sit in a similar chair of opportunity. How proud Linda and I are of our kids. All of them have attended college and are searching out their own opportunities to make the most of their lives.

The continual tug of war on my time remains one of my challenges. First with Linda, she has been very considerate of the time spent elsewhere when she deserved to have more time together. I am trying to play catch up there. Linda and I have tried to compress all the family responsibilities, work, church, and community meetings into one lifetime. That is not easy to do but I guess we haven't done too badly. We are proud of all of our kids. They are wonderful people, and as Linda always says, "It's not only what is on the outside, but what is on the inside that really counts."

We have shared some very special times, but among all the memories, the ones I cherish most are the times we could all return to the place we called home to our little safe haven, and enjoy those simple moments that will long be remembered and treasured.

Pebble 10: The Houses That Became Our Homes

"The most important of the Lord's work you will ever do will be within the walls of your own homes."

~Harold B. Lee

When Linda and I came to live in West Yellowstone we lived in a one-bedroom apartment with a large living room, a warm fireplace, and a front corner window that looked down on Yellowstone Avenue. This was the place where the Wilsons lived when I worked for them my first year, and Linda and I loved the place. Though it was only an apartment, it became a home to us.

Living on site at the lodge, it was convenient to run upstairs to get a sandwich for lunch. But it seemed like it never failed, when I would go upstairs to eat dinner, the bell in the lobby would ding so I would have to run back downstairs (two at a time) to rent a room or help a guest. Linda and I joked that on slow nights, in order to get a customer, all we had to do was go upstairs and eat.

We got along fine in our small apartment until the children started coming along, and then the one bedroom was not sufficient. In time, we used an adjoining motel room as our bedroom and then built on an extra bedroom. We brought Rochelle, Stephanie, and Mike home to that small apartment. But eventually even the additional space was not enough for our growing family.

On June 13, 1978, after 10 years in our first home, we bought some property from Mike Wilson to build our new home. It was on the edge of town, about three blocks from the lodge, right next to the railroad car. In fact, we moved into the railroad car while our new house was being built next door.

It was fun living in the railroad car. Other than Mike and Frances Wilson, who had also lived in the railroad car, very few people knew how elaborate it was on the inside. Linda and I had our bed in the observation room and all the kids had staterooms of their own. There was a large living room with mostly glass walls and the forest was our backyard. It was wonderful.

Through the construction, I acted as the general contractor and hired the building team. We had some contractor friends, Nash and Mitchell, frame the house and other subcontractors do the electrical and plumbing. Then I reserved the finish work for myself.

Once our home was complete, it quickly became a place for guests. It seemed that there were always young friends over to visit or stay the night. After all, we had the railroad tracks with all the train money (round pieces of metal left from the trains hauling timber) as our front yard and a fort in the forest, as our backyard. As our family grew, so did the numbers for dinner. For holidays, our house would swell with as many as fifty-four people.

Some of the most cherished memories made were around the special Thanksgiving traditions that filled our home. I'll try to retell two.

The first was around Mother's special stuffing (dressing) that I grew up helping her with when I was a boy. After filling the turkey with dressing that was moist and sticky, which I never really liked, she made what we called "dry dressing" in her large steamer. She would bake several plump loaves of golden brown bread and let them dry for three or four days.

After the bread was sufficiently dry, we would then break the bread into pieces and rub the pieces together shredding the crust and the rest into fine and slightly larger pieces. Mother, and later Linda and I, would then chop up onions, a tear-wrenching experience, and sauté these in butter with some diced celery. This would be stirred into the large mound of shredded bread crumbs with sage and salt and pepper added to just the right taste. And I was always the official taster.

Then about an inch of water was put in the bottom pan of Mother's steamer. The dressing was placed in the top pan with a lid on top of that. From there, the water in the bottom gave off steam that percolated through the side holes in the top pan and into the dressing in the pan above. The final result was our favorite item on the Thanksgiving table. Always Mother's dressing along with the turkey, gravy, and mashed potatoes was a taste to be remembered and looked forward to until the next year.

As far as I know Mother's dry dressing is still unique compared to the common dressing of the day, which is usually found in a box on the grocery store shelf. Fortunately for our first Thanksgiving in our new home in West Yellowstone, Mother brought along her steamer and thus began this Thanksgiving tradition. Of course, after all these years, Linda's dressing, which is still made in Mother's old gray porcelain steamer, remains the hit of the day.

The other tradition that began that first Thanksgiving involved SkiDoo snowmobiles and an after-dinner ride. In the early years, we rented the equipment, but later, we would eventually get into the snowmobile rental business where we provided clothing and snowmobiles for all. But that first year it was quite an undertaking to get all the little kids and adults outfitted in the right sized clothing and assigned to snowmobiles. On that ride, I felt like a mother hen as I guided about thirty snowmobiles with drivers of all ages.

Through the years that followed, we always started out for Two Top Mountain but seldom made it, as there were always a few mishaps with the teenagers and my two older slowpoke sisters. We also let the sun determine how far we went, since it got cold quickly when the sun went down. Plus once the call of turkey leftovers and homemade pies began to beckon, we heeded the call and turned back for home. Each year, all the relatives looked forward to coming. And upon returning home, none of their friends could top the stories shared about our family's Thanksgiving in Yellowstone.

But over the years, our extended families expanded, and we had to share their time with other sides of families. At the same time, we were also growing out of our house for such large gatherings and our kids were establishing Thanksgiving traditions of their own. Now our family gatherings have shrunk back to about where they were forty-plus years ago.

Overall, during the 27 years we lived there, a lot of fond memories were made. And then it was time for a change. Most of my life, I have wanted to live in a log house, and after purchasing Parade Rest Guest Ranch 10 miles north of town, we decided it was time to build that dream.

I drew out several plans and then made little cardboard mockups so Linda could visualize how it would look. We finally decided on a plan we both liked and Blair Anderson, a master craftsman who built beautiful log homes, had a draftsman draw it up accordingly.

From that point on, the project took three years to complete.

During the construction phase, Blair found the biggest logs he could, some 25 inches in diameter, and pre-built the house on his Highway 20 property. After it was built, the logs were marked, loaded onto semis, and restacked in its final location at the west end of the ranch.

Seely log home overlooking Hebgen Lake and incredible views

I selected and laid the tile in the bathrooms. I also utilized local stone from Graying Creek for the fireplace, and I hauled up huge lava rocks from my farm in St. Anthony for supports for the large pillars and landscaping. Then Blair's crew did the finish work and we moved in during summer 2005.

Some of the things we love about this home are the spectacular view of Hebgen Lake and the surrounding hillside from every window in the house. We also had a cupola built above the roof line so we had a 360 degrees view where we watch the animals that sometimes frequent the grounds.

The children we raised in the West Yellowstone home are now bringing their own kids of similar sizes. Here we have sufficient room for all our grandkids to come and stay with us, and we are building new memories in the log house while still finding ourselves surrounded in the front, back, and side yards by forest lands. **29**

Similar to the house in town, the log house on the ranch has become like a pool where all of us drop our own pebbles— pebbles that have turned this house into a home. This is a place of safety, a refuge from the cares of the world, a place where the

See **29** on the West Yellowstone Map Pages 142-143

little day-by-day memories of childhood and family life are being cherished for years to come.

Much of the legacy of the Seelys began within the walls of these three homes, each one on the doorstep of Yellowstone.

Pebble 11: Loss of Our Daughter, Rochelle

Somehow, across each stretching mile, I feel your touch and see your smile. As though your thoughts had found a way, to reach me with your voice today.

~Author Unknown

It was on August 20, 1994, that we lost our oldest daughter Rochelle. She was just 29 and died as a result of an acute asthma attack. In memory of Rochelle, I will start with her birth and tell a little about the pebble she dropped in the pool of our lives and the lives of others.

Linda and I were living in a little basement apartment in Pocatello, Idaho. I was about to graduate from Idaho State University with my BS degree in education and Linda was taking some graduate classes. Early in the school year, I would drop Linda off at class, while she was still suffering from morning sickness, and we both hoped she would make it through. I can still picture her dressed in a black and white frock as she walked into her school.

I also remember the little kicks and movements when I placed my hand over Linda's stomach as our baby grew. Then, as Linda neared the last stages of pregnancy, she went to see Dr. Wight. He said she was about a week away from labor.

However, that night she became uncomfortable and started having repeated pains. Something was obviously happening. We called the doctor for confirmation. He told us to get her admitted into the hospital and he would come when she was ready. A little after midnight, we were in the delivery room. I was standing at the head of the delivery bed and the doctor was at the action end. I had joked with Linda before by saying, "I don't know why we have to pay for a doctor. I've delivered many lambs, and you've even helped me deliver calves. It can't be much different than that!"

Of course, these jokes were all in good humor. For the reality was, this situation was much more serious than delivering farm animals. We were about to have a little baby, a baby we had been blessed to help create and who was coming to us straight from the presence of God.

The doctor told me I could stand at the head of the bed, but if I got woozy and was going to pass out, I was on my own. A mirror was propitiously placed so Linda and I could see what was happening. The nurse held her hand on Linda's stomach and at the right time said, "Push," and Linda obliged.

Yet each push was very painful, and as I held her hands in mine, she pushed her fingernails into the palms of my hands. I suppose this was a clever way for her to make sure I also felt part of the joy of this whole experience. It was not an easy birth. In fact, when the little head was in view, the doctor took a large set of forceps to help pull, which would leave temporary facial marks. But finally our baby was out!

I watched the umbilical cord be cut, and then we saw that it was a little girl. In that short moment, we rejoiced while our little baby was on her own, and where she should have begun breathing. In an eerie silence, I waited for the typical cry of the newborn, but nothing happened; there was no breath. The doctor picked her up by the feet and smacked her on the bum. He began rubbing her cheeks hard. It seemed the first breath was far too long in coming.

However, the first breath eventually came into her lungs and she began the long-awaited cry. We were so relieved.

Little Rochelle was born about 2:00 a.m. on May 12, 1965. Of course she was the most beautiful baby in the delivery room, little bruised face and all. And although I was beyond delighted, unfortunately, it also was a very short night for me, as I had to be at school in a few hours.

A few weeks later, we returned to Three Bear Lodge for the summer. I had one more year before graduation, but we were going to be short financially, so Mike and Frances helped us out with a loan. We worked the entire summer and then returned to school in the fall.

Linda got a job teaching for a school in Blackfoot, and I commuted to Pocatello. For the weekdays, we would drop Rochelle off at the babysitter's home, which worked out very well. However, during the first eighteen months of Rochelle's life, we noticed she got sick a lot. Then, finally, a doctor determined she had asthma.

As she grew older, Rochelle spent a lot of time in the hospital, which caused her to miss a lot of school. One year she was in the hospital four different times. I believe it is her fourth grade picture that shows how thin and weak she looked. Nights were especially bad for her. I remember when we traveled sometimes we put her inside a shower, as the steam would often help. Other times we just drove around with her mother holding her, since that also seemed to help, and eventually Rochelle's wheezing and whimpering would cease.

During her teenage years, when she had an attack, I found two sensitive pressure points by her shoulder blades and would push hard on them with both thumbs. If I could find that particular sweet spot it would sometimes ease the attack. I don't know if the pressure hurt her so bad that it deflected her attention off her breathing problems, or if it actually triggered something inside. All I know is that sometimes it helped her breath easier again.

Then, somewhere along those teenage years, we finally found an asthma specialist who really seemed to know what to do to help. He indicated that he thought Rochelle would be able to live a long life by being cognizant of her medications and physical limitations. Despite all of her asthma problems, Rochelle always maintained a cheerful personality. She was not one to complain, and she managed to stay very active. She was a cheerleader in high school all four years, and the physical exertion quite often caused her to wheeze. In those cases, she grabbed her inhaler, took a quick puff, and got back onto the floor.

When Rochelle became a waitress at Three Bear Restaurant, she had the same asthma problem. During those years, smoking was still allowed in the restaurant, and the smoke was hard on her. When no one was watching, she pulled out her inhaler, took a quick puff, and then returned quickly back to her tasks. At the time of her death, she was the main waitress, and we had hopes of promoting her to the Front End Manager. She would have done an excellent job.

Rochelle laughed easily and always exuded happiness. She was a cute, little, vivacious, fun girl to be around. As she grew older, this proved especially true with the boys. They wanted to be around Rochelle, which caused Linda and me some worry and led me to a fair share of those little father-daughter talks. Fortunately, Rochelle eventually fell in love with her best friend, Kevin Burns, and they later married.

Kevin was on the police force and was an avid hunter. They loved to go hunting together, sometimes scoping out the area before the season began. Since Rochelle could not always exert herself and keep up with Kevin at the same time, she sometimes sat and waited for him in the pickup. She would say, she "sometimes scoped him out while he was scoping out the game area." Rochelle and Kevin were happily married for five years. They had an enviable relationship.

Though we were anxious for them to bring little grandchildren into our home, it was not to be. Rochelle had another condition that did not allow her to have children. This was disappointing to them and to others who wanted to see this union carried on into future generations. In spite of this, she seemed to have settled down into a rather tolerable lifestyle.

Rochelle and Kevin lived in a small log house we purchased from Iris McNabb in 1989. We remodeled the cabin, which also had a large glassed-in living room that bordered the forest. Their life seemed to be picture perfect. Kevin was really good at police work, and Rochelle was fitting into her responsibilities at Three Bear Restaurant. **25**

In the summer of 1994 as we were building the Holiday Inn (See Pebble 19), I remember a moment as clearly as if it were today. I was looking down through an unfinished third-floor window to see the sidewalk below. Reminiscent of the past, it looked like my little daughters were pushing a baby stroller with a little doll in it. But in reality it was my grown daughters, Rochelle and her younger sister, Stephanie. They were adults now and the little doll was actually Stephanie's baby daughter, our first granddaughter, Shelby. They were both pushing the stroller and giggling as they went along, unaware of whom was watching from above. Rochelle was a perfect aunt; she was so happy for Stephanie.

But soon after that priceless moment, our lives would change forever. On the fateful night of August 20, 1994, Rochelle and Kevin were staying with his folks while they attended the Billings Fair. Linda and I had just gone to bed at 11:30 when the phone rang. On the other end of the phone was Kevin's mother, Rose Mary. She told us that Rochelle had just had an acute asthma attack and that the ambulance was taking her to the Billings Hospital. She said it was a really bad attack, and they didn't know if she would make it.

See **25** on the West Yellowstone Map Pages 142-143

The life of my daughter, which the asthma doctor from our past had indicated would go on for a long time, was now threatened, and we began preparing for the inevitable. We called our friend R. J. from Yellowstone Aviation and asked if we could charter his plane to take us to Billings. Within 20 minutes, we were at the airport and taking off.

In the meantime, we called Kevin. He was sobbing and said, "Clyde, I have lost my best buddy, I have lost my best buddy, I have lost her." Our worst fears were confirmed; Rochelle had not made it.

It was a long, dark flight to Billings. Doug, our sixteen-year old son, sat in the front seat while Linda and I sat huddled together as we tried to understand what had just happened. All our hopes and aspirations for Rochelle were now gone, just suddenly wiped out.

Kevin's mother met the three of us at the airport. We rushed to the hospital and into the room where Rochelle was lying on a table. The long blond hair and the clothes she wore were all still there, but her happy vivacious spirit was not.

We spent some time alone with her, but the realization that we would never see her happy face again set in. It was obvious that nothing we could do could reverse what had just happened. We left with holes in our hearts and wondered how we could possibly cope with this loss.

We spent time with Kevin, who looked so alone. I have always known that we grieve for the loss of an individual only to the extent we have loved them. The grief we shared in that moment with Kevin was incalculable, as was our love. The remainder of the night was short. Kevin couldn't face going back to where he had lost his Rochelle, so he went with us to check into a motel.

What followed in the next few days was the sharing of the grief we felt, mixed with the necessity for arranging for the mortuary, casket, program, and funeral. It may seem inconsequential at this time to talk about the choice of the funeral program, but you will eventually understand. Gary Bidwell, owner of the St. Anthony funeral home, had just received a new program cover on which there was a picture of a deer among some tall trees. It seemed to be looking right at us. Since Kevin and Rochelle had spent so much time in the wilds watching deer and other animals, it seemed fitting that this should be the cover. Then the rest of the program was arranged, and it came time to place the topical phrase or thought-provoking statement on the back cover.

I had never written a poem before but felt prompted to reserve this space for myself so I could write something about the scope of her life. I sat down at the computer and the thoughts began to rush into my head, coming out in a rhyme that expressed a summation of her life.

To Rochelle
I have been honored over the years to speak at funerals galore,
But for some reason this one isn't the same as before.
Because of the person who we honor this day,
I just can't get the words out I wish to say.
So bear with me, my little daughter while I pen a tidbit or two
That only feebly expresses my love for you.
Just 29 years ago straight from heaven you came,
To brighten our lives, that would never be the same.
'Twas 3 in the morning when you first arrived,
After a scare and struggle you finally arrived,
With a prayer on our lips and a doctor's shake,
That first precious breath you finally did take.
With blond ponytails and a happy little smile,
You had special friends and would go the extra mile.
Then came your best friend Kevin, you married;
For the rest of your life with him you happily tarried.
While your first breath was so slow coming,
Your last was too quick to leave,
And we who love you are left here to grieve.
You would have us pick up the pieces and carry on,

And not look back just because you are gone.
We will do our best to follow your happy and positive ways,
Until we have our reunion again one of these days.
This last thing you must always remember,
We love you with all our hearts and will forever.
Dad

The day of the funeral came. On the front page of the West Yellowstone News was a picture of the town flag flying at half-mast, which I suppose was partly because Kevin was on the police force and also because the town wanted to honor the one we all loved.

Cover of Rochelle's funeral program

The funeral was a wonderful time of healing, with so many nice things said about Rochelle. Many friends, from near and far, came to pay their respects to her and lend support to our family in this time of loss and sorrow.

Years later, Rochelle's friend Libby shared her own experience with us that mirrored the comfort offered to us. After listening to Libby, and while I was stuck in a melancholy mood, I wrote a piece titled Dear Deer that recaptured the details, the service, and the events that all seemed to carry a special message for us.

August 2001

DEAR DEER

Seven years have come and gone since you left us. Days turned into weeks and weeks have turned into years. How many times have we thought of you? How many times have others told us they had been thinking of you? How many times have others told us how they miss you and what an influence for good you were in their lives? Too many times to tell. Too many times to record. . . .

On the day of the funeral, it was said that the church had the largest crowd ever assembled in attendance. The service was beautiful. Many attended the graveside service as the grave was dedicated. While we were waiting for that part to begin, I looked across the pole fence. Standing there, as though he had appeared from nowhere, was a young buck deer. Those of us who had the funeral program in our hands looked at the picture on the front, then at the deer, and back again. *Ironic*, we all thought.

The deer watched us, walked around slowly, and nibbled on a blade of grass or two. Then he did what I had never seen a young buck deer do: he sat down on his rump with his front legs still fully extended.

Eventually, he stood up again.

We proceeded with dedicating the grave and the attention of the crowd was diverted to that sanctifying process. When we looked again, the deer was gone. No one saw him come. No one saw him go.

Kevin said as he watched the deer at the cemetery, he had a strange feeling that the deer was there as a sign and Rochelle's way of saying, "I'm all right Kev. I'm all right."

Soon after, when purchasing the headstone we decided that a deer should become etched on her headstone. 26

Years have passed by, and the deer once again returns to the forefront, back into our remembrance. A childhood friend of Rochelle's, Libby Baier, came to visit. She had been gone since high school. This was the first time she had seen us since Rochelle's passing, and she was not aware of the above incident with the deer. Her story was told to us for the first time as follows:

Libby came back into town the day after Rochelle's funeral. She was unaware of Rochelle's passing, and her dad, Harold, told her she better sit down. He then handed her the copy of the funeral program. Rochelle's death hit Libby extremely hard, and she ran out of the house and cried for a long time. The next morning, she was driving out to the cemetery and noticed a deer running alongside of the car in the trees. She was driving slowly, and the deer followed along for what seemed to be a long time. When she arrived at the cemetery, another deer was standing

See 26 on the West Yellowstone Map Pages 142-143

there. Later as she was riding the bus to Billings, she kept seeing deer at different locations.

Now, Libby is a Native American and told Linda of her people's belief that sometimes animals can represent a comfort coming from those who have departed. At least to her it seemed to be so. Libby told us of many heart-warming memories of Rochelle, but some are too close and precious to tell here.

It is not for us to always know or begin to understand the various ways in which comfort can come to those who are left to grieve. While there is nothing to say for certain that the deer involved was anything but a coincidence, we are certain of one thing, that Kevin, Libby, and the Seely family as a whole have been awed and have found comfort as we have looked at Rochelle's headstone with the deer embossed on it. We remember the happenings of those days that were so close to her passing. "God moves in a mysterious way, His wonders to perform" Our thanks go out to that dear deer that has added peace and comfort to the lives of those who have been touched by Rochelle.

Her Dad, Clyde Seely

Many letters and cards of sympathy gave us support during those difficult times and helped us know of others' concern for us.

A few days after Rochelle's funeral, Gordon B. Hinckley, President of The Church of Jesus Christ of Latter-day Saints, was visiting Ricks College. Knowing that President Hinckley wanted to go through Yellowstone on his way back to Salt Lake, President Bennion of Ricks College told President Hinckley of our daughter's death.

That night, President Hinckley stayed at Three Bear Lodge. The following morning, while he ate breakfast with his wife and assistant, Linda and I introduced ourselves. He said, "I understand you have just lost a daughter," and then he expressed his sympathy.

We visited briefly and expressed our appreciation for his life of service. On the way out, we instructed the hostess to buy their breakfasts. A few days later, we received a handwritten letter on the personal stationary of Gordon B. Hinckley.

The letter was dated September 2, 1994, addressed to Mr. and Mrs. Clyde Seely.

I will not quote the letter but he thanked us for our kindness and then wrote:

Thank you for all you did for us.

Our hearts reach out to you in sympathy over the loss of your beloved daughter. We pray that the Lord will assuage your grief and bring comfort to your aching hearts.

Sincerely your brother,
Gordon B. Hinckley

Eighteen years later, standing at the podium of the West Yellowstone High School graduation, I asked my tall, beautiful, dark-haired granddaughter Shelby to help in presenting the annual Rochelle Seely Burns Scholarship. This little doll of 18 years ago, who was being pushed in her stroller by her mother and Aunt Rochelle, now stood beside me in her cap and gown. I asked her to read the inscription on the plaque that had been written 17 years before, when we began giving the scholarship in honor of Rochelle. I have always read it, but this special time I thought it appropriate that Rochelle's niece read it; Rochelle would have been so proud. The inscription reads:

> Life itself is precious, cherish it. Life is a gift of God, give of yourself in return. Life is to be enjoyed, be happy. Life is to be productive, magnify your talents and make a difference. May you be successful in all you do and help others along the way.

~Clyde and Linda Seely

Losing a child is an experience that parents hope will never happen to them. But, no matter how much love there is, no matter how careful and protective parents might be, there are times when such happenings are simply left to a higher power. I may not yet be able to see the reasons why, especially through the earthly glasses that I wear, but I believe the time will come when through a different set of glasses, the plan of Deity will be made known to me in its fullness and I will understand how my life fits into God's eternal plan. It is then that I will understand why loved ones of mine were called home to the other side.

At the time of Rochelle's passing, someone gave to Linda and me a little statement: "Never put a question mark where the Lord puts a period." That thought-provoking statement is still attached to our refrigerator door. We have relayed this quote on to others, those who have also had to struggle with the question, "Why?"

For now, for me, it is enough to know that life continues and that we will see her again. The "Why?" can wait. Still, Rochelle's chapter remains a very influential part of our lives. Her pebble, dropped in our pool, will never stop its ripple affect.

Pebble 12: Seely's Bear Stories

Faith walks in, Fear walks out; Fear walks in, Faith walks out

~Author Unknown

Before bear-proof dumpsters were installed, bear problems in West Yellowstone were quite common. Here are some snippets of a few bear stories that I remember, followed by the most memorable of all.

One early morning when Linda and I were still leasing the Three Bear Lodge, a guest came in all excited and said, "You sure take your name literally. Early this morning I looked out my window and there were three bears just walking by the swimming pool."

Another time our cashier at the Econo Mart bent over to do some cleaning and thought a big dog had walked through the door. Upon looking again, she saw it was instead a black bear. We arrived on the scene in time to watch the police usher the bear back into the woods.

Then there was the bear that discovered a discarded restaurant container full of grease. He must have somehow stepped in the grease, because in the morning, originating from the garbage trailer behind the restaurant, there were greasy paw prints that led a trail through the parking lot.

One night, we awoke to a noise coming from our neighbor's house. We peeked out our bedroom window and there was a large bear standing on his hind legs pushing a discarded refrigerator back and forth. When he had no success there, he resorted to tipping over a garbage can and rummaging through the trash.

However, the most classic Seely bear story was written up in the local paper and an insurance journal. In late August 1986, a huge sow grizzly and her three roly-poly cubs became quite an attraction in West Yellowstone. At night, people would see them foraging for an easy meal of garbage. However, it was decided by the Fish and Game Department that someone would get hurt if the bears were not moved.

A big, round culvert-looking apparatus with a trap door was baited with some meat. Soon after, the mother was caught in this live trap. Next, it was hard to believe, but they also caught all three of the cubs in other live traps. Then, believing the little family was ready for separation prior to "denning up" for the winter, they transported the mother to one part of the park and the three cubs to another part.

About a week later, at 11:30 p.m., Buzz, our collie, and Shultz, our schnauzer, started barking at the door that leads into the garage. I got up and went down, still undressed, to see what the dogs were fussing about. I opened the door and saw a huge bear. It was close enough that I could have reached out and touched it. (Linda loves telling this next part of the story.) Of course, I was a little excited and controlling my vocal chords was the furthest thing from my mind. I half-way called out, "Linda, there is a bear out here." I hadn't heard my voice sound like that since I was a scared, pre-adolescent boy. From the upstairs bedroom, we watched the bear amble across the driveway and disappear.

The next day I had a dental appointment in Bozeman. Linda and I decided to take the boys with us and see a movie. But knowing we wouldn't be home until late, and that our daughter Rochelle would be gone on a date, our second daughter, Stephanie was concerned. She would be working that evening at the restaurant but didn't want to come home alone in case the bear came back.

I said, "Oh, Stephanie, that bear is not going to come in the house, don't worry about it. It may come back and try to get back into the garage where it found the dog food. But just close the doors and you'll be all right."

Well, as it turned out, I had misspoken. In spite of my assurance, when Stephanie came home from work around 11:00 p.m., she was still nervous, so she changed her clothes and left. Yet she returned shortly thereafter, a few minutes before we arrived at 11:30 p.m. She pushed the garage door opener and could not believe what she saw.

The garage was in shambles. Things were all over the floor and some sheet rock had been torn right off the wall. It looked like . . . well, it looked like a big bear had been trapped in the garage. Stephanie called her big sister, Rochelle, who came over with Kevin, her then boyfriend, and local policeman.

Linda, the boys, and I arrived shortly thereafter.

We couldn't figure it out. It was obvious the bear had been in there, but all the doors were closed. So . . . where was the bear? We opened the garage door leading into the house and out ran our two dogs. Neither could bark. They must have barked so much that they'd lost their voice. Then I noticed the door striker was lying on the second stair going to the basement. I said to Linda, "That bear is in the house."

Carefully, I tiptoed down the stairs to the laundry room. It was in shambles. The cactus was knocked out of the window. The clothes, drying on the rack, were all over the floor, but still no bear. The door into the family room was also closed. I cracked the door a little, didn't hear anything, opened it further, and went inside. The TV was on the floor, the drapes torn off the window, the furniture scattered around, and the door leading into the bedrooms and bath was also closed. Now we never closed that door, so I said to Linda, "That bear is in there and I'm not going in."

I retreated, got a flashlight, and carefully went around the perimeter of the house to look into the rooms I had not been in. I fully expected to see the bear caught and caged in one of those bedrooms. I shined my flashlight in Stephanie's bedroom, and, even though the bear had made a mess of the room, no bear was now in evidence. I slowly went around the corner of the house to check out Rochelle's bedroom while feeling a little inadequate, hunting a bear with a flashlight. The window was open, the window screen was lying on the grass, but there was no bear.

So I went back into the house to check it out more closely.

The bear had gone through the door leading into the hall, where the bedrooms were, and somehow closed it behind her.

Stephanie's bedroom wasn't too bad. Except that the bear had obviously gotten into her powder and powdered its nose, because there were nose marks on the mirror. We all guessed it was probably the first time she had seen herself and wanted a closer look.

There was also a bloody paw print on the bed. Later, we discovered that when the bear was tearing off the sheetrock in the garage, she must have thrown her paw sideways into a nail protruding through the stud, because we found blood on that nail.

Rochelle's bedroom door was also shut. The bear must have been really nervous by then. There was bear scat on the floor, pushed up in front of the door on my new carpet.

I went inside.

The room was in shambles. The bed and the nightstand were thrown across the room and one of the full sliding mirror closet doors was lying on the floor, broken. There was a large dirty bear paw mark on the wall.

The window had been left open a couple inches by Linda's mother, who had slept in the room the night before. Somehow, the bear must have swiped her paw sideways at the window, slid it open, and pushed the screen out. Outside, I found nose prints that had been smudged on the outside of the family room window as though she wanted to get back in.

No one knows how long the bear was in her temporary prison, but we know it was between 11:00 and 11:30 p.m.

Linda's mother, Beulah, had been sleeping in that room and fortunately had decided to go home to St. Anthony one night early, since we were going to be late from Bozeman. She was hard of hearing and would have been asleep by the time the bear came into the room. If she had slept there one more night, I shudder to think what would have happened with a seventy-year-old woman and a bear caught in the same small bedroom. Knowing my mother-in-law, I like to think the bear may have come out the loser.

The window the bear escaped through and the bed
Beulah would have been sleeping in

That last door into the bedroom was the fourth out of six doors the bear closed behind her. After each door was closed, the bear was confined into a yet smaller space.

As mentioned earlier, Kevin, the local policeman, was there, and he called the game warden. The next day a bear trap was placed outside our house. It was thought the bear would come back the third night. It didn't. Instead, ironically, the bear was later trapped at the game warden's house and identified.

It was Bear #50, the mother of the three cubs we had sighted about a week before. Since she had been separated from her cubs in West Yellowstone, she headed straight back to West Yellowstone. She was observed by the Park Service from the air on a dead run.

By the time she had come back to town, and I had almost touched her in my garage, she was nearly chest high, but had lost a lot of weight. After being trapped the second time, she was transported into the Teton National Park. We were told by the Fish and Game Department that she had one more set of cubs and was never seen again. The radio collar must have given out.

Our daughter Rochelle was waitressing at Three Bear Restaurant at the time. Since the bear made her escape through Rochelle's bedroom window, a newspaper did a write-up of the story with the caption "Who's Been Sleeping in My Bed?" It included a picture of Rochelle sitting on her bed with the grizzly paw print on the wall in the background. Another newspaper article referred to Goldilocks and the Three Bear Restaurant. Other newspaper articles also followed. We still have the colored photos of the damage done to the house when we shared that night with an unwelcome visitor.

Since that incident, bear sightings have become more rare. Though everyone likes to see bears, it is better if they are seen in the wild in their own habitat. Ultimately it saves many bears' lives and prevents human casualties. All of which comes back to the reason that the West Yellowstone Solid Waste District collects and transfers our garbage to a landfill 120 miles away (See Pebble 23).

Part Two: West Yellowstone

Pebble 13: Three Bear Lodge—
The Beginning of a Legacy

Don't grumble, don't bluster, don't sleep, don't shirk,
Don't think of your worries, just think of your work.
Then your worries will vanish, the work will be done;
For no man sees his shadow who faces the sun.

—Author Unknown

In 1958, when I was nineteen, I started working as a laundry boy at Three Bear Lodge. I stripped sheets from the beds, helped wash the linens, and hung them on the clotheslines to dry. Then I gathered them back up and ran them through the big mangle.

Frances showed me a lot, and although I knew how to make myself scarce whenever she got on one of her rampages, I soon learned how to please her. In fact, I could tell she liked me since she sometimes referred to me, jokingly of course, as a "rose among the thorns" (the "thorns" were the maids). Sometimes after work, she took the maids and me swimming in the Madison River. We dove off the old bridge, roasted hot dogs, and had a pretty good time.

While working at Three Bear Lodge, I slept in a little back room off of the office and was on call for nighttime emergencies since Mike and Frances had bought an old railroad car to stay in. The railroad car sat at the edge of the forest on a stone foundation. It was quiet and secluded, and they liked to get away from the motel for a restful night's sleep. Before they moved in, I helped get this special place ready for them, but little did they or I know the history of that railroad car, or that someday Linda and I would own it; it would become a prized possession to our family.

I also did a lot of the maintenance. Since Mike was my boss, I watched him closely. I learned from what he did, and then I jumped in and did what he wanted. I never left anything for him to do that I could do myself. Soon, he told me what needed to be done and then left me to do it.

He showed me how to install Formica and resurface the older furniture. Soon the room furnishings had a new look. He showed me how to work with Sheetrock, which I had never even seen before. More and more he was becoming confident in what he had entrusted me with. This became evident when I could walk through the lobby in the afternoon and find him having a nap in a chair.

One day, Mike came back from Idaho Falls with a big roll of carpet, a carpet stretcher, and a box of carpet tools. He said, "Here, I brought you something," and he told me I should re-carpet some of the rooms.

I told him I didn't know how to lay carpet.

He said, "You'll figure it out."

With no more instruction than that, I taught myself how to lay carpet.

I suppose I have laid hundreds of rooms of carpet since that time. Every once in a while he walked through a room I had just done, and I could tell he was pleased. This gave me more confidence to tackle more jobs. I still have and use the box of carpet tools.

Mike was a short, stocky guy with a balding head. He served on the Fall River Electric board of directors, was very active in the Lions Club International, and served as the president of the Chamber of Commerce. He was instrumental in helping obtain the railroad property that runs the entire length of town from east to west. He was a strict businessman with a soft heart. When there was no bank in town, he often cashed people's checks and also made personal loans to people.

On many occasions, I saw Mike retrieve the mail, open it with his pocketknife at the counter, get out the checkbook, and pay the bills. If he owed it, he paid it immediately. I learned a great lesson from him, and also from my dad, in that regard. I have always tried to follow their example. Though he was like my dad in that he was never one to vocally give praise, I could tell that Mike was pleased with what I did, and he cut me some slack when I needed it.

***

After work one day, I had an opportunity to go back home for the night. I planned to ride the train back up the next morning and arrive in time for work.

It was fun to be home for the night, and the next morning, I also looked forward to the ride back to West Yellowstone. Dad drove me to St. Anthony to catch the train, and we arrived just in time to see it pulling out. We knew the next stop was in Ashton, 14 miles north. So Dad, in our little old 1950 Chevy truck, started after the train. It was quite a race but Dad beat it far enough so I could run inside the depot, get a ticket and board the Yellowstone Special.

Then the train started off slow and began to wind slowly through the mountain terrain, past Warm River, and through the tunnel in the mountain by Bear Gulch. I kept wondering when the train was going to speed up, above what I thought must be about 20 miles an hour, but it never did. I moved from one side of my car to the other in order to admire the scenery in the early morning sunlight. It was beautiful.

We passed the corrals and loading ramps for livestock at Big Springs. My mind went back to when I was about 16 years old, loading sheep there onto the double-leveled livestock rail car. I relived the experience of loading these reluctant participants at about

4:30 in the morning. There is a trick to loading sheep. They have a characteristic of not wanting to lead but to follow. To push them up the long ramp into the car was like trying to push them with a rope. So, I would grab one by the hind leg and drag it backwards up the ramp and then the rest would "follow like sheep." This was the summer we merged our sheep with Cy Young's sheep on the range along the north side of Mount Sawtelle, just north of Henry's Lake in Island Park.

It was later that I learned of the significance of Big Springs concerning the Oregon Short Line Railroad. I learned that E. H. Harriman commissioned a railroad line to be built from St. Anthony to what would later be known as West Yellowstone. The railroad was built as far as Big Springs the first year. Big Springs, headwaters of the Henry's Fork of the Snake River, became the terminus for the summer of 1907. Passengers could ride to Big Springs on the train and then take a stage about 20 miles north to Yellowstone. Up until then, they disembarked at Monida, Montana, and then rode the stagecoach 60 dusty miles to the sightseeing splendor of Yellowstone. The tracks were extended in November 1907 to the place that was later named West Yellowstone. The first passengers arrived in 1908 and this little place at the west entrance of Yellowstone began to invent itself in order to take care of the passengers of the Yellowstone Special and other visitors.

My ride on the Yellowstone Special ended at 8:00 a.m. I was a little late for work at Three Bear Lodge. I stepped off the train at the large impressive depot and hurried across the street to work. The Wilsons didn't even know I was late.

During my first summer working for the Wilsons, I learned much that put me in good stead for my future involvement in Three Bear Lodge. I worked long shifts and was paid $1.25 per hour with no mention of overtime. Toward the end of the season, Mike called me in and said he was going to raise my wage to $2 per hour. I was dumbfounded.

To begin with, I slept in a little cabin out back of the motel. There were no cooking facilities, and so Frances would have me go over to what is now the Dairy Queen and bring sandwiches home for us. It wasn't long before Mike and Frances took me to dinner with them in the restaurant they had just opened in 1955.

I had hardly ever eaten in a restaurant before and was totally amazed. I felt a little embarrassed to order anything very expensive so I would have a hamburger steak or something that didn't cost very much. At that time, it was about $4.95. Soon, they told me to just eat there every night and to just sign the ticket. Mike told me to have whatever I wanted, but I always ate off the low-ticket items. I was pretty much on my own for breakfast and lunch so I would normally eat cold cereal or something like that for breakfast and cook myself a little something for lunch or build a sandwich. This helped me to save more money.

I sent every paycheck home to Sylvan and the only money I kept was enough to buy a Pendleton jacket from Smith & Chandlers General Mercantile. At the end of the summer, the Wilsons asked me back for the next year. I told them that I would like to, but that I was going on a mission for my Church and would be gone for a couple years.

My goals in life were really quite simple. I would go on a mission, graduate from college, teach school, and farm. Hopefully I could get married and raise a family in St. Anthony. This all started to work out perfectly. According to plans, I returned from my mission, graduated from Rick College with a two-year provisional teaching certificate, and married Linda Fischer in 1962.

I even got offered a job the night of our wedding reception. Since a teacher in Ashton had a retinal detachment, the school needed someone to finish out the second half of the year. Life was great—as newlyweds we lived in a little house in St. Anthony, and the following year I taught in Parker, a little community 3 miles west of St. Anthony with Dean, my brother, as the principal. My salary was $3,200 per year.

My two brothers and I continued to farm in the summer and teach school in the winter. We formed Seely Brothers Partnership and began to increase our acreage. To make use of the land, Linda and I decided to ask her Uncle Clarence if he would loan us $5000. I was a little nervous but got up my courage and explained what we wanted to use the money for: to buy some cattle. To my great relief he said a line that has now become famous within our family, "Clyde, you are sitting in the golden chair of opportunity."

He agreed to make the loan and we were grateful. But on the other hand, how could he refuse the husband of his favorite niece?

In my youth, we often took sheep or cattle to sell and attended the auction sale. But it was quite a different experience now bidding against the big boys and spending money I had been entrusted with. Every time I outbid everybody else, and the auctioneer called out, "Sold," I wondered if I had bid too much. However, I kept that up, until I had spent the money I had allocated, and ended up with twenty-five head of Hereford heifers.

Now I knew that calving out heifers was not easy, but I also understood that an Angus bull would cause the calves to have smaller heads and could be born easier. Linda and I ended up buying a Black Angus bull named Domino. It turned out he was a real find. We backed our little 1950 Chevrolet pickup with my homemade stock rack on it into the coral, put halter on Domino, and led him right into the pickup. It was a tricky ride back to the farm, about 45 miles north, because the little pickup really was undersized to haul a big bull and would rock back and forth.

Domino was about as tame as a big black lab dog. We have pictures of our four little nieces and nephews on his back as I led him around. One warm sunny day, he lay down on the grass in front of the old house where the little bum lamb stood. Domino was lying down, and the camera caught my mother sitting on Domino with Dad standing watchfully by. Then I put my stray hand on him, and helped Aunt Eva take her turn sitting on him. He continued to amaze people with how tame and gentle he was.

Clyde leading Domino with nieces and nephews

However when it came time to do his thing, he rose to the occasion. Calving out these first-time mothers was both a difficult and educational experience, as they often had problems. We started to have the veterinarian come to pull some of the calves that couldn't make it on their own. The cost was $30 each time, so I decided, especially after having my lamb pulling experience, that I could pull calves as well. I rigged up a homemade apparatus, hooked a block and tackle to it, and along with Linda's help became quite proficient at this; even when we had to do it in the middle of a cold night.

Then the next summer came, and I took Linda for a Sunday afternoon drive to West Yellowstone, about 70 miles north, and stopped in to see Mike and Frances and to introduce to them to my new bride. About a week later, they called on the phone and asked if we would come back and work for them. Money to finish college was still a necessity, so we decided that would be a way to make enough to finish my teaching degree and to graduate from Idaho State University (ISU). The following summer, in 1964, we left the farm and cattle for my brothers to take care of and we began working for the Wilsons.

Linda worked in the office checking in people and writing personal confirmation letters to each person that made a reservation. Frances was very meticulous about this process and wrote letters like these people were her long lost friends. Linda was very nervous when Frances was around, but in reality, she did very well, and Frances was pleased.

After working in maintenance all day, I worked the front desk with Linda at night. We worked long hours seven days a week but never thought of complaining or asking for overtime pay.

One day, like Frances had done for my sisters, she said, "Why don't you take my car and go to Bozeman for the day?"

It was the Fourth of July, and we drove her great big, new, maroon Lincoln Continental to Bozeman for our one and only day off. It was a beautiful drive along the Gallatin River and was the first time either of us had been to Bozeman.

That fall we told Mike and Frances we were short on money to finish school and asked if there was any way they could loan us $600. I suppose that was the first I had thought of, or knew anything about, student loans. Without hesitation they wrote us out a check, and we paid them back the next summer when we returned to manage the motel.

I graduated from Idaho State University in spring 1966 and signed a contract to teach school in West Yellowstone for the 1966–67 school year. The salary was $5,175 a year, more money than I had ever earned. While our plan had been for me to teach school in the winter and farm together with my brothers in the summer as well as taking care of sheep and cattle year round. We were beginning to like the motel business and were being wooed over to the thought of changing direction. It seemed "the golden chair of opportunity" was really going to be found in West Yellowstone rather than on the farm.

So we decided to pursue the motel business in West Yellowstone. We were able to sell the cows and calves, and the little farm we had purchased to pay off the loan and break even. I turned my share of the farming operation over to my brothers with no compensation. This cleared the way for our lives to begin in West Yellowstone, Montana.

At this point, Mike and Frances were not only sleeping in the old railroad car, which was away from the lodge, they also had begun spending more time living there. That gave us a little more freedom, as we lived in their apartment upstairs in the motel. We loved the apartment—its view from the corner windows, and the convenience of the lobby below.

Linda and I now had a plan for me to teach school in West Yellowstone in the winters, and instead of farming in the summer, we would manage the motel for the Wilsons. That worked well, and we didn't have to worry about making ends meet. **17**

In 1966, when we were permanently located in West Yellowstone, and before Mike moved back to California for the winter, he asked if we would like to lease the motel the following summer. We were pleased and surprised with the offer. But were greatly concerned that we would not be able to do things right.

Mike expected a lot, but was always fair, steady, and let me do my job without interference. Frances, on the other hand was a different matter. She could be very meddlesome and critical, and when she was in one of her moods *nothing* was right. With her long Benson and Hedges cigarette in her mouth, her tongue could lash

See **17** on the West Yellowstone Map Pages 142-143

out and show no mercy. Linda was very nervous that Frances would be breathing down our necks constantly.

But in the spring, to our surprise, wise old Mike announced that he was taking Frances to Europe for the summer. That was a stroke of genius! Under these circumstances, I felt sure we could do the job and handle the responsibility.

We didn't see Mike and Frances until that fall, after they had returned from their summer-long trip and stopped in to see how things had gone. Well, the motel was still intact.

Our lease arrangement was that we would pay them $25,000 per year, and that we could keep whatever profit there was above that. We had a good summer and were able to make the lease payment to them. Our room rates were $12 for one bed, $14 for two, and $16 for four people. We thought that was a lot of money and tried not to increase our rates so people could afford to stay there.

For two years, we continued leasing. I taught during the day in the winter, then Linda, me, and Linda's mother, Beulah, ran the motel in the summer. During the school year, I often taught in the daytime while my weeknights and Saturdays were spent remodeling some of the motel rooms or shoveling snow off the roof. Meanwhile Rochelle, our first little daughter, was a joy to us as she played in the laundry bins while Linda or Beulah did the laundry.

Mike and Frances returned the following summer but still gave us full rein. I think Mike had something to do with that. They stayed during the summers from then on while continuing to live in the railroad car at the edge of the forest about four blocks away.

But during the summer of 1969, Mike decided it was time for them to sell the motel. I heard them talking, and Mike said he was going to list it with Gene Cheatly, the local real estate agent. Frances interceded and asked Mike, "Why not sell it to Clyde and Linda?" She thought a lot of us, and they both knew that with us the motel would be in good hands. Plus, it would also help us get a start in our life. Mike agreed, and so for the balance of the fall and up until the end of the year, we worked out the particulars. **1**

The problem was that we didn't have any money for the down payment. Dealing with that problem required somewhat of a leap of faith on their part, and a big commitment on ours. They didn't want to receive a big down payment and then run the risk of repossession. We didn't want to invest years into something that might not turn out in the end. They had tutored us for several years and knew of our work ethic, and it also became obvious that we had developed a relationship with them that they were grateful for.

To make a long story short, I came home from teaching school at noon on January 2, 1970 to sign the papers to buy the Three Bear Lodge. I then dropped them in the mail and returned to school. At 2:00 p.m. that very day, someone came into my class and told me the motel was on fire. I ran home to see the fire burning. I felt like I had been hit in the gut. Was this a bad omen? Had we just made a mistake by putting those papers in the mail? For about 24 hours, I felt ill equipped to handle such weighty problems. In Pebble 14, I share the details of the fire and the aftermath that followed. In the end, the purchase served us well and truly has shaped the rest of our lives.

Over the years, we became closer with the Wilsons and deeply appreciated the opportunities they gave us. They continued to come in the summers until it was too much effort, and after that they stayed in California. The last time we saw Mike and Frances was when we made a special trip to Lake San Marcos to see them. We went out to dinner and had an enjoyable time together, yet they were both getting older. Years earlier, we had paid off the seventeen-year contract on the lodge and had also purchased from them five lots on Obsidian Avenue, which abutted the forest. It was on these lots the railroad car sat and we built our first house.

See **1** on the West Yellowstone Map Pages 142-143

Clyde, Frances, Mike, and Linda – Spring 1987

Mike told us he wanted to give us a Chilkat Indian blanket, a prized possession of his, which he had acquired from an old Indian as a pawn for $50. The fellow never returned, and it hung in the office for years. Mike and Frances knew I appreciated it, so they told us they wanted us to have it. It now hangs in a prominent place in the new Three Bear Lodge lobby for all to enjoy in a 5' x 7' glassed-in frame that I made. Alongside it is a National Geographic article and photos of this now lost art.

We asked Mike and Frances about their history, where they were born, and a little about themselves up until the time we met them. They seemed quite eager to tell us what they could remember, and I wrote down the particulars. We were so grateful for the things they told us that night. Some of those things are now inscribed on the historical diorama on the mezzanine level of the new Three Bear Lodge. The Wilsons had no children and thus were pretty much the last of their families. I do not say this boastfully, but I believe we were the closest people in their lives.

Later that night after dinner, when Mike and I were alone near their outdoor pool, he asked if we would take care of their affairs when they died. They had made all of the funeral arrangements, but he wanted to know if we could see that they were buried in the cemetery at Fir Ridge near West Yellowstone. Of course, I told him that we would be honored to do so, and that we would put them in one of our family plots. It was a tender parting as we left them, knowing we might never see them again. These people who had played such an important role in shaping our lives, had dropped a large pebble in our pool.

Mike soon died. He was found by the pool with a bruise on his forehead. Frances spent her last days suffering from Alzheimer's in a rest home. On separate occasions we received packages in the mail containing their ashes. We purchased a headstone, and they were both buried in our family lot.

Pebble 14: Three Bear Lodge, the Purchase, and the Fire

It's not the size of the dog in the fight, it's the size of the fight in the dog.

~Mark Twain

Three Bear Lodge has an interesting history. In 1925, President Calvin Coolidge issued the first land patent to this site. In 1932, the original Three Bear Lodge was built by Wally Bomier. Its rustic wooden cabins were burned in 1941, at which point he rebuilt the new main lodge office. In 1944, Three Bear was purchased by Mike and Frances Wilson for $25,800. Then in the 1950s, the Wilsons converted the lodge into a modern motel. On January 2, 1970, we bought the Three Bear Lodge, and it caught on fire.

Once I heard, I came running home from teaching school to find the back part of the motel and seven rooms on fire. Our little volunteer fire department was there, pumping water onto the flames from the fire hydrant on the railroad property across the street. Everyone worked hard until the fire was finally out.

After the fire department left, I was alone and bewildered, not knowing what to do next. It was going to drop to -20 degrees that night and everybody left except one man whom I hardly knew.

His name was Frank Turner, the owner of the Big Western Pine motel. We shoveled the huge pile of wet laundry to the outside before it froze. Then he said to me, "Well, if we are going to get this rebuilt by the snowmobile races in March, we better get started."

And get started we did. While I resigned from my sixth-grade teaching position, Linda was able to finish out the second semester for me. We had a dear friend, Lois McCray, tend our little daughter Rochelle while Linda taught, and Frank and I worked long hours to get the motel rebuilt.

Frank was another pebble in my pool—as we began to rebuild Three Bear Lodge he taught me many carpentry skills that a farm boy like me would never have learned otherwise. Our goal was to be open in time for the big March snowmobile races. Even though we were typically closed in mid-winter, we were totally booked for those races. We got all the renovations complete except for the carpet the night before check-in. Fortunately, our visitors were good at adapting—they were happy to stay in a brand new room with throw rugs instead of carpeting by their beds.

I don't recall discussing a wage with Frank. He just came and worked, and we settled at the end with what we thought was a fair amount for his labor.

Frank and I became fast friends. One fall, we spent twenty-seven days straight (except Sundays) hunting for deer, elk, moose, and anything else that was legal. We worked together with snow-mobiles and became partners in other businesses until he retired at age fifty-five and moved to Utah. He has since passed away, and I regret he will not read of my deep respect for him; however, his wife and posterity will be able to. Frank was a rock of a man. He took pride in his strength and never left undone what he said he would do. I am proud to have been a part of this mutual friendship and partnership.

***

It was fun to be working for ourselves, able to do as much or as little as we wanted. Linda and I worked well together and enjoyed our work relationship. In those days we had very little business after Labor Day. However, this began to change as more senior couples found that fall was the best time for them to travel. Sometimes we would not clean some of the rooms, because we thought we would not need them that night. But I remember more than one night, when we would fill the last clean room, and Linda and I would say to each other that we'd better go clean a few more. Just as we got those cleaned, Beulah would call and say, "I just rented that room, you better clean another one." We would almost hand the key to the guest, as they were coming in and we were walking out the door on our way to clean another room. We made a lot of beds together, and I still enjoy helping Linda make our bed.

One time someone told me that he wished him and his wife could work together like we did, but they just could not. Linda and I were very blessed. Not only did we work well together, we also enjoyed our free time together.

During those first winters, there were many times when we could leave when we wanted. Since Beulah would always be there to watch the kids, Linda and I skied a lot during the week. We would ski Kelly Canyon Teton Village at Jackson Hole and even at Lake Tahoe.

There never was a better grandma. Beulah's life revolved around her kids and grandkids, because she had lost her husband when he was 45 years old. She loved to talk and visit. She was a real people person, traits her daughter picked up naturally. She worked on the front desk at Three Bear Lodge, tended the kids, and eventually moved from one of our cabins to the railroad car for the summer months.

Three Bear Restaurant/Tepee
Motel/Midtown Motel

Three Bear Restaurant was first opened in 1955. Prior to this, Mike Wilson began talking about a restaurant with Roy Dunlock who was a lead chef at the Camel Back Inn in Phoenix during the winter. During the summer to get out of the Arizona heat, Roy would work in West Yellowstone at one of the local cafés. Together, Mike and Roy decided to remodel one of the main lodge buildings and convert it into the Three Bear Restaurant. The original Three Bear Restaurant could seat 55 people, but it quickly outgrew its little space and was expanded to hold 75 people.

The restaurant business provides great rewards, but it is also fraught with many challenges, chefs being one of them. Roy, the first chef, was quite a showman and would flip the steaks on the broiler behind a glass so the customers could see the flames jump high as their steak was flipped. However, prior to our buying Three Bear, Roy died at an early age. His protégé, Winnie, took over the reins.

When we bought Three Bear Lodge and Restaurant in 1970, Winnie was the head chef; he was young and a good chef. He and his wife basically ran the restaurant, leaving us time to concentrate on other aspects of the business. The year following our purchase, Winnie came in and visited with us and his wife at noon as he usually did. Without saying goodbye or indicating he would not be back, he walked out the back door across the parking lot, and we never saw him again. All of us, including his wife, expected him back, but he never returned.

Other times, I have had chefs who could not stay sober, or who would do pretty good for a while and then blow it. Since we were a small restaurant at that time we only had one chef, and he was pretty much a one-man show. If the chef didn't show up, we would have to close until we could find a replacement. One morning the chef didn't show up. I went to Bozeman in the morning and found a lady who could help us out. Before we left Bozeman, we stopped at Heeb's Grocery to pick up some of things she needed, and she began cooking that night. She stayed on until we could find a permanent replacement. Fortunately for our guests, I have only had to help cook one time.

One time I listed the chef's position with the Utah Job Service. We interviewed several candidates in Salt Lake City. Jim McCabe came in for an interview. He wore cook's pants and a white shirt. I suppose he was about 45 years old. It was obvious that he was very qualified and when I asked him about his personal habits he said, "I am an alcoholic." Now, normally that would have been the end of the interview, but he continued, "You give me a chance, and I will do you a good job." Well, I felt impressed that he would, and since he was open about his problem, it was worth taking a chance.

This was the beginning of a great relationship. I trusted Jim, and he knew it. I discovered that the way he controlled his alcoholism was by working. Jim had his wife with him, which I suppose, also helped. He would open the Three Bear Restaurant at 6:00 a.m. and leave after he put the prime rib in the oven, before closing after breakfast at 11:00 a.m. He would go to his apartment, rest up, have a nap, and then was back at 4:00 p.m. to open for dinner and closed again at 10:00 p.m. He worked every shift from when we opened in the spring until we closed in the fall. He would do the same thing in the winter season as well.

One time we were in need of a waitress and he said, "Well, I know this old gal that would really do you a good job." So we brought her up. Her name was Kate, and she was a perfectionist. She soon began running the front end and was the trainer for the wait staff. Like Jim, she was older and experienced and had a quick wit and sense of humor. It was not until several years later that we found out that this "old gal" was actually Jim's sister. He didn't want us to give her any special treatment or pressure us into hiring her.

We enjoyed many years with Jim without problems. Then one fall, Linda and I were in New York on a sales trip, and I got a call from one of the local bars in West Yellowstone. Apparently, Jim had come in for a drink. Of course, to an alcoholic, there is no such thing as one drink. There is a Japanese proverb that says, "A man takes a drink, then the drink takes a drink, and then the drink takes the man." Jim had passed out sitting in the corner, so the bartender called the police to take him home.

The next morning, after Jim had a chance to sober up, I called him. I asked what had happened and he said he thought he could go over and have one drink and would be able to handle it.

I said, "You know I am back east and cannot be there in time to help." I explained that I trusted him and depended on him. I asked him, "Jim, I really need your help, can I count on you to pull yourself together and get the restaurant open for dinner tonight?"

He did, and by the time we got back everything was running smoothly.

Jim and Kate were two of many people who influenced my life, as I have influenced theirs. Jim eventually retired and was greatly missed. Several years later, Kate fell in the kitchen and broke her hip. We kept in touch with them until the end. Jim died first at about age seventy-four, and then Kate passed away in her late 80s.

As I look back now over 40 years of my life in West Yellowstone, there have been many people who have had a great influence on my life, dropped pebbles in our pool so to speak. I owe a debt of gratitude to many more than I can adequately write about in this book.

***

I have found over the years that learning good business practices is sometimes not as challenging as mastering human relations.

If a company does not have a cohesive group of employees that work together harmoniously, customers can feel it.

Because personnel issues continually surface, there are many times, due to my position, that only I am able to address these issues. Probably the most important qualities in dealing with employees are the ability to empathize with them and to be a good listener. Confrontations often occur between employees, and I learned a long time ago that there are always two sides to every story. Sometimes it is tempting to listen to one person's concerns and make a snap decision, only to have to reverse it when the other side is heard. Through my experiences, I have found that if I take the time to sit down and listen to concerns from both sides, a fair decision can be made and the problem resolved.

Some problems require the wisdom of Solomon. I had a manager at one facility who was really a nice guy, but he would listen to one person and make a decision based on what that employee wanted to hear and seemed best for them. Then he would listen to the other person's side and make a decision that this other employee wanted to hear and seemed best for them. He hadn't really solved anything because he had neither resolved the conflict nor made a sustainable decision. I thought back to my dad's statement, "Clyde, sometimes you just have to put your heart in your pocket and do what has to be done." It is sometimes hard to be firm and make a decision that can't please everybody. It is also hard to release employees, but sometimes that also needs to be done. Our employees are all part of a big partnership, and talking through the problem, in such a way as not to lose respect, helps to make us all successful.

***

With the increasing demand because of the successful winter operation and the need to serve larger groups prime rib dinners, Linda and I along with Bill and Carole, decided to purchase the

Tepee Motel and Restaurant and move the Three Bear Restaurant to that location.

The Tepee Inn was among the early twentieth century businesses in West Yellowstone. It was a charming two-story log structure that housed a bar, dance floor, café, and rooms. The Tepee Inn was built by Val Buchanan in 1921 and the building materials cost $1,750. This rather large two-story log structure was prominent for its time. The impressive rock fireplace and back bar, made from rhyolite stone, still stands today as a sentinel of the lively times that used to happen there years ago.

J.H. Venable sold the Tepee to A. K. (Kayle) Clawson in 1952. A fire caused by a burning grease trap burned the Tepee in 1965. The exterior rock wall and interior back-bar survived the fire. The building was re-built as a single story structure, and Clawson added the Tepee Motel to the building. We purchased the Tepee from Clawson on May 25, 1978, but we didn't begin our remodeling project and relocating the new Three Bear Restaurant and Grizzly Lounge until summer 1984. **4**

I wanted to build a log structure using local logs and retain the historic rock fireplace. Bill Schaap was my manager at Three Bear Lodge at the time and shared my zest for challenging projects. We got a logging permit near the South Fork of the Madison River and were able to cut and load huge logs with my old loader and haul them to town. We were fortunate to get these big Lodge Pole Pines, just 5 miles west of town, just before the Forest Service closed this area to logging. It was fun to be able to cut these trees like the old timers in West Yellowstone did and contribute to the rustic charm of West Yellowstone.

Years earlier, I had noticed that on the inside of the Old Faithful Inn, built in 1903, logs were sawed in half to give a full log appearance, So we had David Rightenour, son of Herk Rightenour who had owned a saw mill in town since the 1920s, saw the logs

See **4** on the West Yellowstone Map Pages 142-143

down the middle and stack them on top of each other. Few people knew that they were not full logs. We used every person who could pull a drawknife to peel the bark off all sizes of logs. The big logs were for the exterior and select areas for the interior, while the small logs were for the majority of the interior décor. We still have people like my nephew Tai come and say, "I remember when I helped peel those logs."

We also honored West Yellowstone's past by gathering photos of the early days from the park's archives and from old timers around town. As usual, there was a deadline we were shooting for. We started construction after Labor Day, and our goal was to be open and operating by the Christmas holidays. The Three Bear Restaurant turned out beautifully, and we opened on schedule in December 1985.

Converting the Tepee Bar into the new Three Bear Restaurant

In addition to the front Tepee building, there was a 16-unit motel operated from an office and a manager's apartment to the north of the restaurant and lounge. We operated this as a separate motel for several years. On January 1, 1982, we also purchased the Midtown Motel across the alley from the Tepee. **5**

See **5** on the West Yellowstone Map Pages 142-143

It is always a challenge to keep an old facility upgraded to provide modern and first class accommodations. This has required continual effort on our part. After purchasing the Tepee and remodeling the restaurant, we remodeled the Tepee Motel and the Midtown Motel, both of which were contiguous to the forty-two units of Three Bear Lodge. For economies of scale, we eventually consolidated the three motels into one. This eliminated the need to maintain three offices. The Tepee Motel and Midtown Motel ceased to exist. They both became part of Three Bear Lodge/Motel. Since they were now part of Three Bear, it was necessary that all three properties were equivalent in quality.

On March 15, 1990, we began a four phase, one-and-a-half-year rebuilding project at Three Bear Lodge. We had made a decision to either tear down or strip to the studs the old sections of the Three Bear Lodge that had not been rebuilt after the fire in 1970. We made an announcement in the local paper that a newly upgraded facility would be ready in 1991. We tore down one section, put in a basement to accommodate snowmobile rental clothing and hot tubs, and put in an all-new electrical and water supply system in another section. This gave a face-lift to the entire property by making the Tepee and Midtown rooms larger, upgrading the exterior, and giving all buildings the same look as the rest of the new Three Bear Lodge.

Over the years I have benefited from a drafting class I took my senior year of high school. With almost every project I have undertaken, I have taken out my inexpensive scale ruler and graph paper to scale room sizes, furniture, and design concepts for the exterior and interior. This has helped me to visualize and design the end result I was looking to achieve and to figure out the steps necessary to get there.

Looking back on things I have accomplished causes me to do a better job on future projects. Any job worth doing is worth doing well. I remember when I was about 11 years old, my family and others were remodeling our church house. I went with my dad to help and was asked to fill the nail holes in the baseboard so the finish coat could be applied. Though it was a simple job, my dad showed me how to push the putty in and smooth it out so it was hardly noticeable. Years later, when walking into that church house, I would sometimes glance down at those baseboards and remember that I had a part in hiding the nail holes that were now invisible. Even today, after all these years in West Yellowstone, I am reminded of installing that tile, remodeling that room, and building that business or structure. There is some satisfaction in knowing that those things are there because of my efforts. Consequently, I have always had a good time producing or building things that can be appreciated by many for years to come.

Pebble 15: The Oregon Short Line 1903 Railroad Car

No one cares how much you know, until
they know how much you care.

~Theodore Roosevelt

In 1975, Linda and I became custodians of a historical treasure, though at the time we didn't understand its full significance. To understand the full story, we need to go back over a century, to 1903 when the Pullman Palace Car Shops in Pennsylvania were commissioned to build a luxury accommodation for the vice president of the Oregon Short Line Railroad. This splendid railroad car, christened the OSL 1903, was built at a cost of $16,850 (equal to hundreds of thousands in today's dollars).

We were ignorant of the car's distinguished history until one day in 1992. While we were out of town, a man came looking for our particular railroad car. Gus Tureman, a friend of ours, let him in to look at the car. His name was Ralph Barger, and he had written a book entitled *Union Pacific Business Cars 1870–1991*. There on page 121 were two pictures of our railroad car.

With this new information, the appointments of the railroad car made more sense to us. There were obviously servant's quarters where the porter and cooks slept which were separated by a door from the VIP section. The executive section was made of beautiful and intricate ribbons of tiny little pieces of inlaid wood (about thirteen per inch), which adorned the Honduran Mahogany walls. There were intricate little decorative railings on top of the cabinets and unique hand sinks that could be pulled down and lifted up so the used water would run out on the tracks below. There were also a couple of little upholstered benches. Under the lids, there was a toilet with a brass handle so one could flush the toilet—you guessed it—onto the track below. One stateroom was made for the ladies out of Birdseye Maple. It was more feminine in design, with a deep red ceiling highlighted with gold brocade and brass colored lamps.

Three of the staterooms had bunks that could be pulled down to accommodate additional guests. One of these classic staterooms had been converted into a tiled bathroom. After we removed the wall tile, we found the big brass key and opened the bunk. There it was, a bunk that looked like it could have been slept in the night before, when in reality it had not been opened for 60 years. It had the original mattress and the gear-and-chain apparatus that lowered the bunk to a horizontal position.

The dining and observation room included a table with leaves so it could be expanded and cabinet drawers lined with a fancy green material to keep the silverware from rattling. Since this was a working vice presidential car, there was also a secretariat in which the secretary could pull down the front to make a desk where a typewriter was undoubtedly kept. This desk had lots of interesting, almost secret, compartments and drawers for important documents.

The OSL 1903 was then retrofitted between 1912 and 1915. At that time it was renamed "OSL 150." Mr. Barger also stated that it was retired in December 1934 "at West Yellowstone?" The question mark indicating he did not know which state West Yellowstone was in (Sometimes that still happens.) On June 15, 1993, Mr. Barger wrote us a two-page letter discussing the condition of the car and indicating how happy he was to finally see it. He said that "of all the old railroad cars I have seen in the wild, they're nothing but a pile of rubble compared to this car."

The pictorial evidence backs up the assertion that this was one of the most sumptuously appointed railroad cars in the county at the time. It just so happened that on the page opposite the photos of OSL 1903, there are photographs of E.H. Harriman's private presidential car, built in 1900. The OSL 1903 was obviously nicer, as was attested by some of the employees who had ridden in E.H. Harriman's car and then after riding in the new OSL 1903 remarked, "We out-bested old E.H. on this trip."

The Oregon Short Line 1903, now changed to OSL 150 was given as a retirement gift to Mr. E.C. Manson, a superintendent of the railroad. We found two large envelopes under one of the drawers in the secretary's desk addressed to him. Since he loved Yellowstone, they pulled this vice presidential car up the tracks one last time, built a spur off the railroad tracks, removed the trucks (wheels) and placed the railroad care on a stone foundation. It sat there for 61 years, from 1934 to 1995, on a lot on Obsidian Avenue. **3**

Oregon Short Line 1903, it's historical elegance once again discovered

See **3** on the West Yellowstone Map Pages 142-143

July 3, 1956, Henry Casper, the original druggist in West
Yellowstone, purchased the railroad car as summer lodging for his
help. In 1958, the summer I came to work at West Yellowstone, he sold
the railroad car to Mike and Frances Wilson. The Wilsons also bought
several adjoining lots on both sides of this property (I believe from
Ken Chandler of Smith and Chandler's store on Yellowstone Avenue,
which is still in existence today). After Linda and I were married, and
came back to work for them, the Wilsons had a large, glassed-in living
room built onto the car. With the forest boundary right out their front
window, there was a wonderful feeling of quiet and seclusion.

In 1975, when the Wilson's ceased coming to West Yellowstone
for the summers, they sold us the railroad car and the six lots that ran
along Obsidian Avenue and the forest. It was on the lot and a half, next
to the railroad car, that we built our new home. **2**

During the summer we built our house, we lived in the railroad
car. Rochelle, Stephanie and Mike each had a posh stateroom for a
bedroom. Linda, our baby Brook, and I slept in the large dining
and observation room in front. After our house was finished, we
let Beulah (Linda's mother) live there. For many years after that,
family members or summer helpers resided there.

However, after we realized its historical significance, we
determined to give the wonderful old car the setting it deserved. We
would restore it and place it on display for all to see at the new hotel
we were going to build, the Holiday Inn.

Yet, it was quite a project to refurbish the OSL 1903. It took
us longer to restore the railroad car than it did to build the hotel
around it. Jim Keeler from Salt Lake was the chief restorer, and
with his guidance we removed and polished over 3,000 pieces of
brass, from screws to the rails on the observation platform.

Through the decades, the old car endured severe winters
and extreme temperatures which created constant maintenance
problems. I had painted it several times on the outside and was

See **2** on the West Yellowstone Map Pages 142-143

constantly patching the roof to prevent leaks (fortunately little water damage ever occurred on the inside paneling). Now in restoration mode, we sanded off many coats of paint in order to get down to the original Pullman green. Then we painted a replica of the original lettering on the sides to replicate the Pullman company photo. It says in Barger's book that the floor plan and elevation drawings had not been found. But when he came to visit the car, there they were, the original blueprint, encased in a decorative, glassed in case. It was standard procedure to place it in this location, just outside the kitchen in the hallway of the servant's quarters. This blueprint was always prominently posted so those planning the train route could make sure the car could fit through the tunnels and openings on the route. Otherwise, if they messed up on this, it would be like a camel trying to go through the 'eye of a needle' at 50 miles an hour.

During the time of transition, between being an old relic to becoming a museum quality executive railroad car in its new location, I made every effort to restore the car in its original condition. The original kitchen equipment could not be obtained, so I turned the kitchen area into a diorama displaying photos of old West Yellowstone and of stagecoaches on the recovered window screens and some old window frames, and covered the walls with pleated fabric.

Today it can be visited in a museum-like setting with a photo display of the restoration process. The car's new setting includes a railroad crossing complete with rails, planks, and an antique marble reflector sign on the west end of the car. Hotel guests drive their vehicles across this on the way to the hotel lobby. On its east end, we built a regular railroad track leading into the building so it looks like we just pulled the car right into where it is permanently located. It was here that I drove in our very own golden spike.

Many guests have enjoyed this rare chance to see this museum-quality executive railroad car. It is truly one of a kind. In fact, this beautiful car now takes its place as stop #10 on the West Yellowstone Historical Walking Tour map (See Pebble 24).

WEST YELLOWSTONE MAP

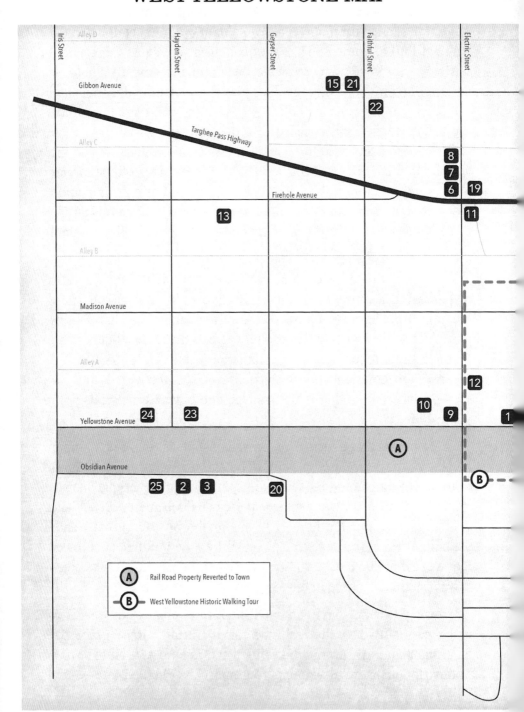

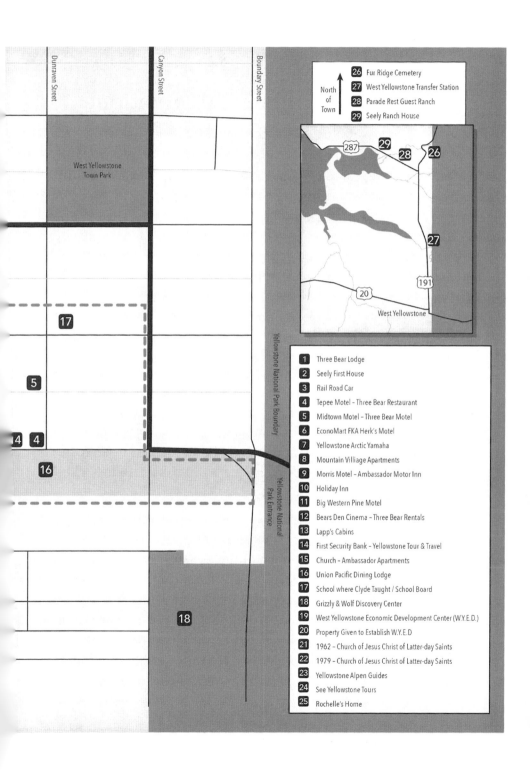

West Yellowstone Town Park

Dunraven Street

Canyon Street

Boundary Street

Yellowstone National Park Boundary

Yellowstone National Park Entrance

North of Town

26 Fur Ridge Cemetery
27 West Yellowstone Transfer Station
28 Parade Rest Guest Ranch
29 Seely Ranch House

287
29
28
26
27
191
20
West Yellowstone

17
5
4 4
16
18

1 Three Bear Lodge
2 Seely First House
3 Rail Road Car
4 Tepee Motel – Three Bear Restaurant
5 Midtown Motel – Three Bear Motel
6 EconoMart FKA Herk's Motel
7 Yellowstone Arctic Yamaha
8 Mountain Villiage Apartments
9 Morris Motel – Ambassador Motor Inn
10 Holiday Inn
11 Big Western Pine Motel
12 Bears Den Cinema – Three Bear Rentals
13 Lapp's Cabins
14 First Security Bank – Yellowstone Tour & Travel
15 Church – Ambassador Apartments
16 Union Pacific Dining Lodge
17 School where Clyde Taught / School Board
18 Grizzly & Wolf Discovery Center
19 West Yellowstone Economic Development Center (W.Y.E.D.)
20 Property Given to Establish W.Y.E.D
21 1962 – Church of Jesus Christ of Latter-day Saints
22 1979 – Church of Jesus Christ of Latter-day Saints
23 Yellowstone Alpen Guides
24 See Yellowstone Tours
25 Rochelle's Home

Pebble 16: Property Acquisitions and Development

*God gave us two ends . . . one to sit on and one
to think with. Success depends on which one
you use—heads you win; tails you lose.*

~Author Unknown

For over 40 years we have been involved in building, purchasing, and running a number of businesses. Time moves ever onward and tends to leave some things behind and forgotten unless they are recorded in a document of some kind to maintain the historical significance. The next three pebbles will bring some of these acquisitions that may even have different names now back to the "Oh, I remember that," phase.

When I came to West Yellowstone, I was a farm boy who had no experience in purchasing land or businesses. However, I was raised with a good work ethic and a level temperament, which is why, I believe, Linda and I were asked if we wanted to buy Three Bear Lodge. From there the opportunities grew. Perhaps it was the right time in the development of West Yellowstone or perhaps it was Uncle Clarence's pronouncement that I was sitting on the "golden chair of opportunity," but for some reason, as you will see in the following accounts, most acquisitions were purchased under rather unusual circumstances.

Time seems to slip by so quickly. Unlike the wealthy nobility of old, we have come to the universal realization that we can't take our worldly possessions with us. As we progress into the twilight of our life, we must make arrangements to pass on to new caretakers our earthly holdings. As you will notice in the following three pebbles, some people had reached this state in life and were looking for someone to be the next steward of their life's work. In some cases it was not the amount of money they received as much as the amount of trust they had in an individual to carry forward a part of their legacy.

EconoMart—Firehole Fill up

One day in 1974, Herk Rightenour, owner of Herk's Motel and West Yellowstone Lumber, came to see me. Herk was aging and apparently was in financial trouble. He said to me, "Unless I come up with [he named the sum] in a few days, I will lose my place."

He asked if I could help him out by buying his two corner lots. I told him I thought I could do it but would have to check with the bank. Within the next few days we were able to buy the lots, which saved the rest of his property from being repossessed. This was a nice corner piece of property on the highway. As part of the deal, we also had the right to purchase the next half lot so as to make the property a complete rectangle.

Because the property was in such a good location, I decided to build the Econo Mart, a little convenience store. It would be the first service station encountered by traffic coming into town from the west. The convenience store concept was still fairly new at the time. Like so many things I have done, it seemed expedient to start small and then expand as the business justified it so there wouldn't be a lot of front end debt.

I began in 1975 by building a small store with gas pumps. We dug the trench for the necessary sewer and water. The next weekend Linda and I took our little family on a trip to Salt Lake City. While eating dinner at Señor Pepe's restaurant, I got pretty ill but didn't say anything until after. By then I felt so bad that I told Linda I needed to go to the hospital. We discovered that I had a ruptured appendix. After the operation and hospital stay, I was pretty weak and was grateful to have Wade, one of my summer helpers, get down in the trenches with me and put the water and sewer pipes together, pull the wrenches, and so forth.

Eventually we finished the store and named it The Econo Mart. We now had a wholesale gasoline source for our snowmobiles. The initial success of the Econo Mart convinced me that there was potential for a more complete facility. Within the next few years, Linda and I purchased the other half lot and built a car wash on the property. We also expanded the store on two different occasions and added a Laundromat. Now at one place, people could come, do their laundry, purchase a few goodies, fill up with gas, and wash their cars.

Husky oil was our branded supplier. The gas price when we opened was thirty-seven cents per gallon. Husky eventually stopped supplying in our area, so we switched over to Phillips 66. Gas prices soared to $1.22 a gallon, and we wondered how those high prices would affect tourism. We found out that even though these high gas prices were a deterrent, people still were willing to give up many things before giving up their vacations. Gasoline prices have continued to rise and fall based on supply and demand. I suppose political forces, whether national or international, also play a role. Prices have fluctuated to nearly 4 dollars a gallon. We still have wondered how gas prices will affect tourism, but because of the popularity of West Yellowstone and Yellowstone National Park, people keep coming and business has always fared well. **6**

See **6** on the West Yellowstone Map Pages 142-143

Mountain Village Apartments—
Yellowstone Arctic/Yamaha

My first experience moving buildings occurred after buying Herk's property. The aging and unsightly individual cabins of this motel had to be either torn down or moved to make way for the new buildings.

We tore down most of the run-down cabins, but there were five cabins that I thought were worth saving. With the forks on my old loader, and other contrived apparatuses, we moved them onto a back portion of the property. We placed them side-by-side and built a room in between each, so we now had two-roomed cabins for our help.

Moving buildings must have been in my blood like it was in my dad's because this was just the beginning. Over the years, I later moved three cabins from town to the Parade Rest Guest Ranch, one cabin from the KO-Z Motel to Lapp's Cabins, and three more cabins from town to the ranch for employee housing. I've also moved a four-unit motel, the house we bought from Gus Tureman, a 1903 executive rail car and the two-story cinder block Ambassador Motel, which was extremely heavy (See Pebble 19).

When it came time to develop a building for a snowmobile dealership (see Pebble 20), I moved more cabins off the lot. On the south half of the back lot behind the Econo Mart, we built the Yellowstone Arctic/Yamaha, our dealership and repair shop. **7**

Also, as a tourism town, I have learned that if we want to attract employees we have to supply housing for them. In 1988, on the north half of the same lot as Yellowstone Arctic/Yamaha, we built the Mountain Village Apartments. For these buildings, we used an innovative, insulated cinder block and a radiant floor heat system. It has served us well. **8**

See **7** on the West Yellowstone Map Pages 142-143
See **8** on the West Yellowstone Map Pages 142-143

Following the first fire at Three Bear, I learned that I could get more mileage out of the available insurance dollars by doing much of the work myself and utilizing the hired help during our off-season.

Architects and general contractors were expensive, and it seemed a lot of time had to be spent with them in order to transfer the vision I had for my project into their heads. Consequently, to start a building project, I'd use my high school drafting class skills. I'd take out my 1-dollar scale ruler, a fixture template, and some graph paper, and I would draw out plans. The more extensive projects were eventually handed over to an architect, but many of these buildings, including our new house in 2007, were initially laid out with this crude equipment.

I acted as the general contractor and contracted out the various phases of the project, like framing or masonry, concrete, sheet rock, and electrical work. It has never been in my nature to stand and talk while other people are doing what I could be doing. I innately learned this even before I heard it from Stephen Covey's principle of "Learn It, Teach It, Do It." I have always been a hands-on guy, teaching my helpers how I wanted things done by working with them and then letting them complete it by themselves.

Morris Motel—Ambassador Motor Inn Precursor to Holiday Inn

Soon after we had completely rebuilt Three Bear Lodge after the fire in 1970, the Morris Motel went up for sale. Since Frank Turner and I had become good friends while rebuilding Three Bear, and we both shared the same work ethic, we decided the Morris Motel was an opportunity for us to go into business together.

The motel was a rose colored, two story, cinder block, 52-unit building named after Ed and Edna Morris. Ed had passed on and

Edna was remarried to Gene Adams. In 1972, they were ready to retire and, they put it on the market.

Frank and I inquired about purchasing the motel and then began serious negotiations. The motel needed a face-lift. Our intention was to purchase it and completely refurbish the interior and exterior. We would even rename the motel, as we wanted to change the image and make it one of the nicest motels in town. I had bought Three Bear Lodge with easy terms from the Wilsons; however, I didn't have the same relationship with the Adamses as I did with the Wilsons, which meant we had a problem: we didn't have enough money for both the down payment and the remodeling work. During the negotiations, we discovered the Adamses also had a problem. If the Adamses were to collect a lump sum down payment, the majority of that money would go toward taxes. They also wanted to carry the contract without pre-payment privileges, which was fine with us. They thought a normal down payment should be $50,000. At the same time, they were equally concerned about selling their motel without assurance that it would be taken care of. They wanted to make sure we were committed and felt we should put money down to show our commitment. They also did not want to have to repossess the motel in case we did not invest sufficient money into keeping it up.

I remember Frank, Gene, Edna, and I discussing all of this while sitting in Adams's apartment, when I was hit with an idea that was so far out I hardly dared mention it. But I have learned over the years that sometimes there are promptings that shouldn't be ignored, so I proposed the following: I suggested that Frank and I put $50,000 into remodeling the motel over the winter months. We would completely redo the interior of every room, paint the exterior, and rename the motel to the Ambassador Motor Inn. This would show our commitment and if we lost the place, they could repossess it in a new and improved condition. The work we would do and the $50,000 that we used for remodeling would be considered the down payment and we would pay off the balance of the contract over the next 20 years.

To our surprise, they accepted the offer. I remember coming out of that meeting with Frank shaking his head and saying, "I do not understand what just happened in there. Did you just say that we would remodel the motel as our down payment and that we would then end up owning it and not pay them anything down?" I assured him that this was what we all had agreed to.

We purchased the Morris Motel April 1, 1972, and began the process of remodeling. As soon as the arrangement was finalized we took our pick-up trucks to Salt Lake City for loads of interior paneling, which was in fashion at that time. We painted the exterior of the motel off-white with a dark green trim and installed a large sign that displayed the new name: Ambassador Motor Inn. When the first real estate payment came due after the remodeling was done, we already had a year's worth of income to make the payment. To this day, as far as I know, this is a unique way of making a down payment on the purchase of a property. **9**

In May 30, 1975, we hired Bill and Carole Howell to manage the Ambassador and to do the marketing for the Three Bear Lodge, the snowmobile operations, and the Big Western Pine (Frank's motel). Realizing that running the Ambassador Inn along with our other businesses was more than we could handle, we began working Bill and Carole into an ownership position in the Ambassador Motor Inn. Soon after this, Frank, my good friend and partner, wanted to start enjoying a more leisurely lifestyle and decided to sell the Big Western Pine Motel.

Big Western Pine—Yellowstone Country Inn

Bill, my brother Sylvan, and I formed a new partnership, Seely, Seely and Howell and bought Frank out of the Big Western Pine Motel

---

See **9** on the West Yellowstone Map Pages 142-143

on December 11, 1975. Included in the purchase were the little Trails Inn Motel (now known as the Moose Creek Inn), the Rustler's Roost Restaurant, and the Arctic Cat snowmobile rentals. **11**

Our purchase of the Big Western Pine eventually led the way to Bill and me buying Frank's share of the Ambassador Motor Inn on May 15, 1992. A few years later, Bill and I decided we wanted to build what is now the Holiday Inn (See Pebble 19). At this point, we had already sold the Trails Inn Motel, and we sold the Big Western Pine to Vernetta Steele. After a few years, she changed the name to the Yellowstone Country Inn. Vernetta eventually sold the property and the Rustler's Roost Restaurant closed.

KO-Z Motel—The Bear's Den Activity Center/Cinema/Snowmobile Rentals

It is surprising how businesses and properties change and people tend to lose track of what was there before. We tend to forget. When I first worked at Three Bear Lodge there were cabins where the pool is now. When I returned from my mission, Mike had moved these cabins to a lot just down the block on Electric Street and sold it as the KO-Z Motel. A few years later, on July 15, 1991, we bought this property from Art Whitmer and again moved the cabins, some to another location.

In 1994, we decided to utilize this property for snowmobile storage and more employee housing. Our kids were teenagers at the time, and we decided to incorporate a youth activity center into the building. We called it the Bear's Den Activity Center. It was a great idea. It gave the kids some place to work and to hang out. We had a pool table, table tennis, foosball, and arcade games. We also had a small kitchen for hamburgers, snack foods, and handmade milk shakes. We also held dances for the kids, complete with a mirror ball and D.J. Jeff Carter painted comedy bears on the walls as a way

See **11** on the West Yellowstone Map Pages 142-143

to brighten the environment while they played pool, drank milk shakes, etc. It was a great thing for the kids.

However, after a couple of years, although our intentions were good, we found the population was not large enough to support the activity center, and we closed it down for a time. Then we began to wonder about another need the town had—a movie theater.

The original movie theater in West Yellowstone was the Chalet Theatre, which burned down in 1980. In those days we fought many winter fires with loaders and snow blowers by dumping and blowing snow on the fire. I helped put snow on the fire with my loader, but to no avail. It was a total loss for the owner. It was also a loss for the town because people had to start driving to Bozeman or Idaho to see a movie, about a two-hour drive one way.

In fall 1996, we learned about a movie theatre that was being torn down in Layton, Utah. We bought the used furnishings and equipment. The most expensive piece of equipment was the popcorn popper at $5,000. The carpeting and floor lighting, sound curtains, chairs, movie projector, and screen were all hauled up on our flatbed trailer.

The original activity center was on the bottom floor of a two-story building. The south part of the building was snowmobile storage. The ceiling was high enough to nicely accommodate the movie screen and the stadium-type seating that I designed and built. We installed all the equipment from the Utah movie theater and opened in the summer of 1997 as the Bear's Den Cinema. People have been very appreciative and supportive of the theater—a movie theater was missing from the town for 15 years and was now back. **12** We double decked the remaining portion of this area for multi-level snowmobile storage.

The need for a youth activity center was soon replaced by the need for a senior citizens' center. Elizabeth Bailey came to see me and asked about using the activity center space as a senior citizen

See **12** on the West Yellowstone Map Pages 142-143

lunch and gathering place. This was the beginning of our town's senior citizen group.

Without having to pay rent, they could charge less for the meals, which were cooked and served there twice a week. They also played Bingo and other games. Over time, the facility became more popular and there was soon a need for a permanent facility. Eventually, thanks to Pierre Martineau and others, the new senior center, called the Povah Center, was built. It was so named because of a large contribution by Ellie Povah and was built on part of the original Union Pacific property.

Lapp's Cabins

Another property purchase sort of landed in my lap, no pun intended. Alan Lapp came to see me and said he wanted to sell me his Lapp's Cabins. He could no longer operate it as a motel and was renting the cabins on a monthly basis. I had known Alan for many years, and we had a good relationship. He had worked for Mike Wilson even before I had. In his later years, he was the local sewer expert and reported the weather each day to the TV stations.

I agreed to buy his place, again to use as employee housing, which was becoming a more critical problem. We got together with the local attorney to draw up the papers. The attorney told him in front of me that he should ask more for it. I indicated agreement, but Alan insisted on the original, lower price and said, "No, I want to sell it to Clyde for (and stated the amount again)."

We closed the deal on the terms he wanted on October 1, 1991. As usual, a lot of work needed to be done. We moved another cabin onto that property from the KO-Z Motel and built another duplex cabin, and now we had ten more employee housing units. **13**

See **13** on the West Yellowstone Map Pages 142-143

Pebble 17: Parade Rest Guest Ranch

*The successful person has the habit of doing the things failures
don't like to do. They don't like doing them either necessarily. But
their disliking is subordinated to the strength of their purpose.*

~Albert E. N. Gray

In October 1979, we learned that one of the jewels in the area, Parade Rest Guest Ranch, was for sale. Retirement age was creeping up on Bud and Lucille (Lu) Morris when they invited us out to have a look around and see if we were interested in purchasing the ranch. Bud must have known what it would take for us to buy it, as he had the horses saddled up and told us to take our family for a ride on the forest trails.

Prior to that time, the property was homesteaded in 1919 by Thomas W. and Katherine (Kate) Rouse. Kate's grandmother was distantly related to Abraham Lincoln and remembered sitting on his lap. This 160-acre piece of property was rather unique in that the Gallatin National Forest surrounded it on all sides.

Original homestead cabin, modernized and still used
as a guest cabin after nearly 100 years

In 1935, retiring army Major John Rodman and his wife, Marie, bought this property. Major Rodman, a veteran of World War I, began to invite some of his friends to the ranch for some good old western hospitality and seclusion. Slowly, additional cabins were built and it became a hit with his friends, and he decided to change it to a guest ranch and named it after the military term "parade rest," meaning a position of relaxed attention, hence the name Parade Rest Guest Ranch. The Rodmans were of the old west mentality and lifestyle, which included a love for guns and even a little moonshine.

Parade Rest Guest Ranch was sold to Wells "Bud" and Lucille "Lu" Morris on July 10, 1957. They owned the ranch for 22 years and operated it in a very low-key way. They advertised in one magazine; had one wrangler, a couple of housekeepers, and a cook; and owned twelve cabins, some situated right on Grayling Creek and some up on a bluff overlooking the corral area. Bill and Carole Howell were part owners with us until 2011. During this time, we thought we could broaden the appeal to clients by emphasizing more family-oriented activities and horseback riding. In order to accomplish this, we expanded the ranch, its buildings, and personnel and made it a great place for families, reunions, and groups. We have now owned Parade Rest for over 36 years.

Still drinking up the beauty and peacefulness of Parade Rest after owning it for 16 years, I was all alone and meandering around the ranch in the fall. I was struck with feelings of awe at the beauties all around me, which continued to leave indelibly imprints on my mind. Upon returning home, I wrote the following poem entitled "Awesome Autumn."

It reads:

AWESOME AUTUMN

A camera, I did not have, so words will just have to do,
As I stood amid the cottonwoods with leaves
of a brilliant golden hue.
'Twas fall at Parade Rest Guest Ranch,
The silence broken only by the rustling of
the leaves and a broken branch.
At my left hand stood our "black as coal" mare,
And under my right hand her little paint
colt was just a standin' there.
The Quaking Aspen had mostly lost their leaves,
With just a little yellow left shimmering in the breeze.
Up on the hillside a jack leg fence ran way up high.
The sagebrush, grasses, and scrub oak were so colorful,
and yet so dry.
To the East the quakies gave way to the pines,
And just to the left Hebgen Lake and Lionshead
were just in line.
I looked on around to complete the horizon,
The mountains of Yellowstone and the grazing lands
for many a bison.
Right in front, Grayling Creek was just a gurgling.
Where earlier this spring it had been raging and whirling.
Across the creek stood the old Homestead Cabin,
Standing like a sentinel and a testament of

things that used to happen.
Now I could not help but stand in the solemnity of awe,
of the beauty all around me just before dark,
And our privilege to live next to Yellowstone National Park.
Even this frame made from the handiwork of God
and shaped by an unskilled hand,
Takes on new meaning as a product of
this almost hallowed land.
But the thing most abundantly clear,
is that we are so blessed by the Almighty above,
To be the caretakers for a decade or so of this
place we so dearly love.
—Clyde Seely, Oct 1996

I made a frame, as spoken of in the poem and it hangs on the wall of the dining room, where guests can relate and enjoy. "Awesome Autumn" represents the passion and feelings Linda and I have for this beautiful peaceful place. In addition to this poem, those staying at Parade Rest will find a detailed history about the ranch that I wrote in 2001.

Not mentioned so far are those same feelings we have for those who have worked at the ranch that we have come to know and appreciate. We enjoy the guests. We enjoy the staff, and we have become attached to and appreciate those who we have relied on to manage the ranch.

Our first managers were Walt and Shirley Butcher, who managed the ranch for 15 years. Walt in his bib overalls and Shirley with her blonde hair and warm personality will always have a place in our hearts. Walt and Shirley are now buried next to our family plot at the Fur Ridge Cemetery one mile east of the ranch. A framed poem hangs in the dining room that expresses our love and appreciation for them.

As has been referred to before, a wise and very successful business man told me how he became so successful; he said "I just hire people that are better than I am and then get out of their way and let them do it." That is just what I did when we hired Marge Wanner. Marge was hired as our next ranch manager. She is also a good cook and often takes her turn in the kitchen. She has been president of the chamber of commerce and chairman of the World Snowmobile Expo in West Yellowstone since its inception over 25 years ago, and, like the energizer bunny, she just keeps going and going and going. Marge is like a mom to the help. She can be stern to them and yet is always compassionate. She is normally the initial contact for the guests and makes sure they feel at home in this awesome place. Larry, her husband, still works for us at Yellowstone Arctic and sometimes provides support for Marge. To them we will always be grateful.

Another unusual purchase was the addition to Parade Rest of the neighboring 160 acres. It was in 1992 that Dick Drew asked if I was interested in buying this parcel of land between Parade Rest Ranch and the highway. While consummating the deal to purchase this property, Dick told me of the time he and his friend Roland Whitman, a well-respected landowner, rode across this property on horseback and both began talking about how nice it would be to own it. Later, Dick decided to buy the land, and in his mind he had always planned on cutting Roland in on the deal. However, that had never happened. Dick also told me that he had always thought when his property was sold, the owner of Parade Rest Ranch should be given first chance to purchase. We were very appreciative of that offer and purchased the property May 1, 1992, and we used it for badly needed horse pasture in connection with the ranch.

While Dick told me about his relationship with Roland, he also said that although nothing had been put on paper, he always considered Roland to be 50% owner of that land. He wanted me to know that if he and his wife Marion (a beloved school teacher in

West Yellowstone) passed away before they had been paid in full for the land, I was to see that Roland got the remaining balance owed.

After both Dick and Marion passed away, the retirement center in which they had been living called and wanted the balance of the property payments given to them. They sent an amendment to the contract that would have accomplished the same. I rejected this amendment and told them of Dick's wishes. After having that settled, which took some doing, we paid the balance of the note to Roland. He was surprised and did not know of Dick's silent commitment he had made to himself in remembering his good friend. To me, that was an example of how deep friendships can run. Roland and Dick were true friends indeed. **28**

See **28** on the West Yellowstone Map Pages 142-143

Pebble 18: Beginnings of First Security Bank and Yellowstone Tour and Travel

The safe way to double your money is to fold
it over once and put it in your pocket.

~Kin Hubbard

It was not until 1966 that West Yellowstone had its first bank. Prior to this, the absence of a bank became a problem especially as commerce increased and large amounts of money were accumulated. Until the early 1960s, during most days of the week, LaVell Coffin, a local grocer at the Market Center Grocery Store, took it upon himself to make a bank run to Ashton, Idaho, a hundred and thirty-mile drive. He became West Yellowstone's first armored car service, without the armored car. My future mother-in-law, Beulah, worked in that bank and almost every morning she saw LaVell waiting there for it to open. He would exchange and deposit money for himself and others before starting on his sixty-five-mile drive back. He would have been a likely candidate for a hold-up, but few people knew the amount of money that was carried in that little personal auto, and people were more trusting then.

When I first started working for the Wilsons in 1958, it was clear that banking in West Yellowstone was not an easy thing. Some businesses used the old combination safes, while others had a secret place to stash money. Mike Wilson, I recall, would cash people's checks for them and make change when he could. I am sure others did the same. Also the Yellowstone National Park Gate normally had extra $1 bills after a busy weekend, which helped out.

Eventually, Mike Wilson and the First Security Bank in Bozeman began talking about building a bank in West Yellowstone. Mike agreed to construct the bank building, which included a manager's apartment, and lease it to the bank on a ten-year contract. My recollection was that it cost $40,000. He built the unique A-framed building with a vault, teller windows, and office space on the first floor, and record storage in the basement. The top two floors made up the manager's apartment. Mike and a few others had stock in the bank and were members of the board of directors. Dean and Betty Nelson managed and ran the bank. The bank building was nearly completed when I went back to work for Mike in 1966. He had me install carpet on the stairs and tile in the two upstairs bathrooms.

A bank in West Yellowstone was a sure sign of the growth of our little seasonal town, a sign to be proud of. Dean and Betty Nelson lived in the apartment on the top two floors of the A-frame. Other than the built-in thick concrete vault, the bank started off with only one room. Dean was the manager and had his desk on the west side of the room where the confidential loan conversations would take place. This always needed to be conducted in low voices so the people in line, just a few feet away at the teller's windows, would not hear and be tempted to divulge privileged information. Still, business continued to grow and the bank had to find more space.

The ten-year lease was about to expire, and the town bank eventually outgrew the A-frame building. A new bank was built on Dunraven Street, where the current library is located. Mike Polkowske took over the reigns as president and has led the bank forward to this day. First Interstate Bank came into town and built a new bank in the Grizzly Park Addition. Yellowstone Basin Bank also built a new bank on the opposite corner. I was asked to sit on the board of that bank. However, it soon became apparent that there

was not enough business for three banks to survive in town. First
Interstate Bank sold their building to First Security Bank and closed
up their operation. First Security Bank then moved into the new
First Interstate building, where it remains to this day.

When the bank outgrew the A-frame building we purchased
it from the Wilsons in 1975. It again became part of the Three
Bear Lodge property. We formed Yellowstone Tour and Travel and
remodeled the building as the office. There was no space for rest-
rooms, so we built them inside the old vault and boasted that we
had the safest Johns in town. **14**

Original First Security Bank became Yellowstone Tour and Travel

Yellowstone Tour and Travel became our marketing and reservation service. The only thing we lacked in order to provide complete package tours was the ability to provide airline ticketing. So
we went through all of the requirements and became a full-fledged
travel agency. Marysue Costello became our first manager. She and
her husband John had come out for several years from Minnesota to
snowmobile with us. They fell prey to the lure of West Yellowstone
and decided to move here. I recommended that John buy Gene
Cheatley's real estate business and he did.

See **14** on the West Yellowstone Map Pages 142-143

We continued to expand our businesses. By now we were operating a number of motels, restaurants, snowmobile rentals, and the guest ranch. We were now able to provide airline tickets and complete travel agency services to the local community as well as our guests. The customer could now make one call to us and we did all the rest. Basically, through our complete vacation packages, we could make arrangements to take someone from their home to West Yellowstone, and back to their home: truly a one-stop shop.

As part of Yellowstone Tour and Travel, Bill, Carole, Linda, and I would travel to various trade shows across the country promoting our complete package: "Winter in Yellowstone." We expanded our marketing efforts and traveled with Western Airlines to their ski market shows from Florida to California. It was fun to tell people about our "Winter in Yellowstone" packages and then later hear them say things like, "it was the best vacation we have ever had." Then we decided to spread the word overseas, and I traveled alone to attend the ten-day London Travel Market. All of these efforts soon generated excitement about coming to Yellowstone and, along with other operators, efforts contributed to the economy of West Yellowstone.

In addition to these efforts, we began marketing to a consortium of private air travel clubs. These marketing trips were very successful, as there were large groups of people coming together looking to travel to various destinations. Some of these travel clubs even owned their own planes.

Once we were allowed to make a presentation in Denver, Colorado, to these large traveling groups. Since other destinations like the Big Sky Resort would sponsor an expensive, fabulous dinner, and try to wow visitors into coming to their facilities, we decided to take a different approach. Quite often, the wow factor is best accomplished by doing the thing that you do best in an extraordinary way. At that time, we were operating 260 rental snowmobiles in the winter and had the lodging and tour opportunities in the summer. So we mixed a western theme into a winter theme. We had buffalo hamburger flown in, bought enough straw cowboy hats for everyone, and served probably the first buffalo burger they had ever heard of, much less eaten. We turned the cowboy hats upside down with the thick burger nestled inside a bandana, which was then removed and used as a napkin.

Off to the side, we had a snowball sitting next to their hat and meal. Yes, a real snowball brought from West Yellowstone, Montana! This was one they could pick up and heft without it melting and running all over. We accomplished this by making snowballs in West Yellowstone, melting about a half-gallon of paraffin wax, then dunking the snowballs into the hot wax. The wax immediately cooled around the snowball, and it came out white, and formed exactly around the snowball. The snowball then melted inside the wax casing and with a little shake you could hear the water sloshing inside. We carefully took those to the presentation dinner and placed one at each setting. We made a big deal about them and told them that they too could make their own snowballs in West Yellowstone and while you are there we will give you an experience that few people have ever had: "Winter in Yellowstone." We explained that we would provide a complete fun-filled and worry-free winter vacation package complete with all meals, lodging, full snowmobile clothing, guides, and snowmobile rental for each person.

The presentation was a whopping success. For a number of years, we had privately-owned or chartered 737 passenger planes flying into West Yellowstone in the summer and to Bozeman, Montana, in the winter.

Pebble 19: Holiday Inn Beginning: The Hotel that Just about Wasn't!

Solomon said, "With all thy getting get wisdom" (See Prov. 4:7). And then someone who must have been a little wiser that Solomon said, "With all thy getting, get going."

~Sterling S. Sill

Bill and I were increasing the winter snowmobile operation and the prospects of a year-round facility were improving. I remember one night in 1980 talking to Bill and saying, "You know, the time will come when there will be a need for a hotel and a large convention facility in this town." At that time, the closest thing was the basement of the Stagecoach Inn.

To accomplish our new goal, we began to purchase the entire south half of the block on Yellowstone Avenue over the next 10 years. Those purchases included Al's Motel, Gibson's Trailer Park (on February 10, 1982), and a house and garage from Gus Tureman. We continued operating those places until we felt the time was right to pursue the hotel and convention facility.

There had already been an independent property assessment of the town. The most valuable property ran along the Union Pacific property down Yellowstone Avenue. The Three Bear Lodge and the Ambassador were both situated on the most prime real estate in town.

Very quietly, we began the process of conducting a feasibility study for the convention facility and talking to people about financing the project. The West Yellowstone's World Snowmobile Expo was becoming successful and was housed in a tent at the old airport. Several thousand people came to the races and West Yellowstone was becoming known as the snowmobile capital of the world. Still the set-up was rather crude: the tent was not adequate to handle the large number of expo attendees, and when the snow and ice melted around the tent, the water ran inside and covered the floor. The portable toilets were also very inadequate. What a nice thing it would be if we could build a facility that would accommodate those needs as well as other meetings and conventions!

The feasibility study for the envisioned hotel and convention facility cost $85,000. We lined up an architect and contractor out of Washington state to construct the hotel. I had talked to Jim Erickson, one of the most regular customers of Three Bear Lodge, and received a verbal commitment to finance the project. I felt confident he had the financial wherewithal needed to build the facility. He caught the vision and said he had some other friends that would be willing to join together and finance the $4 million plus project.

We were excited about how easy it seemed to finance the new facility. We published a rather nice brochure with the conceptual renderings of the proposed West Yellowstone Conference Hotel. This brochure would be used as our initial marketing piece and would announce the construction of this fabulous facility. Crunch time was coming, so I called Jim again to confirm that he and his friends were still committed to financing the project. He said they were. I explained that we were going public at the Snowmobile Expo and that the facility would be built and available for the expo the next year. He said that would be fine and that all was a go.

We had a booth at the expo in March 1994 and, with great colored renderings, announced to the world we would have 10,000 square feet of convention space, 123 hotel rooms, and a restaurant and lounge for the expo the following year. The announcement blew everybody away and they could not believe it. This was a complete surprise to the community and a number of naysayers claimed we could never have it done by then.

Our job was to have all of the property clear of all the current buildings by June 1, 1994, for the building contractor to begin. It was a tight schedule. The day after the expo, when some of the rooms were vacated, we took our backhoe and started demolition of the two-story office and apartment cinder block building.

As the walls were falling, our hopes and dreams also came crashing down. We called Jim to tell him we were starting demolitions and were ready to begin making draws on his financing package. He was sort of nonchalant in his retort. He said, "Well, my friends and I have decided that we are too old to get involved in this project."

Just like that, our hopes were dashed. He was off the hook, and we were out in the cold with our names at stake, the building being torn down, and the June 1st construction deadline looming.

Before settling in with this financing source, that now had vanished, we had surveyed the lending institutions in Montana— and the banks were not capable of financing such a large loan. We thought we were pretty shrewd by skirting around all the red tape and financing requirements with a quick and easy private financing commitment. So once again, we frantically checked all the sources throughout the state. No one was willing or capable of putting together a financing package of this size. The only institution with the slightest possibility of covering such a loan was the First Interstate Bank in Billings, Montana. Meanwhile, we put all of the demolition on hold, so we didn't have to repair what was torn down in case we couldn't finance the project. Prospects were looking pretty bleak.

Then Bill and I set up an appointment with Pete Cochran at First Interstate Bank and went into that meeting with a do-or-die attitude. Pete, at the outset, was not very interested and was paving the way, we thought, for a rejection. As mentioned before, there are times in my life when something from within sort of takes charge, and I say things that surprise even me. This was one of those occasions. I claimed boldly and with great confidence that we were not just a wannabe hotel. We had been in business for almost 20 years and were thriving. We were not coming to him with a pipe dream, but had built a foundation where the risk was pretty well removed. With a snowmobile rental business, we needed more rooms. The timing was right for a hotel and convention center to be built in town. Bill and I were not starting something new but were in the mode of expanding the business we already knew and in which we had already been successful. Pete pushed his chair back away from the table and said, "Well, you have convinced me." Those were sweet words to hear. Bill told me he had never heard such a persuasive presentation.

Starting over with a new financing package for over $4 million when we were already tearing down the existing motel was a daunting task. Because of the size of the loan, First Interstate Bank helped us subsidize the financing package between First Interstate Bank, Montana Board of Investments, and the Small Business Administration (SBA). Lining all this up required several trips to Billings and Helena, Montana. In addition to the above financing package we needed to provide $1,500,000 of private money as well as the land on which to build the facility. In the meantime, with a great deal of faith, we continued to tear down the existing motel, and on April 1, 1994, we finally consummated the loans with these good people.

My plan was to tear down the two-story cinder block motel, salvage the block and the wooden floor joists, and reuse them in building an apartment complex for our employees. We were working rapidly when the owner of Lemons Brothers House Moving stopped in to see me and asked, "Rather than tear this down, why don't you just let us move the building as is?"

I told him, "You can't move a two story cinder block building." He said that he could. If it could be done, it would be far cheaper and faster than tearing it down and rebuilding it block by block, to convert it into the apartments we needed. We were really dubious, but he proceeded to demonstrate how he could do it. Then our endeavors changed from demolition to preparing four different two-story motel sections to be moved.

We separated the building into separate sections that looked something like four different buildings. It was unbelievable to see those large sections, between 40 and 60 feet long, raised. The crew dug with a backhoe deep enough so pocket holes could be punched out on both sides of the building. These were where the large steel I beams (shaped like a capital I) were slid in. When all of them were in place and good footings established under the multiple hydraulic jacks, the Lemons Brothers would gently pull a lever and the whole building began to slowly rise. Truckloads of cribbing were used to rest the beams on as the section was raised high enough for the big bolsters and wheels to be pushed under. The largest section had sixty-eight wheels and trusses made of huge steel beams. Since cinder block and its mortared joints are not pliable, I thought that there would be cracks as a result of the move, but there weren't any.

What followed was the most amazing thing I had ever seen. The sight of the big transit platform that moves the space shuttle seemed no more impressive to me than what happened next as I watched each of the four large cinder block buildings move slowly across the street. They were stored on city property across from our house for much of the summer while we prepared the land four blocks north for their arrival.

We purchased the old LDS church building on Gibbon Avenue, which had been vacated after we built the new church across the street. We also bought an adjacent lot from the Whitmers on April 21, 1994, to provide a location for these four separated buildings. Then we assembled the buildings. On one side, two buildings were placed next to each other, and on the opposite side the other two were placed. We attached them back together with recycled cinder block, and painted them so that no one would know these two-story buildings had been moved from another location. Those buildings, formerly known as the Ambassador Motor Inn, became the Ambassador Apartments. These apartments were hardly finished before the workers who were building the hotel began to move in. We added kitchens and now had twenty-two badly needed employee apartments. Then we converted the old church into a summer dormitory. This would house the employees at our new West Yellowstone conference hotel, Holiday Inn Sunspree Resort. **15**

Moving and recycling motel facilities into employee housing was a very innovative thing to do, and other lodging properties followed suit. By doing this, owners could rebuild or upgrade their nightly lodging and higher income producing facilities, and at the same time provide much needed housing for their employees.

In order to have all the buildings torn down or moved by the construction start-up date, Bill and I had to work rapidly. It was a big project to orchestrate, and it appeared we were playing "musical buildings" as we moved structures around to different locations or recycled structures. We moved the railroad car off its foundation, so we could move Gus's house and garage, which we purchased, to that location. The rail car was then moved onto its new site so the new hotel could be built around it. It became the namesake for the newly built Oregon Short Line Restaurant. Four motel units of Al's motel were moved 40 miles down the Gallatin Canyon. Gibson's trailer park was torn down and the materials salvaged. The old foundations and concrete work from these buildings were used as fill for the old basements eliminating the need of hauling tons and tons of concrete to the dump.

During all of this time, I was the first to arrive and the last to leave the job site. Then at night we would formulate plans for the next day and decide what steps needed to be taken to put the pieces of this puzzle back together. Prior to and during the beginning of the

---

See **15** on the West Yellowstone Map Pages 142-143

demolition stages, my feet began to hurt so badly that I could hardly walk. Doctors could not help and I began to wonder if this was going to be a permanent condition. I wondered how I was going to accomplish the task that lay ahead. For some reason I started taking some antioxidants. I don't know if this had anything to do with it or not, but my feet began to get better and I could finally run at my normal speed again.

We met our goal of clearing the entire half block of buildings by June 1, 1994, and the contractor, White Construction, began their work. Winter came early, and we had ten inches of snow in October. In spite of the inclement weather, all 123 hotel units were completed by the Christmas holidays. ⑩

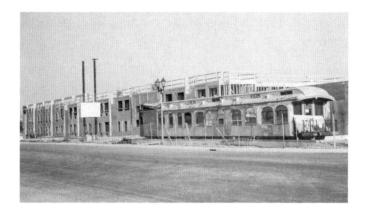

Holiday Inn under construction and restoring the Oregon Short Line 1903

We then concentrated on the interior decorating of the restaurant, conference facilities, and lounge, which was no small job. With the help of some interior decorators, we linked the restaurant and lounge to the Oregon Short Line Executive Railroad Car. Then we purchased conductor's uniforms for our tour guides, to reinforce the railroad theme.

See ⑩ on the West Yellowstone Map Pages 142-143

We named the Oregon Short Line Restaurant and the Iron Horse Saloon after the railroad era that played such an important part of the early establishment of Yellowstone. We made the Oregon Short Line 1903, a museum-quality railroad car, and the focal point of the dining experience. It was fitting, with the old railroad buildings located just across the street.

The conference facility had 5,000 square feet of banquet space. In addition, we designed a 5,000 square foot space that could be used as a dual-purpose trade show/snowmobile storage area. We had reached our goal of providing a facility for the expo in March 1995. However, we were still short on exhibition space, so we rented a 13,200 square foot tent and attached it to the side door of the convention facility. But even after scraping the parking lot clean of snow, we still had melting water running through the carpeted floors of the tent.

After one year, I designed a way to build a removable interlocking floor made out of 5/8" plywood and 1" x 4" boards. We purchased the material from the Westmart Building Center, and they were kind enough to provide some of the labor to build these floor pieces. When we laid it out, it worked perfectly. We removed the floor immediately after the event was over and stored it until the next year's use. Many years later, it is still working fine.

We delayed the grand opening celebration and open house until May 19, 1995. West Yellowstone Town and other regional dignitaries were present. Our chef prepared a wonderful meal complete with an ice carving of the Oregon Short line 1903 railroad car. At the conclusion of the evening I gave a light-hearted speech. I had read a story about a snake pit but could not find it, so using it as a theme, I wrote sort of a fun parody about us building the Holiday Inn and Convention Center. It was entitled "The Allegory of the Snakes in West Snakeville."

THE ALLEGORY OF THE SNAKES IN WEST SNAKEVILLE

It was spring as Cloyd, a little snake, just young in life, with his eyes wide with wonder slithered through the grass as he began to survey the other communities outside of West Snakeville. West Snakeville was a small little commune with only small family pits that the snakes could hiss in. Slithering through the grass, he poked his head between two rocks and, to his great amazement, saw the largest snake pit he had ever seen. He brought his friend Billy to share in his amazement. Inside the lavish snake pit were dozens of snakes gleefully hissing away. First, one would hiss, then the others would hiss back. Then they would all listen to the snake up on a rock in front, who would hiss and hiss to all the others in attendance. They would laugh and laugh and all would hiss and hiss back and forth to each other again.

One of the little snakes from West Snakeville and Billy hissed to each other. "Do you know that we in West Snakeville don't even have a pit to hiss in?"

Cloyd hissed in agreement, "Much less a window to do it out of."

"Well this will just not do," hissed one. "We really need a pit to hiss in, in West Snakeville just like other communes."

"If we just had a Hissing Pit, other snakes would travel far to hiss in our pit," hissed Cloyd. "Why, we not only have West Snakeville to hiss about, we have 'Yellowrock Park' where there are elk, eagles, deer, bison, and now even wolves."

"We even have a Bear Pit now," said Billy, "So why shouldn't we have a Hissing Pit? If we just had a pit to hiss in, all the snakes could come and hiss about what they had seen and learned in 'Yellowrock Park.'"

West Snakeville began to grow and grow but still there was no pit to hiss in. Well, Cloyd and Billy decided to make their dream come true. First, they met with an architect snake that slithered a design in the sand as to how the ideal pit to hiss in should be. After all, he was good at hissing and knew just how to make a wonderful pit to hiss in. Then they went to the banker snake who said, "Well, you've sold me! I'll dig in my pot to find the loot so you can build your pit to hiss in." Well, all this time, you can imagine how much hissing went on in West Snakeville. "This pit is too small to hiss in" or "There is not enough parking for this pit to hiss in." Finally, the plan was hissed to the Mayor Snake and the Council. "All hissed in agreement that a nice spacious pit to hiss in would be a good thing for West Snakeville."

Now building inspector Bit, said, "You'd better put in your pit enough pots to hiss in. There must be the same amount of pots in the one room as there are troughs in the other to hiss in, so there are no discrimination hisses, hissing forth from disgruntled hissing pit participants."

Well finally, it was time to put all the hissing behind, shed their skins, and get to work tearing down the old meager pit where no more than a dozen snakes could hiss in at the same time. The contractor snake and his crew didn't have time to hiss and hiss back and forth at each other. Consequently, they built the Hissing Pit in an unbelievably short amount of time.

So the long and short of this allegory is on the evening of May 19, 1995, the most prominent and most helpful snakes were all invited to gather together in the West Snakeville Conference Hissing Pit to celebrate the completion of one of the finest pits to hiss in in the state. Now the new pit to hiss in is here for everyone to hiss and hiss in for years to come. The two little snakes, who dreamed the dream for the grand hissing pit, hissed to all, "Thanks for being a part of and helping to make our dream come true."

We had accomplished what one person told me was impossible. To remove many buildings from the land and build the largest facility in West Yellowstone in six months did seem a bit aggressive. Later Glen Loomis told others and me that "Clyde Seely willed it to be done."

It was a fun night as we celebrated the completion of the largest hotel in town along with the badly needed convention center. If anyone was looking for a sign that West Yellowstone was coming into its own, they needed only to look to the building of this new imposing hotel complex. There was now a 123-unit hotel, a restaurant, a lounge, and a 10,000 square foot convention facility.

Clyde and Linda Seely, ice carving of R.R. Car, Carole and Bill Howell

We designed the convention center to be a one of a kind in the world. We were running over 120 snowmobiles out of the Holiday Inn and had to store them indoors overnight. Consequently, we designed half of the convention facility, the 5,000 square feet Hayden Hall, with large overhead garage doors on both ends. In the winter, we put about ten inches of snow into this space so snowmobiles could be based there. Then, just a few days before the Snowmobile Expo, we would turn the heat on in the Hayden Hall, and I would take my big front-end loader and plow out all the ice and snow. Within two days we would roll out the carpet on the floor and it became trade show space. Those who came and used the trade show area had no idea that just a few days before; there was 10 inches of snow on the floor and 120 snowmobiles stored inside. This also gave us the ability of holding conventions of up to 500 people. One of the requirements of a convention is to be able to meet and feed in two different areas. While a meeting is in progress, the other room can be set up for meals or banquets. For the rest of the eight months of the year this space was put to good use, and then in December we filled it with snow and the process started over again.

We had initially named the facility the West Yellowstone Conference Hotel. But once the walls were all built and the roof on, a Holiday Inn representative came courting us to join the Holiday Inn network. While we wanted to become affiliated with a brand or a "flag" we wanted to include "conference center" in our name so it would be clear that we were more than just a nice hotel. We found out that if we would become a Holiday Inn Sunspree Resort we could also attach our name to it. The end result was that we named our hotel the West Yellowstone Conference Hotel, Holiday Inn Sunspree Resort. Even though that was a long handle, it seemed to accomplish our goal of identifying exactly who we were and also giving us the Holiday Inn affiliation. We had a large attractive sign designed, built, and installed. Eventually, Holiday Inn did away with the Sunspree Resort brand and we became simply the Holiday Inn.

***

We wanted to do some special things in the lobby so people would come in and say "Wow." We had Jeff Carter paint a panoramic view of the Grand Canyon of Yellowstone. Jeff spent weeks on this 5' x 25' painting. For full effect, we framed it and mounted it above the reception desk in the lobby.

We also had a statue of a seventeen-foot-tall dead tree, representing a burned tree from the '88 fires of Yellowstone and two eagles. The male eagle, with wings spread to full length, is swooping down to encourage the female perched on the old spare tree into romantic flight. The base of the sculpture has the skull of a bison laying between the tree roots as they spread out into the blackened ground. We built a 40" x 40" base for the statue and a plaque that referred to the new birth that would come back to Yellowstone like the green of spring that emerges when the winter snows recede. Governor Marc Racicot came down for the unveiling and the raising of the seventeen-foot-tall tribute to Yellowstone's wild heritage.

We employed the interior decorators who had done such a fabulous job decorating our Three Bear Restaurant with historic memorabilia to decorate the Oregon Short Line Restaurant. We used the 1903 Museum Railroad Car, now situated just across the hallway, as the namesake and the theme setter for the restaurant. Between the railroad car and the restaurant, we built a walkway out of fir and elevated it on two-inch strips, so when the floor was walked on it sounded like you were walking on a train station platform just outside the depot.

I have always liked to create and build things. It is fun to be able to stand back and look at a completed project and know that the town is better as a result of this creation. I remember being on a sales trip and relaxing in an outdoor hot tub at a rather large convention hotel and thinking, "Wouldn't it be nice if we could one day build something like this in West Yellowstone?"

At that point, a large convention hotel was one of the missing links to creating West Yellowstone as a destination town instead of just an overnight bedroom community for Yellowstone Park. Although it seemed like a pipe dream at the time, it eventually became a reality.

Starting up an entire new operation of this size was an undertaking that we had not done before. First of all, it started with hiring a general manager, Doug Smith, before we ever completed the construction. Fortunately we had our employees from the Ambassador Motor Inn as the core of this new facility. Everybody thought it was pretty cool to be able to work in this new landmark hotel. To that crew we added a restaurant staff, additional housekeeping, and a full-time marketing person. It was like we had expanded our family

178 Clyde Seely

multiple times over as we got everybody organized in their new positions and hired additional people. We would hold weekly staff meetings in the new board room and forged ahead. Bill and I each slid into our own areas of expertise as we had 24/7 communications.

It is a wonderful thing to be able to create a facility and fall in love with it. It was also a wonderful thing to gather together a staff of people willing to work together as a unit for the good of all. A bond was created that we will always remember. We had designed a facility to work exactly as needed and everything really worked well. We started a tradition of having all our employees and families come to a big Christmas dinner. This was a time when we could get them all together and express appreciation for them. We would also express a thought or two to set the tone reminding us all why we were really there and whose birthday we were really celebrating.

The Holiday Inn became a pace setter for future hotels and generated revenue for the town as a whole. Millions of dollars have been pumped into the community through conventions and up-scale functions held there. Building the Holiday Inn could well have been another example of the embodiment of what Uncle Clarence referred to as the "golden chair of opportunity," and we were proud to be a part of it.

However, after the major fire at Three Bear Lodge (See Pebble 28), I needed to devote 24/7 to its rebuilding. My full attention was required at Three Bear in designing and overseeing the construction, and Bill and I thought it would be best to divest our financial interest in the Holiday Inn.

We sold the Holiday Inn to Delaware North Corporation on May 15, 2009. The 15 years since the opening of the Holiday Inn Sunspree Resort and Conference Center passed ever so quickly. It is easy to remember so many things, too many to include here. I can clearly remember working with Pete White, the contractor, in making sure things were done right and making changes as needed. Many decisions had to be made. I was not able to just sit back and let someone else build and finish out a new hotel without being involved. As our first manager, Doug Smith said, "You are not only going to decide what chair will be purchased but also where it should be placed."

Selling the Holiday Inn was a difficult thing to do. I could no longer have a say about where that chair should be placed. Nor could I have any say when the name of the Oregon Short Line Restaurant was changed to simply "The Branch." We loved the old railroad car from which it was named. A relic that was once a mystery, which we cared for and preserved for 40 years, only to discover it was built by order of E. H. Harriman himself. How do you walk away from a 113-year-old museum-quality railroad car like that? How do you just sign a piece of paper and walk out the door for the last time on a project that was a dream brought to fruition? How do you leave behind the memories of turning the stud walls, trusses, rafters, and sheet rock ceilings into finished, beautifully furnished rooms? And especially, how do you say good-bye to the new family of devoted employees that have been there all the way through those 15 wonderful years.

As the years have passed since the sale, whenever I walk into the restroom at the hotel, I remember when Linda and I went to Salt Lake and picked out the tile and then laid it. The memories and sense of pride remain. It was a dream that involved risk and hard work, but it was like creating another pool for more pebbles to be dropped into, where the ripples will continue for another century and beyond.

Pebble 20: The Impact of Snowmobiles on my Life and West Yellowstone

The 3 Cs of failure are criticism, condemnation, and complaining.
The 3 Cs of success are compassion, courage, and commitment.

~Author Unknown

Early in winter 1964, I turned up the lane to the old farm house where I was raised. My brother's father-in-law, Owen Jensen, was there with a machine that I had never seen before. It had an aqua-green hood that covered an engine. There was a bright orange seat and a set of handlebars to hold onto. "Johnson Skee Horse" was written on the side. I was told it was a snowmobile, and Owen told me to sit on it. He pulled a rope and the engine started. He told me to push on the lever with my thumb to make it go. I did, and to my amazement, off it went. I steered it down to the cow pasture, which was covered with about eight inches of snow. With the wind on my cheeks, I went up and down the gentle hills of the pasture, and the feeling was exhilarating. This was the first time I had ever heard of, much less ridden, a snowmobile.

After graduating from Idaho State University in 1965, Linda and I moved to West Yellowstone, and I began teaching school. Snowmobiles were becoming more common in town and some of the local guys would get together to go snowmobiling. It looked fun, so in 1968 I bought a used snowmobile from Ehlert Koski for $600. It was a Johnson Skee Horse, like the first one I had ridden. After school I would get dressed and was off for a ride. I normally stayed close to town because if I ever got stuck, I would get really stuck and it could be a long, deep walk for help. The machines then were heavy and not very powerful, with very little clearance between the running board and the bottom of the track. However, when I could find a drift I would hit it at full throttle (the maximum speed was about 20 mph) and try to catch a little air.

In order to make this a family affair, after school I worked on building a pull-behind sled to pull the kids. It ended up looking more like a Santa Claus sled, but color coordinated with the Johnson colors of aqua green and orange.

Linda pulling Rochelle with the Johnson Skee Horse

Eventually, the Johnson became too tame, and I couldn't keep up with the rest of the guys, so I bought a used Polaris that I thought was pretty hot. It had a narrower track and could do about 40 mph. Now that I had more power, my friends and I could get through the deep snow and up the steep hills to the top of Two Top Mountain. The view was spectacular. We called the trees at the top snow ghosts because they were totally encased in snow, and it was easy to imagine them as ghostly figures. My favorite was the one

I called "Old Man Winter" that looked like a man with his cheeks blowing out, like he was blowing the wind. I took a picture of "Old Man Winter," along with other scenic photos of Old Faithful and other Yellowstone features and eventually took them on a road trip with me to Minneapolis.

The West Yellowstone Chamber and Snowmobile Club sponsored snowmobile races in December and March. This was a way to bring winter business to town and many places would open just for the races. The people that came to the races also discovered unbelievable snowmobiling outside the park and a few ventured into the park.

Since I already loved the mobility snowmobiles offered, and since I knew where to share the rare beauty that few people get to see in the winter, I was excited to offer a unique vacation experience to our guests. But at that time, in 1971, when I first started renting them, I couldn't have imagined the impact that snowmobiles would have on my life and that of the town.

During these early years, a trip inside the park to Old Faithful was rather adventurous since there were no facilities open, poorly groomed roads, and snowmobile technology that was still in its infancy. Outside the park, the three national forests, Gallatin, Targhee, and Beaverhead, had snowmobile trails, but we had nothing to groom trails with. I remember one time I took the leader of a group who had brought about twenty other snowmobilers to show her Two Top. We had a deep snowfall the night before and I wanted to see if we could make it up the mountain. We worked and worked, digging out the machines too many times to count in the soft powder. Finally we decided we had met our match. We eventually turned around, admitting the mountain had beaten us. If we just had a trail groomer, it would have been no problem.

In order to have people come and enjoy the surrounding areas on a snowmobile, we needed to find a way to groom the trails. The first groomer was provided by Bombardier and was marketed as part of their "Operation SnoPlan." Jerry Schmier (sometimes accompanied by his wife Verlene) was the first to groom the trails with the SV250. The West Snowmobile Club eventually purchased this early groomer for $12,000 at 6 percent interest.

The groomer was a small yellow machine, and a driver would sit inside to drag a small groomer attachment, leveling out the snow as it went. This was an improvement over no groomer at all, but the number of people that began to come in the winter made the necessity for improvements clear.

I thought we could just widen the area the snowmobiles could ride on and diversify the traffic without grooming. I was wrong. It was decided by the Chamber, the newly formed grooming committee, and the Forest Service that we needed to cut down some trees in order to make a snowmobile trail that would be maintained by the small groomer.

The Forest Service was very helpful in making the forests user friendly. I remember one time Claude Coffin from the Forest Service and I cut down many trees to widen the trail coming down off Two Top, on the South Fork side.

Of course, grooming the trails wasn't free, so the funding for it came from trade dollars. These were attractive gold-colored coins the size of a silver dollar designed with West Yellowstone and the trail grooming program featured on the coin. Visitors could purchase them as a collector's item and memento of their snowmobile experience in West Yellowstone. The idea was to sell $2 souvenir coins and end up netting $1 that would be used for the funding of the grooming program. This project only ended up netting us about $2,000 per year, not nearly enough to cover the cost of trail grooming. So the Snowmobile Club and others met in the Firehole Room of the Dining Lodge to discuss how we could increase revenue. One suggestion was to make a West Yellowstone snowmobile patch that could be sewn on snowmobile jackets and caps.

My suggestion was to discontinue the trade dollar program and to sell these patches to the lodges and other merchants for $5 each. They, in turn, could sell them to their customers. By reselling the patch for what they paid for it, there was no cost to the merchants and the grooming program would receive the full amount. We adopted that program and the grooming fund received about $40,000 a year from these patches. The patch program morphed into the Fair Share program that put us in a position to purchase and operate some grooming equipment ourselves. Coupled with the state gasoline tax that Bill Howell and others championed at the State Legislative level, we now have the funds to operate four groomers and groom about 400 miles of trail. The state contributes less than one penny of tax per gallon to the statewide grooming fund of about $400,000. We received a portion of that, about $76,000, and another $35,000 from the Recreation Trails program, totaling around $140,000 to help with our trail grooming. The state now owns three state-of-the-art groomers, and West Yellowstone owns one.

West Yellowstone has become known for its hundreds of miles of groomed trails and is looked to by other areas as a model to follow. All of this was done to help the visiting public have smooth rides and unsurpassed experiences while in Yellowstone country. Now the chamber of commerce and the state own the groomer equipment and are responsible for the groomed trails. The chamber is responsible for the financial end, and the trail grooming committee is responsible for the operational side of this effort. All of this effort transformed the forest trails outside the park into award winning places to snowmobile in the United States.

***

Yellowstone first began to grow its over-snow use in 1955, when Harold Young and Bill Nichols of West Yellowstone received permission to take Bombardier snowcoaches into the park. Soon news of winter access into Yellowstone by snowcoach began to spread to adventuresome folks who wanted to see what only a few winter keepers had seen in the past: Yellowstone in the winter. In

1963, a few personal snowmobiles (six total) were allowed into the park. My first ride was to Old Faithful in winter 1966. No facilities were open, and we sat under the abandoned porte-cochere of the Old Faithful Inn to eat our frozen sandwiches. Early over-snow travel without groomed trails made for a long, hard day to Old Faithful and back. In 1971, with the increased appeal of winter tourism, the park began grooming the roads for over-snow use. This was also the year we began our snowmobile rental operation.

At first, in 1970, I decided to keep the motel and the restaurant open in the winter and acquire some rental snowmobiles for the next winter. I contacted Howard McCray, the Scorpion snowmobile dealer, and we struck a verbal partnership. I told him "If you'll fix 'em, I'll rent 'em," and we did just that. We went in together to purchase fifteen shiny, new, metallic red Scorpion snowmobiles and rental clothing. We would split the profits at the end of the year—if there were any.

Early in fall 1971, I flew to Minneapolis in search of customers to come experience winter in Yellowstone on a rental snowmobile. Armed only with my 8" x 10" photos of Old Man Winter on Two Top Mountain, a few photos of Old Faithful and some wildlife, and a hand-typed itinerary copied onto light blue paper, I boarded a Northwest plane and flew to Minneapolis, a hotbed of snowmobile activity. To this day, each time I land in Minneapolis, the feelings of that first time flood back as though it were just last year. As we slowly descended into the city, the plane just seemed to hang there. I could see the tall buildings in the distance and the lakes below. I hadn't a clue about what I was going to find, what I was going to do, or even where to begin. I wondered why I was doing such a crazy thing with no direction or experience. But I knew firsthand about the beauties of the Yellowstone area, and I knew if I could just find people to talk to, I could convince them to come. Undeterred by my lack of marketing experience, I felt confident I was doing the right thing and that it would all turn out for the good.

The plane landed, and I checked into a motel in Bloomington. I got out the Yellow Pages in the phone book (no websites then) and started looking up travel agencies and snowmobile clubs. The next day I started cold calling these agencies. It was surprisingly easy to get people interested first by showing them my 8" x 10" photos and then by explaining the proposed itinerary.

On that first trip, I contacted the Lake Minnetonka Snowmobile Club and convinced the leader to bring her group. Also as a result of this trip, I met Chuck Ericson who ended up bringing John Holme and his employees and friends from Wilmer Minnesota who had their own snowmobiles and traveled around to different destinations to ride them. Because no one had heard of it being accessible in the winter, they were all impressed with the thought of seeing the majesty of Yellowstone under these circumstances.

I assured them that their every need would be taken care of. We would meet them at the Bozeman airport, have rooms waiting for them, and have Three Bear Restaurant open for them. I would guide them and show them the time of their lives (and I was not exaggerating). These first two groups hauled their own machines out using semi-trucks and had such a phenomenal experience and ended up coming back for 25 years straight.

During those early tours, our guests had a great time, and Clyde the Guide, as I was soon to be known, was having the best time of all. I loved to turn around as we came up on a bend at Two Top and stop and watch the faces and smiles of those that followed. It was a whopping success, and there was no doubt in my mind that in time we would be overrun with business.

As far as I know, I was the first to begin offering and aggressively marketing complete winter snowmobile packages in West Yellowstone. As a result of that trip, the Lake Minnetonka Snowmobile Club came and was followed by others. We kept the motel and the restaurant open and provided snowmobile rentals, clothing, and personal guide service. Friends began to tell their friends, and pretty soon we couldn't take all of the groups, so I told my neighbor that he ought to consider staying open in the winter. Pretty soon, many businesses began to open for the winter. We had opened up a new winter economy and a new reason to come to West Yellowstone in the winter.

During the first year of winter operation, we also began working with the Boy Scout troops from Salt Lake, Ogden, and Provo. They brought boys and leaders all during the Christmas holidays. We would eventually take 1,200 boys and leaders into the park or outside of it over a period of ten days. Our scout package included two nights lodging, five meals, a double riding snowmobile, and complete clothing. We rented the snowmobiles for $25 each, and the complete package cost them $55. We would house them at our three motels: Three Bear Lodge, the Big Western Pine, and the Ambassador Motor Inn. We fed them in our restaurants, Three Bear and Rustler's Roost, and took care of the rentals at Yellowstone Arctic and Three Bear. Since then, those boys have become men and fathers, and many still remember coming up on our scout snowmobile trips.

Since the 1971 opening of our snowmobile operation, snowmobiles have played an important part in my life and in the history of West Yellowstone. For a number of years, my partner Bill Howell and I operated 260 rental snowmobiles in West Yellowstone. In addition to that, we had a fleet of 60 snowmobiles at Flagg Ranch, then at Signal Mountain Lodge near Teton National Park. We started a rental fleet at Wasatch Mountain State Park at Midway, Utah, and operated that for six years, managed by John and Jo Ann Lawrence. After we closed that operation, we brought them to West Yellowstone, where they worked for us many more years. We also opened a snowmobile rental operation in Big Bear Lake, California. In order to provide income for those employees year-round, we rented three and four wheelers in the summer. It was difficult to start, operate, and sustain these satellite operations, although we enjoyed the challenge. However, we eventually pulled back and concentrated on other interests and businesses in West Yellowstone.

***

Some visitors brought their own snowmobiles and others rented from us or other outfitters, but people were intrigued! Initially they came to see the magic of Yellowstone in the winter, but while they were here, they also wanted to see the spectacular scenery and ride through the deep powdery snow in the national forests outside the park. Consequently, while people from long distances away came to Yellowstone, they also wanted to stay longer to ride in the wide open spaces surrounding the park. Trail counters in the national forests indicated that as park visitor numbers grew, there was a commensurate increase in riders outside the park. With our big increase in winter tourism, we began to tout ourselves as the snowmobile capital of the world. West Yellowstone in the winter was booming.

After we built the Holiday Inn, ten new hotels were built. During the holiday periods there could be as many as 1,300 snowmobiles going into the west gate of the park on any given day. Winter in Yellowstone had been discovered.

Snowmobile Halls of Fame

I was inducted into the International Snowmobile Hall of Fame in 2006. It was a nice event, and I was honored to meet and be recognized by Elmer Cone, the founder of the organization, who has since passed away.

The International Snowmobile Hall of Fame (ISHOF) was founded in 1984 in Grand Rapids, Minnesota. ISHOF was founded to promote and preserve the historical aspects of snowmobiling and to include recognition of individual achievements made on behalf of the sport. Inductees into ISHOF are nominated and honored from the following categories: designers and manufacturers, explorers and adventurers, trail and program developers, volunteers and club organizers, and publishers and journalists. Among other prestigious people was Bill Howell, my partner, nominated in 1991.

Three or four people are recognized each year for outstanding contributions in these areas. Such people as Edgar Hetteen, co-founder of Polaris Industries in 1956 and founder of Arctic Enterprises in 1960, Ralph Plaisted, who was the first to successfully travel to the North Pole via snowmobile, C.J Ramstad, a founder of the Snowmobile Hall of Fame, as well as a journalist, editor, and publisher for popular snowmobile magazines and several books, and none other than my partner Bill Howell in 1991. In 2009, the ISHOF moved from Bovey, Minnesota, to Eagle River, Wisconsin, and is now located in the World Snowmobile Headquarters building. Interested folks can check out the following website: www. ishof.com.

Four years after being inducted into the ISHOF, I was inducted into the Snowmobile Hall of Fame on February 10, 2010. These two halls of fame should not be confused as they are separate organizations. The Snowmobile Hall of Fame (SHOF) was actually conceived and had its organizational meeting in 1983 with Loren Anderson, C.J. Ramstad, and others as founders. I was, I believe, only the second person to be inducted into both halls of fame. C.J. Ramstad had nominated me to be inducted into the SHOF, but unfortunately he was killed in a tragic car wreck before I was able to be inducted. I considered C.J. to be a friend of mine. He came to West Yellowstone many times doing work for his magazine. He was an energetic fellow and loved to follow snowmobile events and cover new products of the industry. We will all miss him.

It was a fun time when we inductees were considered the champs and went on a ride on vintage snowmobiles. I picked out and rode a 1971 Scorpion like we had used when we started our operation. Each rider was given a racing bib and a hat and during the banquet the inductees signed the bibs of all the other participants. We also had our picture taken, and it will always hang in the Snowmobile Museum (www.snowmobilehalloffame.com).

People began coming from around the world to experience this winter wonderland. Eventually, however, the drums of overuse began to beat by some environmental groups. We decided early on to obtain a commercial use authorization (CUA) issued by the park allowing us to operate commercially guided snowmobile tours into Yellowstone. That was a smart thing for us to do, as eventually only those who had those permits could operate in the park.

In 2004, we received a ten-year contract authorizing us to operate snowcoaches (See Pebble 21) in the winter and sightseeing tours in the summer. However, because of the litigation (See Pebble 22) that unfolded regarding snowmobiles in the park, these type of contracts were issued on a one- or two-year basis.

The overall result was a severe decline in winter visitation. For West Yellowstone, some of the lodging facilities, which were built based on winter income, ended up closing for the winter and relying solely on a summer operation. West Yellowstone, however, has been adept in dealing with change. And fortunately, like most West Yellowstone folks, we found a way to meet all of our obligations and to continue to employ a broad base of West Yellowstone residents. In spite of the difficulties due to the limitations on snowmobiles, we were still able to operate a viable operation.

Pebble 21: Snowcoaches in Yellowstone: Past, Present, and Future

Someone once said, "If at first you don't succeed, try, try again."
Someone else added, "If at first you do succeed,
try something harder."
I might add, "If at first you don't succeed, you're about average."

~Clyde Seely

In 1955, Harold Young, a local businessman, was the first to take snowcoaches into Yellowstone. The original snowcoaches were made by Bombardier. They were made for over-snow travel and were single, purpose-built vehicles traveling on tracks and skis. These unique looking over-snow vehicles looked as if they were equipped to go to the North Pole; and people naturally wanted to ride in them as a means to effectively see the park.

Harold Young's and Bill Nichols's first trip to Old Faithful

Harold Young and his contemporaries were extremely influential in helping visitors see the beauty of Yellowstone's winters. On the day he received permission for this unique venture, he dropped a pebble in the pool of West Yellowstone and Yellowstone National Park.

Although our focus had begun in snowmobile tours, over the years we also began to see an interest for our guests to see the park in a snowcoach. In 1991, Bill Howell and I purchased a SnoBuster track and ski system from Jim Hobbs that could be fitted under a van. The track system allowed the van to go over the snow and was the beginning of our snow coach operation that we operated under the name of Yellowstone Tour and Travel.

In 2000, we bought four new vans and put them on tracks and skis. Then in 2004, we applied for and received a ten-year concessions contract with Yellowstone Park to conduct snowcoach tours in the park. We were approved to operate six vehicles and provide summer and winter sightseeing tours in Yellowstone. (However, due to maintenance problems, we always had nine available as backup.)

2000 homemade conversion to a snowcoach

Originally we started booking the snowcoaches out of the small shops at Three Bear. But it was obvious very soon into our operation that we would need a larger facility. In May 10, 2006, we bought the property that was the original West Mart Building Center. We made it into a shop and four storage bays where we handled the fleet's maintenance, storage, and staging needs.

The original Bombardiers, which Harold Young used, were a single purpose-built snowcoach. These became an icon for winter use in Yellowstone, but have long since ceased to be manufactured. Since then, we, along with many other operators, have tried to come up with ways to retrofit regular off-the-shelf vehicles and make them work as snowcoaches. Our goal has been to resourcefully locate a type of vehicle that would have sufficient power to plow through the heavy Yellowstone snows and also mechanically stand up the rigors of over-snow travel.

We have tried various types of track-and-ski combinations, but the result in most instances has been less than satisfactory. The track system we purchased in 1991 required more maintenance and power than was practical. When we purchased a new fleet of vans in 2000, we replaced most of these inefficient track systems with the Mattracks system. The Mattracks system is a triangular looking track that replaces each wheel. Again, these required more power than an off-the-shelf summer vehicle could easily provide. Consequently, new motors and transmissions and the cost of the track replacement, required us to keep looking for other solutions.

Over the course of this business endeavor, I bought Bill Howell out of our partnership. See Yellowstone Tours became the new name under which we operated and we purchased the old West Mart property on Yellowstone Avenue. This has served us well for vehicle storage and a mechanics shop for See Yellowstone Tours. **24**

We acquired two new 13-passenger and two new 20-passenger high profile vans. These have large viewing windows and are much roomier. We have used the Mattracks systems on the smaller vans and designed a totally new concept of tracks and skis for the 20-passenger vans. But these have also proven largely inefficient.

Meanwhile, within our snowcoach business, ridership has continued to increase. While snowmobiles have by far been the most popular mode of transportation in the park, I could also quickly see that the snowcoach offered a legitimate alternative for those who wanted to see the park in a more temperature-controlled environment.

While some people enjoy feeling the wind on their cheeks and the opportunity of driving their own snowmobile, there are also those who want to sit back in the warmth of a snowcoach and leave the driving to the informative driver. So, in order to provide the complete gamut of experiences in Yellowstone, we decided early on to provide both experiences and let the customer chose which they would like to do.

***

With the shared use of Yellowstone, the local snowmobile operators and local snowcoach operators cohabitated just fine

See **24** on the West Yellowstone Map Pages 142-143

while serving the needs of their guests. However, the drumbeat by the environmentalist groups to eliminate snowmobiles began to be heard. Multiple Yellowstone winter use studies were performed, which generated hundreds of thousands of public comments. The underlying issue was the difference between continued mixed use of the snowmobiles and the snowcoaches vs. a snowcoach-only plan. The environmental groups threw their support behind the latter.

Throughout these winter use studies, many meetings were held about the snowcoach-only alternative. I felt strongly that this option could not successfully address the current needs of those visiting the area. There simply was not a viable snowcoach on the market that could effectively replace the snowmobile. The snowcoaches we were using were too expensive to operate and would not work as a sole alternative to snowmobiles. Operators could not afford to provide snowcoaches that did not work effectively. Contrary to what we were told, there was no way the existing snowcoach technology could handle the numbers of people who had previously come to snowmobile. It was a losing proposition.

Yet it was obvious that the National Park Service (NPS) was leaning in the direction of snowcoaches only within the park. However, we were able to convince them that they could not require operators to provide vehicles that were prone to expensive break-downs and dissatisfied customers. So, they appeared eager to listen to our requests.

Since I wanted to help the snowcoach industry succeed, in all the meetings and in lobbying Washington and the National Park Service, I was a strong advocate of government funding going toward developing a new snowcoach built from the ground up that would withstand the rigors of over-snow travel. Once we, the snow-coach operators, were heard, we were asked to come up with a wish list of what needed to be included in such a vehicle. I submitted my list.

In fact, I was asked to accompany a group to Washington to help come up with the funding for such a vehicle. We succeeded in our request and a company was hired to develop this vehicle. Then, after much time and expense, the new vehicle was unveiled in Washington within sight of the Capitol. I was there during the press conference and unveiling.

But unfortunately, during this whole process, some of the key ingredients of our wish list were either left out or altered. The new vehicle was designed again to be an all-purpose vehicle that could be used for summer tours on wheels, and tracks for over-snow travel in Yellowstone in the winter. Six of these vehicles were built at the cost of millions of tax payer's dollars.

I am sorry to say, in my judgment, that this whole project was a failure. They made the vehicles large enough to carry sixteen passengers. Because of the size and weight, they were required to use extremely large tracks. We had said the vehicle needed to have 4-wheel drive. They failed to do that; it was only a push system instead of a push-pull system causing breakdowns and other related issues. The solution they came up with just didn't work.

The park tried to use these big yellow coaches for a couple years, but in the end they were not practical. You can now see these yellow vans providing a public transportation system in the city of Bozeman, Montana. So, there still has not been a practical solution to a single, purpose-built snowcoach.

But in 2010, SnoBear USA, based out of Fargo, North Dakota, brought a very interesting vehicle for me to look at. This was a small, lightweight vehicle built on a similar design to the Bombardier snowcoaches from Harold Young's days. I was impressed with the design and had a gut feeling that this could be the answer to the snowcoach problem.

I indicated to SnoBear that I would be interested in using the SnoBear based upon the following agreement: that they would use this basic design but would be willing to build an expanded version for our use in Yellowstone. I would provide them with my "wish list" and consultation services and they would do the research and development to construct a functional 13-passenger snowcoach. They were already successfully producing the SnoBear ice fishing vehicle and an eight-passenger over-snow vehicle called a Grizz. I committed to buying a SnoBear and a regular Grizz, if they would develop the extended Grizz.

I received delivery of the new SnoBear ice fishing vehicle in December 2011. This is a fun vehicle that I can take out on the lakes and ice fish. It lowers onto the ice so you can fish in your shirt sleeves at 20 below zero while watching videos and tending the fishing lines. I have never had much desire to sit outside on the ice and freeze hoping to catch a fish. The SnoBear, however, seemed to change all of that.

During winter 2013–14, the extended Grizz, which I named the Yellowstone Grizz, was delivered for testing in the park. More work still needs to be done on it in order for it to meet my requirements. At a maximum it could turn out to be a viable alternative to reliable snowcoaches in Yellowstone. At a minimum it could be that I have spent much time, money, and mental capital all for the fun of trying to make a new cutting edge snowcoach technology available for everyone to enjoy. Either way, I have had a good time trying to solve the ongoing snowcoach problem.

***

In addition to the Yellowstone Grizz, there is another possible viable solution for snowcoaches to view the park. This solution may be through Yellowstone Alpen Guides. In 1984, Yellowstone Alpen Guides was formed and became known for their unique old Bombardier snowcoaches patented in 1939, which Harold Young had first taken into the park. This company had refurbished the Bombardiers, painted them a bright burgundy color and used them specifically to take cross-country skiers into Yellowstone.

Since Bombardier ceased making these coaches in the early 1960s, Yellowstone Alpen Guides bought what they could find. We understand that the original snowcoach taken into the park in 1955 by Harold Young was also purchased at that time. Affectionately known as "bombs," these Bombardiers were built as a single-purpose vehicle for going over the snow in Canada and Alaska. In the hands of Yellowstone Alpen Guides, these machines rapidly became known for their dependability and the ability to travel long distances throughout the park.

So in 2014, we purchased Yellowstone Alpen Guides. There was some risk in this, as we knew it would be a huge and expensive endeavor to replace motors and improve interior sound according to park standards, but we were excited with the challenge. **23**

I have always appreciated and wanted to preserve the history of West Yellowstone as witnessed by the Historical Walking Tour (See Pebble 24), the preservation of the Executive Railroad Car and preserving the history of Three Bear Lodge by bringing it out of the ashes and preserving all the historical wood and recycling it (See Pebble 28). It is somewhat ironic that life has opened up a rare opportunity with these snowcoaches as well.

I have been credited for being one of the first to market and provide complete "Winter in Yellowstone" snowmobile packages. However, I consider Harold Young to be the real pioneer of showing people Yellowstone in the winter. I appreciate this new opportunity to carry forth the legacy that began 60 plus years ago when Harold Young first introduced these wonderful, iconic snowcoaches into Yellowstone.

See **23** on the West Yellowstone Map Pages 142-143

Pebble 22: Yellowstone / Snowmobile Winter Use Controversy

You can't win a war unless you are willing to fight the battle.

~Author Unknown

With the opening of new hotels and snowmobile rental operations in the mid-1990s, West Yellowstone became a two-season town with a vibrant two-season economy. West Yellowstone was the first to successfully apply for and receive the authority to implement a resort tax in the state of Montana. Cal Dunbar and the town council members worked hard with the state legislature and deserve much credit for lobbying the key legislators in Helena and also for explaining and acquiring the support of the local citizenry. Until that time, the town was severely impacted by thousands of tourists and the infrastructure of the town, police, and other public services had to be funded by the local people. Consequently, while we appeared to tourists to be a charming little town, we were dealing with some ugly realities. We were struggling with potholes, had no public water supply, and had limited sewer services. Private wells, troublesome septic tanks, no street drainage, and inadequate police and medical services also caused great difficulty.

With the passage of the resort tax, we were able to install new streets complete with curbs and gutters, a municipal water and sewage system, and enforce regulated signage. The town had more than just a facelift. It became an attractive municipality capable of handling over two million tourists per year. Tourism began to flourish as never before and West Yellowstone began to take its place prominently in the state and nation as a major tourist destination.

However, in the late 1990s, at the peak of the snowmobile era in West Yellowstone, a movement was begun by the environmental groups, the Fund for Animals and the Greater Yellowstone Coalition to ban snowmobiles from Yellowstone. The chamber called a meeting with the National Park Service, the rental snowmobile operators, and each of the four snowmobile manufacturers. That 1995 meeting was the first official meeting held in the new conference hotel. I was asked to chair the meeting. The NPS explained their belief that snowmobiles were causing too much air pollution in the park. Superintendent Mike Finley stated that it was his responsibility to establish a carrying capacity for snowmobiles in the park and that he was mandated to enforce it. I said, "Then you should do it now rather than later, when more hotels and businesses are built based upon a strong winter economy. After new facilities are built, a cut-back would be devastating."

Well, nothing was done at that time to establish a carrying capacity for snowmobiles in the park. Based upon a strong year-round economy, a building boom took place and ten lodging facilities were either newly built or remodeled. At that point, much more was at stake for the owners and employees as the threat of banning snowmobiles loomed ahead.

It seemed that the main concern was the amount of haze and exhaust fumes that hung around the west gate on those cold mornings. At that first meeting I proposed the use of Gasohol, a 10% blend of ethanol added to gasoline (E-10). I had just been to a public lands meeting in Lake Tahoe where a report was given about this new concept. I talked with the ethanol people presenting the concept and discussed the logistics of being able to use and even sell Gasohol. I had a report just released by Howard Haines of the Montana DEQ that found that with the use of Gasohol, carbon monoxide emissions could be reduced between 9% and 38% and particulate emissions could be reduced between 24% and 55%.

The *Billings Gazette* front page article entitled, "Gasohol promoted for Yellowstone use," dated December 4, 1997, shared this, "'We've been under the gun for some time,' said Seely, who along with Howell has 260 rental sleds and a gas station. But until the DEQ report came out showing that pollution could be reduced by using the mixture of 90 percent gasoline and 10 percent ethanol, suppliers were reluctant to switch over."

We proposed that all rental operators begin to use Gasohol and that we would now sell it at our Econo Mart Service station. This was a new challenge for the fuel suppliers, as they had to obtain the ethanol and blend it with regular gasoline at their site. However, I convinced them there would be a good market. This was the beginning of the across-the-board adoption of E-10 fuel in snowmobiles. The park people admitted that this would help, but they remained determined to push on for more controls. However, the E-10 fuel has become the fuel of choice, not only for snowmobiles but for many cars as well and is sold year around in West Yellowstone. We were the first to sell it at our service station.

The new Record of Decision (ROD) was finally issued November 22, 2000, by the National Park Service. As published, it would have eliminated all private snowmobile use in Yellowstone and Grand Teton National Parks within three years and relegated winter visitors to mass transit by snowcoach.

On an unforgettable night, the day before the park was to open to the public, December 17, 2000, we were having our Christmas party with about 200 employees and their families. At the beginning of the party, I was informed about Judge Emmet Sullivan's ruling to basically close the park to snowmobiles the next day. Not wanting to spoil the excitement of the evening, I waited until after the party to relay this terrible news. Stillness fell over the group as no one knew what this would mean to their jobs, family, and future. There were many people already in town planning on us taking them into the park the next day. What a disappointment to them and to us.

Around this same time, snowmobile groups filed a suit against the ban, and litigation continued with vastly reduced numbers of snowmobiles allowed. So we also started down the path of litigation. The National Parks Conservation Association, the Wilderness Society, the Natural Resources Defense Council, the Winter Wildlands Alliance, and the Sierra Club had joined forces with the Fund for Animals and the Greater Yellowstone Coalition, to become co-plaintiffs, and sued the NPS. Their objective was to ban all snowmobiles from Yellowstone. This huge environmental coalition, which appeared to be encouraged by the Park Service, became a formidable opponent to our little group of snowmobile rental operators.

This little group of rental operators joined up with the Blue Ribbon Coalition to help finance the Yellowstone Legal Defense Fund. We lent our on-the-ground experience and support to the efforts of the American Council of Snowmobile Associations (ACSA) and the International Snowmobile Manufacturers Association (ISMA). Both of these groups were key in leading the charge to keep snowmobiles in the park. The banning of snowmobiles in Yellowstone would just be a precursor of additional restrictions to come in other public lands. Our group of rental operators hired Aubrey King as our lobbyist and we began a long uphill fight that has lasted 15 years and counting. Without the cohesive support of these four groups the end result would have been vastly different.

The biggest reason for pushing to get snowmobiles out of the park was air and sound pollution. News media sometimes visited the west gate on a cold morning and photographed park rangers wearing gas masks. We tended to think those photos painted a distorted picture and were basically a publicity stunt to gain the support of the advocates of a snowmobile ban. These photos were blasted across the media and did tend to gather support for the snowmobile ban.

Bill and I knew that Arctic Cat was working on a new concept 4-stroke snowmobile. They were hesitant to release it but we explained to them if they didn't get it out to us quickly, the park would be closed to snowmobiles and their efforts would all be for naught. They listened, and the first week of January 2000 they delivered two unbelievably clean and quiet 4-stroke snowmobiles. These new machines did not burn oil as did the 2-stroke machines and were also much quieter. The news media was quick to pick up on these new snowmobiles and we received a lot of positive publicity. We thought for sure these would be the solution to the noise and emissions problem.

First 4-stroke Arctic Cat snowmobile, which led the way
in keeping snowmobiles in Yellowstone

My association with Don Berry is worth noting. Don was the Assistant Secretary of the Interior and came to speak to the Greater Yellowstone Coalition meeting held in the U.P. Dining Lodge across from Three Bear Lodge. He basically vowed to remove snowmobiles from the park. We asked for a meeting with him the next day. At that meeting we explained our plight and asked him to empathize with our situation. The park was claiming that the snowmobiles were too noisy and polluted the air with blue smoke and high particulates. I asked Don if the problem would be solved if we could get rid of those two difficulties. He indicated that it would. We asked him to come across the street where we performed a little demonstration.

Bill and I showed him the new Arctic Cat 4-stroke snowmobile and a 2-stroke snowmobile sitting side by side; we started the two-stroke machine and left it idling. Then I asked Don to walk away from the machines with me. As we walked, I asked Don to tell me when he could no longer hear the engine. He said at one point, "I can't hear it anymore." Then we went back and started the 4-stroke machine and left it idling. He admitted that the new technology 4-stroke snowmobile could be heard less than half as far. That answered the noise issue .Then we showed him the engine. It was a little automobile engine that did not burn oil. He was visibly impressed.

I continued to meet with Don from time to time. We were diametrically opposed in our positions, but we maintained a cordial relationship. I really believed we were making progress with him. Then one day I received a phone call. "This is Don Berry," he said. "I am resigning my position as Assistant Secretary of Interior and I wanted you to be the first to know." He told me that he had only told two other people. He went on to say that he would make it possible and embed into some of the documents recommendations to adopt a more flexible Park Service snowmobile policy. I was flattered that he would tell me first and that he had already taken some steps to help.

I was in Washington with Aubrey King and was invited to Don's retirement party in the Secretary of Interior's lavish office. It was a large office with probably seventy-five of his friends and coworkers present. It was time for the "roast" and gifts were given and tributes given to Don. I was in the other room on the phone when Aubrey came running in and said, "Hurry, Don is talking about you." He thanked everyone for coming and said, "But, the person I am most pleased to have here tonight is Clyde Seely. We have opposed each other but are still friends." At the end of the party I shook his hand and thanked him for saying those nice things about me. I told him I was sorry to see him leave because I felt we had established a bond and were making progress. He agreed.

Don accepted a position as the executive director of the Wilderness Society. It was now his job to continue his anti-snowmobile role. About six months later I received another phone call from Don. He said he would like to come to West Yellowstone and meet with me. At the meeting, with just his aid and me present, he again tried to talk me into giving up snowmobiles. I said, "You know you are paid to get snowmobiles out of the park, but the way the town survives and the way I make my living is through snowmobiles." He then said something that really shocked me. He told me, "We (the Wilderness Society) have some funds that we could use to help you get set up with snowcoaches so you wouldn't need to rely on snowmobiles." That sounded a lot like a bribe to me, and it rankled me to think of what they were trying to do. I told him, I suppose you will never recant your position, and I assure you that I will not go back on mine. I again reminded him of the progress the 4-stroke snowmobile was making and asked what had happened with the things he had embedded in the Environmental Impact Statement (or EIS) documents. He said his successor had taken them out.

***

Our relationship with the Department of the Interior (which supervises the NPS) was somewhat adversarial. As evidenced by Don Berry, they wanted to remove snowmobiles from the park. Fortunately for the snowmobile issue, the Bush administration replaced the Clinton administration and we now had a fighting chance. The new administration appointed a different and more sympathetic Secretary of Interior and National Park personnel. Several times our friendly Republican legislators were able to get riders placed on other bills that effectively, if not explicitly, prevented snowmobiles from being banned in Yellowstone for that budget year.

The introduction of the first two 4-stroke snowmobiles in January 2000 proved to be the thing that began to change the minds of members of the opposition. We had Arctic Cat name this machine the "Yellowstone Special." The next winter season Arctic Cat agreed to build and lease to Bill and me fifty 4-stroke snowmobiles for the 2000-01 season. Photos of the new Yellowstone Special and us went out over the Associated Press (AP) and to newspapers in Atlanta, New York, and other places—too many to mention. I am not alone in saying that if Arctic Cat had not produced the Yellowstone Special that year, we would not have snowmobile access in Yellowstone today.

On February 10, 2003, I was asked to testify in Federal District Court in Cheyenne, Wyoming, presided over by Judge Clarence Brimmer. As a result of this hearing, Judge Brimmer issued a preliminary injunction against banning snowmobiles that counteracted Judge Emmett Sullivan's earlier order to ban all snowmobiles from Yellowstone.

At the time of Judge Brimmer's hearing, I was in the hospital in Idaho Falls with blood clots in my lung. Knowing I was supposed to testify in court the next day, I talked the doctor into releasing me early. Glen Loomis picked me up at the hospital that evening. We spent the night in Jackson, were picked up by the state's plane, and flew to Casper, Wyoming, the next morning. When called to the stand, the strain of walking up caused me to be short of breath and I had to explain why I needed a moment to catch my breath. Our testimony was successful, and snowmobiles were allowed to continue in the park.

Rules have been published and litigation has stayed the implantation. Washington DC and Wyoming courts have jostled back forth the future of winter use. Judge Sullivan and Judge Brimmer pushed for different alternatives and created what became known by some as the "battle of the judges."

Some of us got to know the people in Bush's Department of Interior and had a good relationship with all of them from the Assistant Secretary on down. Aubrey King, our lobbyist, would set up meetings with congressional people in the appropriate positions of power who could help us. Others and I were able to speak with passion and authority, and I knew we were in the right and were making a difference. The Park Service has completed the last EIS. As will be seen in Pebble 30, we have weathered the storm, so to speak, badly bruised perhaps, but still renting snowmobiles as well as snowcoaches that meet all the park's requirements.

I have always said that in the end right and reason would prevail. Over the years we began to see a gradual change in the position of the NPS. At one time, John Sacklin, Chief of Planning in Yellowstone, and I would make diametrically opposed statements in TV and newspaper interviews. Later, those interviews became more closely aligned. I have always pushed for a balanced winter use between snowmobiles and snowcoaches. The NPS was pressured by the environmental organizations to do away with snowmobiles. With the implementation of 4-stroke snowmobile technology and many studies indicating big declines in noise and air pollution, the NPS has finally agreed with us that the snowmobile and the snowcoach are very similar in the amount of impact they produce on the park resources. The "Winter Planning Update" by John Sacklin, Kevin Franken in *Guides and Outfitters,* December 2009 nicely summarized the situation:

What we have learned from recent studies:

- BAT snowmobiles and modern snowcoaches contribute similarly to impacts from oversnow vehicle use.

- One vehicle type is not necessarily better than another. Each has advantages and disadvantages.

Over the years, I have gone to Washington many times, sometimes with Bill and some of our local rental friends, and sometimes alone. We have testified in a Senate hearing with Senator Craig Thomas and in House hearings on the impact of banning snowmobiles inside national parks on small business on July 13, 2000, conducted by Representative Donald Manzullo, and again on January 26, 2002. I have been on television shows such as *Face the State* in Montana and NPR—both radio and television—all trying to arrive at a balance of use and defend keeping snowmobile access in Yellowstone National Park.

The Yellowstone gateway communities, especially the operators of over-snow vehicles, have often been accused of wanting to profit from the park and overuse its resources. Such is not the case. I am reminded of Aesop's fable "The Goose with the Golden Egg":

> One day a countryman going to the nest of his Goose found there an egg all yellow and glittering. When he took it up it was as heavy as lead and he was going to throw it away, because he thought a trick had been played upon him. But he took it home on second thoughts, and soon found to his delight that it was an egg of pure gold. Every morning the same thing occurred, and he soon became rich by selling his eggs. As he grew rich he grew greedy; and thinking to get at once all the gold the Goose could give, he killed it and opened it only to find,—nothing.

The beauty and remoteness of Yellowstone are what draw visitors to the area, and the opportunity to experience Yellowstone in winter is a unique opportunity that few experience. I believe we must do what we can to ensure that visitors are able to see and experience Yellowstone as those in the past did but with a minimal impact on the environment and the fragile setting winter offers. Protecting quality visitor experiences and preserving the natural environment can easily be compared to the golden goose. Yellowstone will keep on laying golden eggs for all to enjoy unless it becomes sick or is killed. These are also key components of the success of Three Bear Lodge's snowmobile and snowcoach operations and other businesses in the gateway communities.

I also believe that we should not carry the wish to protect a precious resource so far as to deny people the right to enjoy and visit the park. Herein lies the crux of the problem: how to protect the park's resources and still be able to enjoy them for future generations. It seems to me that the answer lies somewhere between both ends of the spectrum or, in other words, balance. That is the purpose of the lengthy winter use studies that have been conducted over the past years. That is why I have passionately tried to push for a balance so we can enjoy and still respect this special place. I believe in part it has been achieved.

So far we have been able to ward off complete closure of Yellowstone to snowmobiles. A likely analogy is a four-legged table that is holding up snowmobile transportation in Yellowstone. Without any one of those legs, the table would fall. One major leg is the International Snowmobile Manufacturers Association (ISMA), comprised of all four snowmobile manufacturers and led by Ed Klim. Another leg is the American Council of Snowmobiles Association (ASCA), led by Christine Jourdain, along with the Blue Ribbon Coalition and its legal defense fund, led by Jack Welsh. A third leg is Arctic Cat, which was responsible for creating the first 4-stroke snowmobile. Another, and certainly not of least importance, is the local snowmobile rental operators group that I have been able to help guide. In conjunction with these efforts, state snowmobile associations, individual snowmobilers, and supporters of keeping snowmobiles in Yellowstone have written thousands of letters of support to maintain snowmobile access in the winter. Without any one of these support legs, the table would have fallen and snowmobiles would have been banned from Yellowstone Park years ago. It has taken a collaborative effort to keep all four legs firmly in place.

I believe we have a reasonably balanced conclusion to the winter use issue. I found the following in a newspaper article years ago and have always been amused by the wisdom found therein. As the two jackasses in this story finally realized, there must be some give and take and compromise. I hope we have become as smart as they.

Two Fool Jackasses

Two fool jackasses say, get this dope—We're tied together with a piece of rope. Said one to the other; "You come my way while I take a nibble from this new mown hay."

"I won't," said the other. "You come with me. For I too, have some hay, you see." So they got nowhere, just pawed dirt. And oh by golley, that rope did hurt!

Then they faced about, those stubborn mules and said, "We're acting like human fools." Let's pull together. I'll go your way, then you come with me and we'll both eat hay." Well, they ate their hay and liked it too and swore to be comrades good and true, as the sun went down they were heard to say; "So– this is the end of a perfect day."

Part Three: Developing West Yellowstone

Pebble 23: West Yellowstone Incorporation / Boards and Committees

A man went to the doctor who said, "You're burning your candle at both ends." The man said, "I already know that; what I want from you is more wax."

~Author Unknown

West Yellowstone was born when visionary people saw an opportunity to provide necessary services to the summer visitors of Yellowstone National Park. There was no official town organization and no local taxes to help provide public services, such as streets, police protection, and all the other resources that are available today. Things were accomplished out of necessity as needs arose.

The town of West Yellowstone has morphed from a few businesses with no public resources to a nationally renowned destination. No longer is it just a place where people can spend the night before going into the park in the summer. It has become a destination—a hub, if you will—where people come not only to enjoy the park in the summer but also in the winter. West Yellowstone is now a vacation destination where people can enjoy the many town amenities and use it as a base for day trips.

West Yellowstone started because a small group of business people joined together to help promote their businesses.

Long before it became an incorporated town in 1966 with Billie Smith as the first mayor, the National Forest Service managed the town site of West Yellowstone. The Lions Club had an influence in the town, along with law enforcement provided by the Gallatin County Sheriff's Department, a volunteer fire department, and most predominantly by the chamber of commerce. In those early days, the chamber of commerce was the closest thing we had to government. I remember when Mike Wilson was the president, with Jan Dunbar as secretary, and Cal Dunbar and others on the board of directors. We looked up with wonderment and awe to the leaders of the community. The Eagles, Stuarts, Whitmans, Wilsons, Dunbars, Smiths, Hadleys, Coffins, Bert Fields, Rightenours, and others too numerous to mention had earned a place as mentors to many. I wished to pattern my life after their example of service to the town and their spirit of cooperation with each other.

Today few will remember the name Mike Wilson. Without this man, in my estimation, West Yellowstone would not own the Union Pacific property and all of its buildings that are the focal point of the town.

In the 1950s and '60s, Mike Wilson was an important community leader and president of the chamber of commerce in West Yellowstone. Since the town was not incorporated and was mostly run by the chamber and volunteer organizations, Mike held a very important position. By 1960, passenger trains had ceased to run into the town. The 1959 earthquake caused some damage to the Dining Lodge. The buildings were repaired but never reopened. The question then became, what would happen to the property and the beautiful buildings that belonged to the Union Pacific in West Yellowstone? Mike felt the town should take ownership, and that it would be too bad if the property ended up in the hands of private enterprise or even the Forest Service. That would have been a great loss for this little town.

I remember Mike got all stirred up about this, and while he was in California for the winter, he uncovered an old federal law and gave me a copy. (*As codified at 43 U.S.C. § 912, the 1922 statute provides that upon forfeiture or abandonment, the lands granted to any railroad company for use as a right of way for its railroad etc. would pass to a municipality if the right of way passed through one...*) This statute made it clear that the town needed to incorporate, so that the railroad property could pass to the new municipality of West Yellowstone. With the incorporation of the town, it seemed that there could be a windfall of other advantages.

However, according to the minutes of the newly incorporated town, there was a lot of disagreement among several entities (BLM, State of Montana, Union Pacific, and West Yellowstone) as to how to deal with the railroad property.

The BLM also recognized receiving several letters requesting that the buildings be torn down. Others said that since the state of Montana owned the street, which ran alongside the property, there was a case that could be made that the property should be donated to the State. And at this time the land was under consideration to be transferred to the state of Montana, but the town made it clear that they would protest this action.

Even though arrangements had been made with Union Pacific to use the dining lodge for various functions, the town did not have ownership of the railroad property. It was not until October 8, 1968 that an official resolution to request ownership and accept the donation of the Union Pacific Railroad property and a portion of the right of way to the Town of West Yellowstone that the destiny of the property was finally determined. Finally, on May 27, 1969, the law Mike found finally prevailed and the town received the Quit Claim Deed to the railroad property. It was recorded later and has become a focal point of town.

Not many know nor will remember how close we came to losing this railroad property to private enterprise. In my opinion, if Mike Wilson had not dug into the law books and found an old, obscure law, West Yellowstone would now be a vastly different place. We would have lost this showcase of railroad history.

In order for the town of West Yellowstone to take ownership of the Union Pacific property, the town had to incorporate. It was officially incorporated in 1966. The unbelievable strip of land is over 300 feet wide and runs the entire length of the town from east to west. In the end, all of the buildings and land were eventually donated to the town of West Yellowstone. **(A)**

Mike Wilson and the incorporating leaders dropped a pebble that caused positive ripples, which are still being enjoyed today.

It was not until 1976, after the tracks were no longer used for hauling pulpwood, that the tracks were removed.

Eventually, the Union Pacific depot became the Yellowstone Historic Center Museum, the baggage building became the police station, and the newly elected town council met in a part of the magnificent 1920's dining lodge. The dorm for the railroad's female summer employees burned down in 1980, and the men's dorm became the Guy Hansen Medical Clinic. Since that time, the city office and fire station, a town public works facility, the chamber of commerce and public lands building, and the Povah Center—a senior citizen/community center—have all been built on this property. A garage was built in 2011 by the West Yellowstone Foundation to store the senior citizen's bus and house its office. In 2012, an emergency service building was completed and the historic forest service cabins built in 1906 were moved to the east end of the property. In 2013, a new city office and city court center was built. Before our little town was even named, the Union Pacific terminal was the arrival and departure point for thousands of tourists and the focal point and heartbeat of the town. It continues to play that role today.

See **(A)** on the West Yellowstone Map Pages 142-143

If you want to have a seat on the train, you must first get on board. If you want to determine the destination of the train, you must get involved and contribute to the cause. You may even be asked to drive the train with others help in order to arrive at the desired destination. Like my mentor Mike Wilson, I have always stayed involved in community organizations as they are a great way to accomplish things that are above the ability of a single individual.

The success of my business ventures in West Yellowstone and the fact that I have always surrounded myself with good people have allowed me to reach out and spread myself a little further by serving on local committees. I have always enjoyed doing things to help others. I was raised that way. After all, what is the point of having blessings if you don't share them with your friends?

Groups of volunteers and committees have been a driving force in getting the town to where it is today. As mentioned earlier, the Chamber of Commerce has always been a dominant force in the town. Mary Sue Costello has been the executive director and has served with dedicated presidents and board members for many years. Since the town was incorporated, it has been lead by elected mayors and council members who have given years of service. They are the governing agency on which the community members and millions of tourists rely. I would like to recognize all of them individually but that would be impossible. To all of those individuals and their spouses and families, I am grateful.

Though we now have an organized town government and have acquired resort taxes to fund municipal services, volunteer committees still play a crucial and innovative role in securing the things that many take for granted. I would like to mention a few committees with which I am familiar and have been involved with. Many of these committees or assignments have overlapped. The following are some of the committees or assignments I have been involved in. I have thoroughly enjoyed the years of service on these committees and boards:

* School board, 1971–1983 and 1992–1995 (15 years)
* Branch president, West Yellowstone Branch,
  LDS Church 1968–1981 (almost 14 years)
* High council and stake presidency 1981–1990 (9 years)
* Fall River Electric board of directors
  1980–1995 and 1998–2010 (27 years)
* Chairman/board member of the Solid Waste
  board 1980–present (35 years)
* Organized the West Yellowstone motel association (8 years)
* West Yellowstone chamber of commerce
  director (off and on for 20 years)
* Board Member West Yellowstone Snowmobile
  Expo Committee 1989–present
* West Yellowstone Economic Development
  Council (WYED) 2005–present
* Instrumental in spearheading the painted
  "Buffalo Roam" Project-2006
* Spring and fall cycle tour, instigator
  and chairman, 1996–2002
* Leading role in Snowmobile Access in Yellowstone in
  conjunction with the local Snowmobile Rental Operators
  (many trips to Washington D.C. beginning in 2000)
* Involved in response to Yellowstone 1988 fires,
  initiator and lead of the sprinkler installation
  for defending West Yellowstone, Old Faithful
  power line, and Duck Creek subdivision.
* West Yellowstone historical walking tour—
  began leading this effort in 2010 to preserve
  the history of West Yellowstone.

I have tried not to be just a flash in the pan when taking on an assignment. I have felt a lot of passion for achieving the goals of these various committees and meeting the challenges they present. I have always believed the time spent working for the common good of all is necessary and will pay great dividends. Serving on these committees has become a part of my life. I have served on some of them for decades and have enjoyed doing so.

Working together as a committee creates a synergy that lends strength and perseverance that an individual lacks by himself. Those who have a vision are often called upon to lead. Meeting together, thinking outside of the box, speaking up and discussing the issues at hand, and having passion and belief in a common cause generates action. Many good things have transpired and have helped to make this place that we live in and love so much a better place. It is a great location to raise our families and the quality of life here is envied by many. That is because what is good for the goose is good for the gander or, said a little more eloquently by President John F. Kennedy, "A rising tide lifts all boats."

I could not have been as involved in community events if I did not have a qualified staff to run each of my businesses. Because of the competence of those who are devoted to their jobs, I have been able to divert my attention to other projects. When I asked a very wise businessman how he became so successful, he told me, "I hire people who are smarter than me and then I get out of the way and let them do their job." That is what I have been able to do. Those good people are the ones that have allowed me to devote as much time as I have to community affairs. I, of course, can't name all of the people that have been pebbles for good in my pool; however, I will mention two, Bill Schaap and Bill Howell.

Like I followed my sisters who worked at Three Bear when I was a kid, Bill Schaap, a vice president of one of the Banks in Utah, followed his kids Jody and Jayne who had been working for me. Bill had been bit by the same bug that brings so many of us here, and when it was the right time for him, he approached me about a job.

For many years, he managed Three Bear Lodge and became another pebble in my pool. At his retirement party in 2001, I wrote and read a poem about Bill. I share a portion of it here:

Bill Schaap

'Twas twenty some years ago when the
Schaaps came on a family vacation.
Who would have guessed that Bill would
start a whole new vocation.
It was in the hallway at the old church
When he asked if at Three Bear he could work.
He had a family he wanted to raise in
Yellowstone, well just west,
To live here 'til they were all pretty well out of the nest.
Marty, Julia, Jayne, Jody, and Donna were all part of the deal;
To us in West Yellowstone, it was really quite a steal.
It was at Three Bear Lodge that Bill began to run.
He did a good job too; he seemed to have so much fun.
Nothing was ever impossible or out of his realm
As he guided his ship while standing firmly at the helm.
I told him he was like a bulldozer with wings on the side
For there was nothing he wouldn't do,
no job he would let slide.
Guiding snowmobiles was to him a great delight,
People would come year after year; he
would show them such a sight.
They all loved it when he didn't quite make it across a creek.
By his snowmobile they took his picture
with a big smile from cheek to cheek.

It seemed Bill and I were made out of the same mold. Like me, he enjoyed physical work. We got a permit to cut and haul big logs for the new Three Bear Restaurant and together we used my front-end loader and trailers to acquire sufficient logs and to complete the project. There are people, like Bill Schaap, whom I would trust with my life, who I know would never take advantage of a situation. People like him have become my dear friends. Because of them, I have been able to turn away from my trying businesses and devote more time to committees and community projects.

Bill Howell has been a stalwart and trustworthy partner with integrity that is unequaled. Throughout this book I have mentioned operations that Bill Howell and I have forged through together. Although he is no longer with me in most of these operations, he and his wife Carole have been like other meaningful pebbles that have been dropped into my life's pool.

In addition to my community service, I have also encouraged others to get involved. Bill Schaap at Three Bear Lodge, Bill Howell, and other managers and employees of the Three Bear Lodge and Restaurant, the Holiday Inn, Econo Mart, Parade Rest Ranch, and our snowmobile and tour operations also devoted untold hours to the community organizations. That is just what we do.

Western States Governors' Conference

I took on my first committee assignment in West Yellowstone when I was just 27 years old. While I was managing Three Bear Lodge in 1966, I was given the responsibility of raising funds for restoring the Union Pacific Dining Lodge, which would render the space usable for the Western States Governors' Conference. This all came about while attending a chamber of commerce meeting. I made the mistake of raising my hand and was put in charge of forming the committee and then became the chairman.

Later I read this poem entitled "Committees," which seemed very appropriate. Over the years this little poem keeps popping back into my mind as I keep raising my hand at the appropriate time.

It seems whenever I go to a public meeting,
I slip quietly into the back of the house
Pretty soon things begin to start heating,
No longer can I sit quiet as a mouse
This could turn out to be a real pity,
Reluctantly, I raise my hand and open my mouth—
And "Bam," there I am on another committee.
~Author Unknown

Few people may remember all of the necessary repairs needed to complete the transformation of the beautiful 1925 Union Pacific Dining Lodge for the conference. The 1959 earthquake caused considerable damage to this building. Union Pacific repaired the damage to the Dining Lodge, but the building never returned to full operation.

Even though the Dining Lodge was not officially deeded to the town until 1969, it lay idle from 1960 until the town had the opportunity of hosting the Western States Governors' Conference in 1967.

The Dining Lodge, with its rustic atmosphere and charm, had the potential of becoming a showcase for such a prestigious event, with others major events to follow. But we needed to retrofit the building, repair broken windows, remove pigeons and improve it for the conference. We held a number of meetings to decide how to raise the $60,000 needed for the renovation, but no one could figure out how to raise that large sum of money in a short amount of time. I was only in my twenties, and even though a little timid, I stood up in a meeting and suggested that we contact all the motels and see if they would contribute up front 90% of their estimated proceeds for this one-time event and "bam," just like the poem, "there I am on another committee."

After I had made many individual contacts, the motels agreed and completely supported us. The $60,000 was raised from these contributions, and the town ended up with a beautiful and functional building, placing it on the map as a place to have meetings in an impressive, rustic setting.

Ronald Reagan, who was the governor of California at the time, with his white Levi jacket and cowboy hat seemed to be the focus of attention at the conference. The Northern Hotel in Billings was contracted to cater the banquet and it was quite an affair, including ice carvings and elaborate meals. I remember talking to the chef, who was at the height of his glory because of the opportunity to cook on the huge, old, wood burning stove and ovens. The cold storage rooms behind the kitchen also came back into service in order to handle the large amount of food needed.

The event was held in June, when the town would have been rather quiet. Twenty brand new Mercury station wagons were brought in for the governors' use. Later these vehicles were sold at the reasonable price of $6,000 each! Thanks to the motel owners' contributions, the new vision for that beautiful historic building was realized.

Dining Lodge Remodeled for Convention Facility

Later, the chamber of commerce tried to figure out a way to make better use of the Dining Lodge. We had a large building, plenty of cold temperatures, and a concrete floor with a roof, so we decided to line the edges with plastic, flood the floor during the winter time, offer ice skates for rent, and have an indoor ice skating rink. This worked fairly well for the community, but getting the ice out during the spring was a rather daunting task. In the end, we decided that the effort wasn't worth it. Neither was this an appropriate use for such a magnificent building. An exaggeration would be like roller-skating in the Sistine Chapel.

The chamber of commerce, remembering the Western States Governors' Conference, decided to convert the Dining Lodge into a convention facility. Once again, in order to accommodate our needs, a major remodeling was needed. I was again appointed chairman, and Gene Adams was my co-chair. During remodeling, we divided the large kitchen in half, put in new ovens and ranges, installed bathrooms by the dining court, made another meeting room out of the west half of the original kitchen, installed overhead electric heat, and put tile over the entire concrete floor. We named the rooms for easy reference and marketing purposes. The east room with the fireplace was named the Firehole room, and the large dining area was the Mammoth room. The new yet smaller meeting room was named the Rainbow room. **16**

Dining Lodge prior to being remodeled for the 1967
Western States Governors' Conference

The chamber of commerce hired Roger Carvallo as the convention and marketing manager. It was his responsibility to promote and operate the facility as a convention center, thereby bringing more revenue to town. However, it was quickly discovered that a single, large meeting room was not adequate to host large conventions. While the meeting was going on, tables needed to be

See **16** on the West Yellowstone Map Pages 142-143

set up and preparations for the banquets needed to be carried out. We discovered that for conventions, a place was needed to meet and a place was needed to eat. A large meeting couldn't be interrupted while the banquet arrangements were being set up and then taken down. It became obvious that to be successful, we needed at least twice the space. At this juncture, realizing the need for the town to have a well-planned convention facility, the initial plans for such a facility began to germinate in my mind. Even though it took a few years, Bill and I began to plan building the West Yellowstone Conference Hotel, which is now called the Holiday Inn.

West Yellowstone School Board

Shortly after I stopped teaching and was keeping the motel open year round, the chairman of the school board, Guy Hansen, asked if I would run for the school board. He told me that if I did, he would recommend the superintendent be replaced. I taught under that superintendent and had witnessed firsthand a lack of professionalism and an apathetic attitude. I agreed to run. Guy had been chairman for a long time and because of his relationship with the current superintendent he did not feel he could make that change. He wanted to step down and, for the betterment of the school, recommended that the replacement be made. I was elected and, along with the other board members, went through the difficult process of notifying and replacing the superintendent.

It soon came time for salary negotiations with the school. When I was teaching, the school did not belong to a teachers' union, but since I left, the union had come to the school and proposed their model contract. Under the oversight of the school board and the superintendent, who we had just replaced, they had "swallowed hook, line, and sinker" the model contract that was now firmly in place. I went to seminars at the State School Board Association and consulted with our attorney and learned what a risky position the town and school had been placed in. I had been a teacher and therefore believed in being paid fairly; however, the demands of this model contract were weighted too heavily in favor of the teachers. We felt the union contract would have limited the local control of the school board and the administration, all at the expense of the community.

I became chairman of the negotiations committee, opposite my previous fellow teachers, making it hard to maintain the relationship I once had with them. Many meetings were held to work out a settlement. It was a difficult process, but over a period of time, we finally found language that restored a balance between the administration, the school board, and the teachers.

In 1915, the town's first elementary school was built and then was moved across the street so the second larger school could be built in the 1920s. This second school underwent several renovations and expansions over the years and became the town's first high school in 1966, which was the first year that I taught. That winter, the high school students could stay at home instead of having to board for the year with friends or relatives in other towns. It wasn't too long, however, before the school was again outgrown. It needed a kindergarten room, a music room, a shop, and more space. We knew we weren't in a situation to pass a bond for a new school, but we badly needed a larger facility. I began to formulate a plan, and over several days used my trusty quarter-inch scale ruler, and drew out a proposed addition to the building that I thought would be adequate for the time being. The board approved my plan and took it to an architect. The school was expanded again, and it served us well for several years. **17**

When the town was thriving with winter business, the time soon came that we needed a still larger school. I was off the school board for a while, but when I came back we were building a new K–12 building in the Madison Addition. The property was donated thanks to Lewis Robinson, the developer of the Madison Addition.

See **17** on the West Yellowstone Map Pages 142-143

There was some discussion regarding whether we would have to pay for the land or if it would be donated, but ultimately it was donated. We now had a beautiful building and an athletic field. Nevertheless, that first winter ceilings leaked, windows and doorframes sagged, and many other problems appeared. These building errors sprang from a combination of architect and contractor mistakes. It is my recollection that it cost over a million dollars to make the corrections. Construction in West Yellowstone, with extreme temperatures and heavy snow, is challenging if not considered thoroughly. The school has functioned marvelously since then.

Solid Waste District

When I was a laundry boy, one of the favorite evening attractions for locals and visitors alike was going to the garbage dump and watching the bears come in and eat. It was widely known that the bears fed on the garbage. Tourists would often ask us, "Where can we go watch the bears being fed?" Well, the bears weren't intentionally being fed; they just knew where they could find an easy meal on human garbage.

At night, we would go to the dump with a car full of kids and turn out the lights (it was a good time for the girls to act scared and the guys to act brave). At the right time, we would turn on the lights and the smaller black bears would be rummaging through the garbage. Then, as though on cue, the black bears left and the big grizzlies came into view. The black bears didn't want to mess with the grizzlies, especially the huge, locally famous "Old Snaggletooth." He was so named because of a lower incisor that protruded out of his mouth. When he stood up, he towered at 10 feet tall. He definitely ruled the roost. Eventually, a poacher shot him and he currently resides in a full, upright position in the West Yellowstone Historical Center Museum.

Since the arrival of the Union Pacific Railroad in 1908, bears and geysers had been used on advertising flyers and posters. The bears were portrayed as playful characters, encouraging people to come and see Yellowstone. When we built the Holiday Inn we incorporated some of these Union Pacific posters (obtained from the Union Pacific Museum in Omaha, Nebraska) as displays next to the Oregon Short Line 1903 railroad car. These advertising posters were from the 1920s–1940s. Since that time, one of the main attractions of Yellowstone was the bears. People took photos of bears with people in rather precarious situations.

When I first came to work in West Yellowstone, bears could be seen on a nightly basis in and around town. The tourists fed the bears and even the local folks unintentionally contributed to their demise. The problem is that when humans fed bears they became too friendly and dependent on human food. When they did not get that food, they became aggressive and dangerous, all of which resulted in them being trapped, and in some cases euthanized. The Park Service and Fish and Game Department started trapping bears that became too aggressive and moved them to the backcountry, normally into the isolated parts of the park.

It was common for black bears and grizzlies to come into town at night and tip over garbage cans and containers with restaurant scraps for an easy meal. The garbage used to be hauled to the garbage dump 2 miles north of town, but over time, a decision was made to close the garbage dump and start a landfill.

This landfill was the third garbage disposal area that I can recall. It still remains in this location today. A huge hole was dug and the garbage would be dumped into it and covered over each day. It was on forest service land and was fenced to keep the bears out. That was the end of the bear watching at the dump. These big holes, roughly 30 feet deep by 300 feet long, and filled with garbage, were called cells. This practice continued for many years. When one cell was filled another would be dug.

Eventually, it became clear that leachate, a toxic solution resulting from the surface water filtering down through all the garbage cells, was creating ground water pollution, which threatened to contaminate the nearby Madison River. Of course, no one wanted that. Because this was mainly West Yellowstone garbage, the town was given the responsibility of cleaning up the problem. The apparent solution was to haul all the garbage to the Ennis landfill, which was 70 miles away. A few years later waste was hauled to the Logan landfill, 120 miles away! Mayor Larry Binfet called me into his office one day and asked if I would be the chairman of a committee to help find (and fund) a solution to the garbage problem.

We established the West Yellowstone Hebgen Basin Solid Waste Refuse District. This covered not only the town but the complete Hebgen Lake Basin. We formed a volunteer committee with two responsibilities:

1. Fund and build a transfer station at the landfill site 5 miles north of town and establish a system for collecting garbage and hauling it to a different site. The transfer station consisted of a facility where people could drive up on a ramp and dump their garbage on a concrete floor. It would then be pushed into a 40-ton trailer below and hauled to a safe landfill. In preparation for the designing and building of a new transfer station, we traveled to different operating transfer stations to observe their set-ups. Then we hired Barry Damschen as our engineer.

2. Close and cover the cells, as well as monitor and clean up the ground water pollution. We worked with the Montana Department of Health, and under their direction, we drilled and monitored wells and checked the ground water until the leachate dissipated. The monitoring happened for many years. We finally received word that the threat had passed and were cleared from continuing testing.

Simultaneously, we went through a very complicated process of proportionately assessing and placing on the tax rolls funding for the completed building and the ongoing hauling of garbage to the landfill. We worked through each tax payer's assessment.

We considered one house a household unit (based on one ton of garbage per year) and grocery stores, restaurants, and other businesses multiple household units. After nearly six years, in 1983, we held the ribbon cutting for the new facility at a cost of $224,000. We contracted a company to pick up the local town garbage and haul it to the transfer station. Those who wanted to bring their own garbage to the transfer station could do so for free, as the taxes were paying for it. After the pickup and transfer of the local town garbage, the contractor hauled it to a licensed landfill out of the Greater Yellowstone Area. **27**

Ribbon cutting ceremony at the transfer station
Left to Right: Clyde Seely, Shirley Butcher, Mayor Larry
Binfet, Frances Kawakomi, Ralph Meyers

We purchased four-yard, bear-proof, dumpsters to keep the bears from ransacking the town people's garbage. This was necessary to wean the bears off of food provided by humans. Many dumpster-diving bears were caught and transferred to a different habitat, some way back into the park areas.

See **27** on the West Yellowstone Map Pages 142-143

In the early years of the 21st Century, composting became a big buzz. After much work and many, many meetings, in conjunction with the National Park Service (NPS), Montana Department of Environmental Quality (DEQ), and others, we decided to fund and build a composting facility near the transfer station. On June 13, 2003, we held a ribbon cutting ceremony for the $4.2 million compost facility. The facility can process only the amount of garbage generated by Yellowstone Park; the rest of the districts' garbage still has to be taken through the transfer station and hauled to Logan, Montana. Yellowstone has made a good effort to reduce plastics and other non-compostable solid waste, but a high percentage of the garbage still has to be hauled to the landfill. Yellowstone has received funding and has paid off the cost of the composting facility. However, some of the equipment is reaching its life expectancy of about 10 years and will have to be replaced.

The transfer station itself needed a major remodel after 30 years. We have found it necessary to expand and, for the most part, rebuild the facility with a larger tipping floor. This is the concrete floor where the garbage is dumped into and then pushed into the large trailer situated below. In 2013, we completed the new facility, which cost a little over $500,000. After nearly 35 years and three major construction projects, I am still on the board. The local bear problem has been pretty well resolved.

Fall River Electric Board Member

I remember first appreciating electricity as a small boy. We had electric lights and outlets in the house, and eventually we got indoor plumbing and an electric water heater. We also had a couple of drop-down electric lights hanging in the barn. My job was to read the meter, which was about 12 feet up on the power pole. I would bring the meter reading back to the folks and they would subtract the previous month's numbers from the current month to figure the bill. It normally totaled about $10–$12 per month.

I mention this because years later, when West Yellowstone installed a public water system, the board discussed how they could get the water meters read. One thought was to hire a meter reader and have someone figure the bill. Of course this would be an administrative expense. I relayed my boyhood experience and suggested they initiate a self-reading system like we did on the farm and do a periodic spot check for monitoring. That concept was eventually adopted and has worked very well over the years. It saved the town hundreds of thousands of dollars. Now the electrical and water meters are read remotely.

My association with the Fall River Rural Electric Cooperative whose main office is in Ashton, Idaho, began one day in 1980, when the general manager and two of the board members came to see me. They asked if I would complete the term for Dutch Spainhower, who had just passed away. Fall River is a cooperative business owned by its members. Members in each of the nine districts elect a representative to the board. There are nine board members, one of which represents West Yellowstone. Mike Wilson had served on this board when I first worked for him. I completed Dutch's term and then was elected, serving from 1980 to 1995. Then I was re-elected in 1998 and served 12 more years until term limits prevented further service in 2010.

I saw much progress over those 27 years. At the beginning of my service, the board was sort of like an old boys' club that met once a month. One of the board members had served 40 years. The National Rural Electric Cooperative Association (NRECA) provided classes and training seminars for new board members. It is an overwhelming thing to come onto a board that deals with unfamiliar acronyms, budgets, rate structures etc., so by taking the offered classes, a board member could become certified. Though schooling for the board members had been available for years, I was the first to become certified by attending the recommended classes. I pushed for board certification to be required within the first three-year term for new board members. My proposal was adopted, and the requirement is now in place.

When I was still new on the board, we were asked to approve a capital expenditure budget. I said that I could not approve it because what had been submitted was only a partial budget. We needed to see income, expenses, and a complete budget all presented at one time to see the complete picture. Without that, an informed decision could not be made. From that time on, we were presented with a complete budget. I was surprised that, after all those years, that was the first time such a practice had been implemented.

> The co-op was formed in 1938. In 1941, the co-op purchased the diesel generators and power plant in West Yellowstone, which had previously been owned and operated by Bert Fields. The Union Pacific Generator House was built in about 1910 and remodeled in 1918 and 1927 to blend with the Rustic Style of the new dining hall next door. The Union Pacific diesel generators provided backup service for the town. When Fall River Rural Electric Cooperative purchased its facility in 1941, they began providing 24-hour electrical service to West Yellowstone. When the power line was put in from Ashton to West Yellowstone in 1947, the generators were no longer needed. Even though the generator house is no longer used, it is listed as a historical building and has been restored for public visitation. The large shiny generator remains inside. It stands across the street from Three Bear Lodge and is listed as site number 7 on the West Yellowstone Historical Walking Tour.

Fall River Electric owns and maintains power lines that run from West Yellowstone to Ririe, Idaho. Since this is a rural cooperative, many of the board members are local farmers. Most of the time I served on the board, I was the only board member who had owned and operated a business. I keenly took on the responsibility of looking after the commercial consumers as well as the residential and irrigation consumers. The board was able to work out a fair rate for each of these classes of consumers.

During my tenure on the board, Fall River Electric became increasingly involved with hydroelectric plants in order to achieve some independence from Bonneville Power and other big suppliers. When I came on board there was one little generation plant in Felt, Idaho. The board later decided that the Island Park Dam and Reservoir had great potential for generating electricity. The dam had been built in 1939 for irrigation control and is located in the Targhee National Forest near Island Park. Its potential for generating electricity was not being utilized. Cost studies were done and we discovered that the project would be financially feasible only if we could get a $1 million tax credit.

I was asked to go to Washington DC in 1991 and ask Max Baucus, the senator from Montana, to plead our case. He listened and eventually stood on the floor of the Senate and asked for the tax credit. It was granted. We began breaching the top of the dam in 1992 and completed the project in July 1993. Since that time we have retrofitted and built the Buffalo River Dam and the Chester Idaho Hydro. I also helped lead the way to turn our local Hebgen Dam into a hydro plant, but that project ultimately failed, which is unfortunate as it would have been a great asset to West Yellowstone.

Serving as a board member for 27 years has ingrained an appreciation in me for co-ops and the fact that these organizations are nonprofits with the purpose of serving its members. With Fall River Electric, I held several board positions over the years, including chairman of several sub-committees, and vice president and president. When serving as the president, Three Bear Lodge had its fire (See Pebble 28), and I had to resign as board president so I could devote sufficient time to rebuilding. I found I had too many responsibilities on my plate to do justice to the job, so I resigned from that position and continued on as board member until the end of my term.

Periodically, we have had to increase electrical rates. One of these times in particular weighed heavily on my mind and on the minds of others on the board. There were people who were having trouble paying as it was. My personal goal was to come up with a solution to help those individuals.

I felt that there were members with the means to help others who were not as fortunate. So we needed to come up with some kind of a vehicle to help make this possible for those in need to have energy assistance in order to meet their power and heat requirements. This was not a problem unique to our co-op, and we looked at some programs that other co-ops had in place. Then I wrote up a presentation to the board, and with their support, we established the "Fall River Electric Helping Hands" fund.

Now there are three ways people could contribute:

- Rounding their bill up to the next whole dollar each month

- Sending an additional fixed amount each month

- Making a one-time large contribution

We formed a non-profit corporation, established a separate board, and began the program. I was chairman of the Helping Hands committee and stayed on for several months after term limits prevented me from staying on the regular board. We got the bugs worked out and set the direction for the program. It was very gratifying to help those who were having trouble paying their bill and who would otherwise have had their power cut off because they couldn't make their payments. All they needed were some helping hands. The response from the membership was good, and I am sure the program will continue for years to come—just another pebble in the pool that will continue to cause ripples into the lives of others.

Yellowstone Avenue Street Lights

Even before I came to West Yellowstone, Lon Hadley, owner of the Madison Hotel, and some other businesses had joined together and bought about half a dozen street lights to be installed on Yellowstone Avenue, the street that runs straight out of the park. You can imagine many years ago, coming out of the park at night into a little town with only a few twinkling lights in local stores, indicating there was a town there.

It was a wise thing for a group of innovative individuals to work together to install streetlights down Yellowstone Avenue. But the rest of the town was dark. Lon Hadley would come around every fall and collect the lighting fee from the businesses that had agreed to pay for the electricity. When Lon died, I took over that responsibility.

In 1988, the town was in the process of putting in new streets and gutters and paving all the streets. There was no money in the budget to install street lights. I then contacted the folks on Yellowstone Avenue and around the corner on Dunraven Street, asking if they would be willing to come together again as a group, and pay for new street lights. Most were willing.

The total cost of the project for fourteen streetlights would be $42,567. We allocated this cost to the businesses according to the number of feet that fronted Yellowstone Avenue and Dunraven Street. Each agreed to pay their share. This little lighting district was eventually taken over by the town.

As time goes by, fewer people remember how dark our little town used to be or what an effort it took to make our streets bright and inviting. Probably most don't care, but behind so many things that have been accomplished in our little town, there is an interesting story. There are many people who have dropped a pebble in the pool of West Yellowstone, the result of which has not been recorded. The Yellowstone Avenue Street Light District is just one example as to how the town grew into the wonderful place that it is today. Efforts such as this would long be forgotten unless they are recorded.

The Community Water Ad Hoc Committee

The town looked like a war zone during the time its new infrastructure was being installed. The sewer system had been installed previously, but in 1987, with payments from the resort tax being instigated, the town began to make major changes. New sidewalks, curbs, and gutters were being installed in addition to a new storm drainage system, fully paved streets, underground water lines, and other utilities. The old sidewalks and streets, many of which had never really been paved, were torn out. Many of the big commercial signs were moved. Tourists coming into town that summer probably wondered how to get where they wanted to go.

Most signs were installed prior to the town being incorporated. With no guidelines, many of these signs had been placed on town property and would be right in the middle of the new sidewalks. It would be a real head knocker had they been left in the middle of a new sidewalk. But with a new sign ordinance in place, these signs had to be torn out and moved back. Three Bear's forty-foot-tall sign was no exception; like the rest, it had to be moved. At whose expense? Of course, you guessed it, ours.

The town council had asked the citizens to support a bond for $1,800,000 for a culinary water and firefighting grid system. Ideally this would be installed prior to the surface infrastructure being installed. However, the residents didn't support it. Left with no other choice, the town council planned to move forward with the sidewalks and gutters without the water system. In my opinion, this would have been a horrendous mistake.

In a matter of a few days, a group of us formed the Community Water Ad Hoc Committee and offered an alternative. I chaired that committee and proposed that a firefighting grid system be installed for $515,000. This would provide the piping needed for the fire hydrants and later, when funding could be obtained, the culinary water could be added. We also told the council we would carry petitions to the residents to show the support.

It was not easy to knock on the doors of those who voted against the town water system. But necessity is the mother of invention, and we felt it was necessary to put the water system in before the streets and sidewalks were put in so they wouldn't have to be torn out later. After much legwork, we came up with enough support from the town so the council could proceed and eventually the complete water system was installed.

As a result, the underground water system ended up being charged by Whiskey Springs, a spring 4 miles away, which required no pumps, as the water was gravity fed. At the owner's discretion, individual wells were closed and people began to use the municipal water system. An excellent fire hydrant system was installed, and we had the complete water system. This system was installed prior to the installation of the complete sewage system, the storm drain system (with curbs and gutters), and the new streets and sidewalks. Had we not done this when we did, one can only imagine the additional cost it would have been to install a water system after the streets, gutters, and sidewalks were installed.

Gone are the times when I had to get the well fixed because of a burned-out pump. Gone are the times when I would have to dig into one or another of the makeshift septic tanks with their wonderful aroma to find out why it was backing up. Sometimes I miss the good old days, but in respect to these experiences, I am glad those good old days are gone forever.

Board of Directors—Averting a Crisis at the Grizzly and Wolf Discovery Center

An eighty-seven-acre parcel of land just south of the town was deeded to the Union Pacific Railroad. In the beginning, it was deeded for the purpose of building a $1 million hotel to accommodate the influx of Yellowstone Park visitors. However, the hotel was never built. This land south of the railroad tracks and buildings abutted Yellowstone Park on the east and for many years was used as a stud mill.

In 1990, the land was sold to the Firehole Land Corporation, which developed the Grizzly Park subdivision. The eighty-seven-acre parcel was purchased, the infrastructure put in, and the land sold in various lot sizes for commercial development. An IMAX Theater, the Silver Tip Restaurant, McDonald's, Hibernation Station, and Kelley Inn were among the first businesses built in Grizzly Park. Later two banks were built, and the local post office was relocated to a new building in the development.

After the land was purchased and preliminary plans presented, public zoning meetings were held. There was some disagreement about the viability of the overall project. The plan was rather grandiose, and I, for one, was concerned that if it got into financial trouble the town could have a white elephant on its hands. I was wrong.

The Grizzly Discovery Center (GDC) was built as the flagship and main attraction for the newly developed Grizzly Park in West Yellowstone and opened its doors in August 1993. It provided the opportunity for visitors to see and learn about live grizzly bears. No cost was spared to create a first-class facility. The town folks supported the GDC as it provided another attraction that was memorable and caused people to return to town or to stay in town longer. In 1995, the facility was sold to Ogden Entertainment out of New York.

In early fall 1999 at a chamber of commerce meeting, Dr. Gale Ford and Nancy Heideman, who represented the GDC and who had put their heart and soul into it, made a startling announcement: Ogden Entertainment had decided to close its holdings west of the Mississippi. They were looking for a buyer or they were going to close the GDC before the snow fell. Gale and Nancy said that unless they could come up with the down payment in the next week, the bears would be euthanized and the GDC would be shut down.

At the end of the meeting, Bill Howell and I talked briefly and then asked to meet with Gail and Nancy. We asked what they planned to do about it. They said they were in the process of obtaining non-profit status and the financing to purchase the facility, but if they couldn't come up with the necessary down payment there was nothing they could do. They were in need of an additional $150,000. We told them that they couldn't just let it close up, as it would be bad for the town. I was also concerned about having a dreaded white elephant that would sit there unused and be a symbol of failure in the town. So Bill and I presented them with our quickly drawn-up plan. Though it would be hard, we would write them a check for $150,000. They could then do what was needed to save the animals and carry the GDC onward.

The end result was that we purchased $150,000 of GDC tickets in advance in order to sell them to our guests at Three Bear Lodge and the Holiday Inn or build them into our packages. We could recoup our money in that way, so that is what we did.

It took us several years to sell that many tickets, but it ended up being a good thing for the GDC because it sent more people to see the bears. Until then, only a small percentage of our patrons went to see them, but now we had an incentive to push it hard. Our risk, however, was that if the GDC did not make it financially, we would be out our money. There was no signed agreement, which was kind of like how my dad used to do business. We did, however, get a "First Right of Refusal" agreement, so if the facility was to be sold again, we could possibly step in to purchase it to save it from closing.

To ensure that we were kept appraised of what was going on; Bill and I had one seat on the GDC board; we alternated every other year. The reorganization took place, and the bears were not euthanized. The GDC operated quite successfully as a non-profit, so it was able to continue operations. Many improvements and additions, including a wolf habitat, were made, and plans were in place to make it even better.

As a board, one of our first responsibilities in late 2003 was to hire a new director of the GDC. The Director of the Boise Zoo, my partner Bill Howell and I were put in charge of the hiring process. We received résumés from a number of very well trained and experienced individuals. We asked two of them to come for an interview, along with John Heine, then the GDC Animal Curator. As successful as the center was, it was still in its infancy and had to become financially viable. The GDC had much more land to utilize, which required large expenditures. Not only would this person need to be able to manage the facility, he or she would need to secure grants for the future operations and GDC expansion.

Nancy Heideman, Dr. Ford, and John Heine were excluded from the hiring process. Our selection committee reviewed all the information available and made a very difficult decision. We called a meeting with all of the Grizzly Discovery Center employees and announced that we were offering the job to John Heine. There was an outbreak of applause, and we knew we had made the right choice.

Something I have learned from serving on many municipal boards is that one of the most important things a board can do is to hire a good manager. The board can direct and set policies, but the manger is left to carry out those directions. John lived in the area, his heart and passion was in the GDC, and we believed he would continue to do a great job. The GDC has now come into its own and is a credit to the community. With the addition of the wolf habitat, it was renamed the Grizzly and Wolf Discovery Center. **18**

See **18** on the West Yellowstone Map Pages 142-143

Pebble 24: The West Yellowstone Economic Development Council Inc. (WYED)

When a man has put a limit on what he will do,
he has put a limit on what he can do.

~Charles M. Schwab

The formation of the West Yellowstone Economic Development Council Inc. (WYED) was originally an unintended consequence of dealing with another issue. As was mentioned in Pebble 21, our snowcoach business had continued to grow, and in 2006 we realized we needed a larger garage and storage facility. I owned the property on both sides of the new Rendezvous Ski trail building. I determined that the east side of that building would be the most logical spot to expand. I requested a building permit from the town, but my plan did not sit well with the cross country ski people (some of whom were on the town council), and they met with me to express their concern about having a snowcoach barn right next to the pristine entrance to their ski trail. I could understand their concern but didn't know what else to do. **20**

The town offered to buy another piece of property and trade it for mine so I could build elsewhere. I agreed, as the location was

See **20** on the West Yellowstone Map Pages 142-143

not important to me. However, the search for property was unsuccessful, as all available options were extremely expensive. At a
special meeting called by the town council to discuss the dilemma,
I explained my situation: I owned the property and needed a snowcoach facility. They could not find an affordable piece elsewhere, so
I had to build next to the ski trail entrance.

Then they asked if I would sell the property to the town. I
thought about it and decided to sell it to them for $100,000. They
thought that was a lot of money and asked if I would take less. I
said, "No that is as low as I can go." They swallowed hard and discussed it among themselves. Their decision was to come up with
the money because they really did not want a building right next
the new cross-country ski building. By this time, I had an ulterior
motive for selling, but gave no indication of what it was. They came
back with a unanimous decision to pay the $100,000 for the land.

I thanked them and then told them I would accept the
$100,000, but that I would turn it back to the community and estab-
lish an entity that would be used for the marketing and improvement of West Yellowstone. I received the $100,000 and, along
with the new board, established the West Yellowstone Economic
Development Council Inc. (WYED), a non-profit organization. The
articles of incorporation were signed in June 2006 and the bylaws
and mission statement quickly followed.

The formation of WYED was a response to a longstanding
problem in the community: dealing with the lack of town money
for marketing and promoting tourism. As I explained to the council,
you can't expect to harvest a crop unless you fertilize. I thought it
was also important to create a new and interesting image for West
Yellowstone. What could I do that would make West Yellowstone a
more memorable place—more than just a bedroom community to
the park? I believed that such an organization as WYED could help
find ways to accomplish this goal.

The winter economy had been thriving because of the popularity of snowmobile access into the park, but because of the lawsuits

by environmental organizations and the environmental impact statement regarding winter use, the National Park Service was considering doing away with snowmobile access (as mentioned in Pebble 22). The threat of reduced snowmobile access in the park began to loom like a dark cloud over our heads.

The chamber of commerce began to hold what we called visioning meetings. The purpose was to brainstorm ideas that could help supplement revenue for the town and help ward off the impending slump in the winter economy. About a dozen people were present and were considered part of this committee. (In West Yellowstone, if you show up, you usually end up on a committee.) We were assigned to think of ways to create new sources of revenue for the town.

Late one night while sitting in the hot tub, I came up with three ideas that seemed rather ambitious but I thought doable. Then days later, when our committee reconvened, a lot of ideas were written on whiteboards. In order to prioritize the items listed, each person took a sticky dot and placed it on the project they thought would be the most effective and achievable in West Yellowstone. Those with the most dots would be pursued. My three contributions rose to the top: 1) create a painted buffalo street display, 2) develop a historical walking tour (like the Freedom Trail in Boston), and 3) pursue establishing a local based college program.

Buffalo Roam

The first major community project that WYED undertook was the Buffalo Roam project. This idea came from a vacation Linda and I took to Calgary more than 25 years before. One evening, we decided to do a little window-shopping and were amazed to find a number of cows scattered around the downtown area. They seemed to be spread in no particular order or location, but as we walked along, we saw one, then another, and another. These were not full-sized cows, they were rather docile, and they let us take pictures of them—since they were all inanimate objects made of fiberglass. They all looked alike except they were each adorned with different colors of paint and artistic renderings. We took many pictures, sometimes with Linda standing by the side, sometimes with me posed in some contorted position next to them. It appeared this project was something the city had done to generate interest in their downtown area, and for us it had been a hit. We had fun finding these cows and seeing the various colors and designs.

All these years later, I called the city of Calgary and asked if the painted cows were still on their sidewalks. They explained that the painted cows had been a summer project, but that some of them could still be found, displayed by the merchants that had purchased them, and were now protected inside some storefronts. I envisioned a similar project in West Yellowstone in which we would have cows all right, but in this case cow-buffalo. What could be more appropriate than buffalo, who, in days gone by, roamed down the streets of West Yellowstone?

Three million people a year passed through West Yellowstone, but they were just passing through. Even if they stayed overnight, they left with little recollection of our town. But the town was working hard to change that. The goal was for our town to become more than just a stop on the way, but also a place that would be remembered. Since most visitors had cameras, it made sense that the painted buffalo project could increase our town's intrigue.

This project did not just happen overnight. In fact, in the beginning, it was only three or four of us that began putting meat on the bones of the painted buffalo idea. With me, it became a passion; although, I had no idea how to proceed. Then I learned that the summer before, Great Falls had a painted buffalo project. At the time, Linda and I happened to be in Salt Lake City, and I awoke early one morning and decided I should go check it out for myself. So I hopped on a plane with my camera and landed in Great Falls a couple hours later. There, in the terminal, was the first big, full-sized bull buffalo. It was amazing. I rented a car and drove around the city, looking for and taking pictures of every bull I could find.

It turned out a volunteer group had held a fundraising project for the C. M. Russell Museum. They spent a year planning and creating twenty fiberglass forms, which became 3D canvases for the artists. Each buffalo had a sponsor. After the painted buffalo were completed, they were on display all summer. In the fall, there was a bull sale, and many of the buffalo were bought locally and stayed in the town. After just one summer, I believe, nearly $300,000 was raised for the museum.

I looked up the people who had successfully completed their project, which they named the buffalo hunt. They gave me contact names and shared with me the procedures they went through to complete the project.

A similar project could be done in West Yellowstone, so I wrote out a bullet point plan from start to finish and then approached the newly formed WYED board with the proposal, and they approved it. We then approached the town council for their approval to create and place the painted buffalo on the sidewalks and received their blessing. With the infusion of $100,000 into WYED from the sale of my lot, we now had the money to proceed without having to rely on any financial solicitations or assistance from the community other than from willing sponsors. Permission was granted, and we were off and running.

Even though WYED utilized the information gathered from Great Falls, we formulated our own plan. I made up a timeline for completion of the project, which we followed precisely. We decided to have twenty-seven cow-buffalos produced and have twenty-five of them painted. On the day of the unveiling, the twenty-sixth buffalo, a collage of fifteen artists was painted. We made a verbal contract with Joe Halko, a sculptor and artist, to create the buffalo. First of all, Joe created a wax model about eight inches tall for our approval. He used this model as a pattern from which to create a near-life-sized cow made out of Styrofoam. After approving it, we shipped this Styrofoam buffalo to Fiberstock in Buffalo, Minnesota—a fitting location name. They used it to create a mold, which they used to create twenty-seven near-life-sized fiberglass, gray cow-buffalo. These were then shipped back to us. In the meantime, WYED had advertised for artists from neighboring states to submit their proposed art sketches.

We formed an artist selection committee to judge the artist applicants to paint these 3D canvases and ended up awarding twenty-five contracts. Then an invitation to sponsor a buffalo for $3,000 was sent out to the businesses in West Yellowstone. The sponsor's name, along with the artist and the name of the buffalo, would be placed on a plaque at the base of the buffalo, which would be placed in front of their business. Their business name would also be placed on a walk-around buffalo location trail map. Rather than charging $3,000 for one year, the sponsor received these benefits for three years. But in order to keep interest high, we moved the buffalo, or had them roam around, to different sponsors each spring. Hence the name, Buffalo Roam.

One evening in November 2005, we invited all the winning artists to meet their sponsor and pick up their unpainted cows, which were corralled behind jackleg fences in the conference room at the Holiday Inn. From there it became a labor of love, with artists painting during the winter months. One artist said she had the buffalo in her bedroom, where she painted on it whenever she could.

We had allowed the artists to choose from three themes: Yellowstone, Historic West Yellowstone, or the Native Americans. It was like Christmas the next spring when these beautiful masterpieces of 3D art began coming home to West Yellowstone. We stored them in my warehouse so no one could see them until the grand unveiling in June 2006.

I asked the *Bozeman Chronicle* to donate $10,000 to the project. They agreed to contribute by printing separate tabloids and inserting them in their papers in Montana and Idaho. The WYED wrote up a background piece on the project and submitted photos of all twenty-five of them for the insert.

The buffalo were randomly placed inside our specially made jackleg fence on the lawn of the Yellowstone Historic Center Museum and were veiled with white motel sheets. We hauled in bleachers from the rodeo ground and the school football field.

Then the big day finally came. The bleachers were full of people. The anticipation was high! After recognizing the appropriate people, on my signal, all the sheets came off. Oohing, aahing, and clapping followed. It really was an unbelievable sight. We had the Playmill Theatre lead the people in a snake dance going through the buffalo to Roger Miller's song, "You Can't Roller Skate in a Buffalo Herd."

Grand Unveiling of twenty-six painted buffalo, ten calves followed the next spring.

In addition to unveiling the painted buffalo, we introduced and served free samples of our very own Buffalo Chip ice cream. I had contacted Wilcoxin's Ice Cream Company in Livingston, Montana, and explained our project, asking him if he would consider making a signature ice cream for our Buffalo Roam project.

He agreed and came up with what he later said became one of his bestsellers. It is made with chocolate ice cream, caramel swirls, and Snickers pieces. I thought, perhaps, he would stop making it after our three-year Buffalo Roam project, but Wilcoxin's is still making it because it is one of their most popular flavors.

After the first summer, the WYED decided that where there was a herd of cows, there was normally a bunch of calves, so we organized a calf committee and went through the whole process again. I took a picture of a calf buffalo, Joe sculpted it, and, low and behold, the next spring we had a crop of ten calves. These were cute little guys, some of whom had the same theme and looked like their mothers.

In addition to our WYED general board and the calf committee, we organized others committees. We had an artist selection committee, a marketing committee, and a merchandizing committee. Each of these committees worked very hard. Also, in conjunction with the grand unveiling for the calves, we sponsored an art show in the Union Pacific Dining Lodge, where some of our Buffalo Roam merchandise, such as cups, T-shirts, ball caps, and other clothing items were on sale.

At the end of the third summer, we began a two-day event (August 28–29, 2009). It was the West Yellowstone Regional Art Show in conjunction with the painted buffalo auction. On August 28th, potential bidders along with the public could come and preview the buffalo. On the 29 , people were invited to a pancake breakfast, and that evening at 7:30 p.m., the cow auction was held. The convention room at the Holiday Inn was nearly full. Many of the artists were able to attend, but unfortunately, Joe Halko, the sculptor, artist, and by now a good friend, had just passed away.

Before the auction began, I took time to pay tribute to Joe Halko and his good wife, Martha, with a slide show of the progression of his work. He was a great guy. I ended up buying the two buffalo he had painted. They will always stand in front of Three Bear Lodge, and Joe will long be remembered. Stephen R. Covey also bought a cow buffalo. I had explained to him about the project at its outset, and he was also a generous contributor. He has also since passed away, and I also honor him in memorial. His buffalo still stands at the family house west of town.

The sale that followed was exciting! Not only were the people in the room bidding, but Sam Korsmoe bid by proxy for people he had on the phone from across the country. We ended up selling buffalo to buyers from the East Coast to California. Most however, were bought locally. The sale prices of the buffalo ranged from $2,700 to $17,500 each, and we took in over $160,000.

Many thousands of photos were taken. These photos and fond memories of West Yellowstone's very own Buffalo Roam project have traveled worldwide. Of all our volunteer community projects, surely the Buffalo Roam endeavor was one of the most successful.

It is still common to see people stop their cars and take pictures of these unexpected, beautifully painted buffalo on various sidewalks around town. There are still eleven buffalo that can be seen in the business district, with their locations shown on the walking tour map that was developed later. Three more, including Stephen Covey's, are located in the surrounding residential areas. Some buyers purchased the buffalo, not only because they wanted to have a keepsake, but also because they wished to continue supporting the project. Some of the money collected went to pay the artists, some was earmarked for small WYED grants, but most was set in reserve to support subsequent WYED projects, such as the West Yellowstone Historical Walking Tour.

The West Yellowstone
Historical Walking Tour

Just as Linda's and my visit to Calgary years ago was the impetus for the Buffalo Roam project, our visit to Boston and the Freedom Trail made me start to ask, "Why can't we make a similar historical experience in West Yellowstone, even though it would be on a vastly smaller scale?"

While in Boston, we picked up the Freedom Trail walking tour map and started to follow it on our own. There were helpful and easy-to-follow red lines painted on the sidewalks, which led us from one historical site to another. At each site, the main stories were told by signs. Linda and I gained an appreciation for the many things that happened in Boston that helped formulate our country, which we love so much. By following the red line, reading the plaques, and seeing the historic buildings, we could relive, in a sense, the sacrifices that were made for us all.

Move ahead to 2010, and you will find in West Yellowstone, Montana, a spin-off of the Freedom Trail. I have always been awed by the sacrifices of those who have gone on before and paved the way so we could enjoy what we have today. Their pebbles dropped in pools along the way and created ripples that have joined together in making our lives what they are today. West Yellowstone has a rich but much younger history than the events depicted on the Freedom Trail. Much of our history centers around the magnificent 300-foot-wide Union Pacific Railroad property, which runs the entire length of the town. After the railroad abandoned the property, it was deeded to West Yellowstone.

Most people recognize 1908 as the arrival of the railroad and the beginning date of the town. If we consider this to be true, the town was just 50 years old when I arrived there as a young man. With just a few businesses in the town at that time, many people of my generation will remember the changes that our little town went through during those years. As I have often heard said, "There is nothing as constant as change." This certainly has been true in the case of West Yellowstone. Since over the years I have seen the transformation of this town, I wanted to help preserve the memories of how things used to be and recognize how we got to where we are now. No wonder then that one of the projects I wanted to accomplish with the WYED was to create a historical walking tour for West Yellowstone.

Working in conjunction with the Yellowstone Historic Center to ensure accuracy, we decided to incorporate some of the ideas of the Freedom Trail into the West Yellowstone Historical Walking Tour. The WYED board chose buildings and businesses that were of historic interest and then invested research time to come up with interesting and factual information regarding these places.

The Union Pacific property, with the depot and Dining Lodge, was the arrival and departure point and the main attraction for the town's thousands of early visitors who came to see the wonders of Yellowstone. Businesses sprang up across Yellowstone Avenue, which ran parallel to the railroad tracks to accommodate visitors' needs. Visitors came by stage, train, or horse and buggy, and eventually touring busses and automobiles. We thought it fitting to begin our historic walking tour with the railroad buildings and then feature the other early businesses that served visitors in those early years.

The WYED board asked for authorization to establish a walking tour on town property and on the sidewalks in front of the historical buildings. Permission was granted, and we were off and running. We had to establish the criteria used to qualify the sites chosen. It was decided to incorporate some of the existing historical signs authorized by the Montana Historical Society and make new signs for the facilities that we wanted to add.

After we decided to name the tour the West Yellowstone Historical Walking Tour, we decided to design and place weather-proof plaques outside each place of historical significance, showing original photographs and telling a snippet of its past. We then made a walking tour map brochure to direct visitors from one place to another in a sequential order. Though the Freedom Trail had a red line painted on the sidewalks leading from place to place, the WYED decided to use a bear paw trail painted with green spray paint to lead from site to site. We paid for the signs and brochure maps with proceeds from the Buffalo Roam project, thereby putting back into the community another long-term benefit. We approached those whose names were on the map and who were to have a plaque placed in front of their business to finance the printing of the brochure map each year. Other than that, all the funding came from WYED's proceeds of the Buffalo Roam.

We were willing to invest a lot of time, effort, and capital to make this experience intriguing and user friendly. Hundreds of volunteer hours were spent, mainly by John Greve, Glenn Hales, and me, researching and writing up the copy for the plaques and for the information on the historical walking tour map. We engaged Scott Bevan's design firm, Attune, to design the logo, plaques, and map. We contracted with Fossil Industries of New York to create almost indestructible outdoor signs. Then I designed and built metal mounting brackets and attached the signs.

We had plastic templates made with grizzly bear paw cutouts about 3 feet apart, and we got down on our hands and knees and spray painted over 1,100 green paw prints. I used the wood salvaged from Herk Rightenour's old 1920s sawmill to make 22 three-pocket brochure racks. These were given to the sponsors to display and distribute the walking tour maps. We printed 20,000 West Yellowstone Historical Walking Tour maps, which were distributed in the unique brochure racks and have continued to reprint that number annually.

Fires played an important part in changing the face of Old West Yellowstone. Though never welcome, they caused West Yellowstone to rebuild and to modernize some of the old buildings. The little town, mostly made of wood, was a tinderbox in which wood stoves, electrical wiring, and later propane leaks often caused fires. The Three Bear Lodge, for instance, has burned three times. Interested folks can follow the map with its fire icons and see some of the photos of buildings that used to be.

Also included on the walking tour map are the buffalo icons that identify the places where the Buffalo Roam statues are located. It is interesting to watch families take the tour with kids trying to step on every bear paw and parents taking pictures of the attractive plaques, buildings, and the now famous Buffalo Roam painted buffalos. **(B)**

You can go to www.wyed.org to find a copy of the walking tour map.

Tourism Business Improvement District (TBID)

As was mentioned earlier, West Yellowstone was confronted with a declining economy in the winter because of the snowmobile restrictions. We needed a way to fund promotion of the off-season in West Yellowstone or find another way to offset the loss of winter revenue.

The WYED board, led by Sam Korsmoe, felt we could receive legislative approval to establish a Tourism Business Improvement District (TBID) in town. We were only the second municipality in the state to apply for this status. The TBID planned to charge $1 for every occupied hotel room in hotels of ten or more beds located within the city limits. The TBID anticipated raising in excess of $250,000 per year to be used mainly for marketing and promoting the town.

We met with the town council to get their blessing and then with the hoteliers to get their support. In order for this initiative to pass, we needed 60% of the major hotels' support, based on the square footage of the building footprints, as well as parking and landscaped areas.

The initiative passed, and the TBID became a reality. A board was set up representing small, medium, and large hotel properties that became the operating entity to administer the funds. At the successful completion of this entity, WYED, the initiator of the project had to divest itself of any control.

See **(B)** on the West Yellowstone Map Pages 142-143

We had reached the goal we set out to accomplish. With these projects we have learned that to get to the top of a mountain, you need to take one step at a time in a steady climb, and we had reached the top of another mountain.

Purchase of the West Yellowstone Economic Development Council (WYED) Building College Satellite Programs

For many years, I had been struck by what an amazing resource the park could be as a site for academic research and teaching. Right in our own backyard was one of the greatest laboratories on earth to pursue studies of geology, seismology, biology, ecology, and many other disciplines. The concept was not to have a big formal college with buildings of bricks and mortar but to utilize the local facilities that already existed. One of the first things we did was to form a college committee. Then we invited local universities to come for a roundtable discussion about the potential for such a program and those who attended were very enthusiastic about it.

Two college personnel surfaced as the main drivers of the effort, but eventually they retired or were transferred to different locations. Finally, there were only three local diehards that continued on: Heidi Roos, Pierre Martineau, and myself. After several years, even though the WYED board still believed in the college concept, we decided it would be better to put it on hold and revisit it when we were better prepared.

With the completion of two out of our three goals, the Buffalo Roam and the Historic Walking Tour, we decided to once again reinvigorate the college concept. With some money left over from the sale of the painted buffalo to put toward that effort, we had a college feasibility study done.

In December 2010, the WYED was approached about buying an 11,500 sq. foot building. This building had been remodeled and expanded to include a beauty salon, a fitness center with two racquetball courts, and two apartments. The facility was still nearly new on the inside, as it had only been operating a couple years.

I was determined not to go to the community and ask for money for the building. So we decided to take a leap of faith, and on December 15, 2010, we purchased what would later be named the WYED Center. The purpose of establishing WYED was to add to the economic vitality of the community, not to cause a drain on it. Linda and I came up with half of the money to be paid off in four years. We found a benefactor who wished to remain anonymous to match our payment for the first two years. Another local lady, who also did not want to be personally recognized, graciously contributed money for furniture and equipment and for renovation of the first classroom. Included in the building were rental spaces for physical therapy, a restaurant, a catering facility, and a large private apartment. These rental spaces have pretty well carried the operation and maintenance costs of the building.

We named the building the WYED Center with the full name written underneath: The West Yellowstone Economic Development Council. The main purpose of the building is to provide educational spaces and badly needed sleeping quarters for high schools and colleges. There are classrooms and breakout areas with the necessary audio visual equipment and lounge area. Students can go on field trips to the surrounding Yellowstone Country for experiential learning and then return to their home base for study and sleeping time. **19**

We renovated the two racquetball courts to provide basic dormitory spaces for students of both genders. Both male and female sleeping areas are equipped with 25 cots, sleeping pads, and lamps with device charging ports by each cot. Male and female restroom and shower facilities are available as well as a food preparation area. This educational side of the building is referred to as the

See **19** on the West Yellowstone Map Pages 142-143

Yellowstone Study Center (YSC) and is being used successfully by high schools and colleges for a rather minimal pay-as-you-use fee.

WYED/YSC center

The Yellowstone Study Center Consortium (YSCC) is an organized group of colleges that uses the same facilities but with a different purpose and application. Multiple university administrators have joined together into a consortium for an annual fall meeting to which their professors are invited to experience firsthand what is available for their students.

They can utilize all of the YSC aspects, or WYED can assist them with local lodging since cot sleeping isn't very appealing to college administrators. WYED also helps to provide local speakers and arrange transportation into the park with interesting and knowledgeable guides for extended field trips.

The response of high schools and colleges has been terrific. They go back and tell their friends and associates and word spreads like another pebble in a pool. It has taken time, dedication, and perseverance by the board of directors but we are now seeing the rewards as people realize that Yellowstone is what we tout as the greatest classroom on earth.

Pebble 25: Growth of the Local LDS Congregation and the Roles I Have Been Asked to Play

Don't get so heavenly minded that you are of no earthly use.

~Author Unknown

On September 22, 1968 I was called to be the branch president of the West Yellowstone Branch of The Church of Jesus Christ of Latter-day Saints. A small unit of the Church is called a branch, presided over by a branch president. When the branch becomes large enough, it becomes a ward and is presided over by a bishop. A stake is comprised of about seven to ten wards and branches. We were part of the St. Anthony, Idaho Stake. I was 29 years old at the time I was called to be branch president, and like me at that time, the Church in West Yellowstone was fairly young.

The branch in West Yellowstone was originally part of the Western States Mission, headquartered in Billings, Montana. It began with a small group of members who met together in the Union Pacific Dining Lodge. Meetings were held in the summer months only, under the direction of missionaries. Stephen L. Richards, an apostle of the Church who had a summer cabin on Hebgen Lake, was influential in starting these meetings. The first officially called branch president was Lee Jacobsen, who served for 11 years. The second branch president was John Olsen with Steve Blomquist and

me as his counselors. John served for two years. I was called to be
the third branch president and served in that position until 1981, for
almost 14 years.

The first LDS chapel was built between 1959 and 1962 as a
visitor center and chapel. This picturesque building was made from
black obsidian stone quarried and hauled from the south plateau, 5
miles to the south by volunteer members. The largest stone in the
building weighed two tons. In total, the chapel's stone weighed
about 1,500 tons. The stone, high ceilings, exposed fir trusses,
knotty pine walls, and ten-foot roof extensions made this the only
building of its kind in the world. **21**

First LDS chapel in West Yellowstone, dedicated in 1962

Sometimes people would stop in to inquire about the unique
building or about the Church. There were paintings hanging on the
walls, and the missionaries would discuss these as they took interested people through the building. When the building was no longer
used as a visitor center and chapel, we got permission to hang these
paintings in the hallways of the new chapel. They are still hanging
there for all to enjoy.

See **21** on the West Yellowstone Map Pages 142-143

When called to be branch president, I felt extremely inadequate. A branch president has many responsibilities. He is the spiritual and administrative leader of the branch. He is responsible for seeing that all the functions of the Church are carried out and that the spiritual and temporal needs of the people are taken care of. This was a heavy responsibility and required a great deal of time. However, my service in this position was one of the most rewarding and fulfilling experiences of my life. Today, bishops are usually called for about five years, as opposed to my almost 14 years. A branch president normally has the same two counselors throughout his tenure, but because people were moving in and out a lot and the length of time I served, I had thirteen counselors, as if matching my years served.

The main difference between the callings of a branch president and a bishop is relative to the size of the congregation. When the group gets large enough, it becomes a ward and a bishop is called. A few years after I was released, the West Yellowstone congregation was large enough to become a ward. Consequently, a bishop now serves as West Yellowstone's ecclesiastical leader.

When I was branch president, our numbers were rather small in the winter. Attendance would be around 30 people while in the summer it would swell to about 300. Filling leadership positions in the branch presidency, priesthood quorums, Relief Society, Primary, Young Men, Young Women, and scouting programs was a challenge. We reorganized these leadership positions almost twice a year in order to accommodate the difference in summer and winter attendance.

We, who have been here for many years, look back with fondness on those years we spent in the old chapel. That building was difficult to heat in the winter. We would winterize it by climbing up and closing off the open loft above the big trusses with two-inch, white Styrofoam sheets. It was fun going back and forth on the rafters, like a monkey, being careful not to fall, and placing each piece of sheeting to cut off the cold from seeping into the chapel.

The temporary low, white ceiling seemed to make the chapel cozier and warmer.

In preparation for the winter months, we stored a lot of firewood on the back entry steps.

Sometimes when it was forty below, we would close off part of the chapel by closing the folding wall and build a huge fire in the massive, free standing diamond shape fireplace. The glassed-in fireplace was in the middle of the activity area and was the focal point. On such occasions we would hold sacrament meetings there. Other times we held classes, square dances, parties, and potluck dinners (our favorite). Eventually, when building the new chapel across the street, we held various kinds of fundraising activities that went toward the building fund.

In the spring we would reverse the process and get ready for summer crowds. We became fairly proficient at doing this, and the whole branch would turn out for the task. Sometimes a party was held in conjunction with this event. Along with other preparations, we stuffed fiberglass insulation in the openings of the walls that was used for natural air conditioning in the summer.

Those were good times. We were few in number but lent strength to each other. At that time, multiple meetings were held during the week. Primary for the younger children was held on one day, young adults and Scouts on another. Sundays started off with priesthood meetings and Relief Society women's meetings in the morning with the main sacrament meeting in the evening. In addition to those meetings, since we were part of the St. Anthony Idaho Stake, various afternoon leadership meetings were held at our stake building. Every Sunday, I drove that 150 mile round trip either by myself or with other branch leaders. We had just enough time for dinner back home before the sacrament meeting started at 7:00 p.m. During most months there was a meeting in St. Anthony every week. This would require driving about 600 miles per month or 7,200 miles per year. Of course most other units in the stake were closer to St. Anthony, so it was easier for them. Eventually the stake was divided and Ashton became our stake center, which was only 57 miles away.

By the late 1970s, our numbers had grown to the point that we were outgrowing the building we so dearly loved. Our building had a dual purpose. Originally it was built as a meeting facility and a visitor center, where visitors passing through could come during the week and learn about the Church. Because of its multipurpose design, it was not very conducive for multiple classes and activities. In the summers, when tourists swelled our congregation, we had to set up chairs out both side doors for sacrament meeting and some classes had to be held on the lawn. I accompanied the stake presidency to meet with Brother Baker, the head of the Church Building Department in Salt Lake City, to see if it was possible to build a larger meeting house.

When the first church building was constructed, it was the practice of the Church to allow in kind contributions of labor. Members did a lot of the work, which cut down on the overall expense of the building. In the case of West Yellowstone, Glen Goff was hired as the main contractor and the members volunteered their time to haul many loads of obsidian stone. Herk Rightenour milled the unique tongue-and-groove interior wood. In the wake of the 1959 earthquake, the building was built to withstand severe earthquakes. A 14-inch slab of concrete was poured at ground level and the building was constructed on top. The theory was that if one part of the earth moved or shook, the building would just float on that slab of concrete. In addition to the in kind labor of the members, the overall building was completed for $168,000.

It was 1980 when the Church introduced the block program and some of the meetings were consolidated into three-hour blocks of time. This was good for us in West Yellowstone. Since the Church was increasingly becoming an international organization, there were many countries in which travel was expensive. It seemed to me to be a practical change so more time could be spent with family and less time and expense on travel. Also the number of stake-level meetings was reduced, which gave us more valuable family time.

It is interesting to note the difference between now and 40 years ago in respect to the responsibilities of the local units for funding new buildings. Today, the cost of new buildings is paid by the tithing funds of the Church with no building assessments. Back then, wards were assessed 30% of the cost of the buildings and branches were assessed 20%. It was hard to raise that much money, and yet in retrospect, it was a great blessing. The new chapel cost $857,000 to build, so our share was $171,400.

I have always said "we ate our way into this building." The ward members brought food every month for a potluck dinner and then turned around and paid to eat it. Those monthly dinners and fundraisers tied us together even more closely as we worked without one grumble to raise the money.

Also the Quilting Queens (as I called them) of the Relief Society quilted and sold beautiful quilts. We intentionally held the quilt auction in the summer, when the crowds were there to purchase them. We always knew that Lynn Richards would buy several, so we would intentionally bid the price up, just enough. The summer folks—Garffs, Smiths, Richards, Wilkinsons, Coveys and others—too numerous to mention, helped by contributing one way or another to help satisfy our building assessment.

There is also a great difference between then and now in the involvement and decision-making authority of the local leaders regarding a new building. Today, when a new meetinghouse is going to be built, the local bishop and members have little input in design or facilities. But back then, to explain the difference, I will relate some of my responsibilities as branch president in building our new chapel in the 1970s. I am the first to say, however, that I could not have done it without the collaborative effort of my counselors and the local members.

Land needed to be purchased. I knew Gene and Edna Adams, from whom we had purchased the Morris Motel, also owned the land that would be ideal for a new church building. I approached them and negotiated a purchase price. The LDS Church approved and closed the deal. There was also an adjoining lot to the south belonging to the Welshes that we purchased in the same manner.

The stake president and I met with the head of the Church Building Department in Salt Lake City and explained our proposal for the visitor center and chapel combination. After we explained the inadequacy of the current chapel, Brother Baker called in his staff and announced to them, "We are going to build a chapel in West Yellowstone; give President Seely what he wants." I was very pleased and grateful for what I thought was unusual latitude.

First, we chose an architect. Earl Booth was a summer resident who had done some work for me at Three Bear Lodge and we eventually chose him. After completing the work on this unique chapel, he went to work for the Church full time.

The Church had five or six master plans we could choose from, including interior room layouts and rooflines. All of the approved plans had sloped roofs. Because of my experience with the heavy snows and the danger of snow sliding off metal roofs, I requested a flat roof and it was approved. As far as I am aware, this flat roof design is unique within the Church. I do not know of another chapel with a flat roof. As a consequence of a flat roof, we had a non-vaulted, flat ceiling in the chapel. This, I believe, adds to the closeness and warm feeling that is felt there. Most chapels have a higher vaulted ceiling. Many people comment that there is just a special spirit when they come to visit our little ward, even though it can swell to over 1,000 people in the summer.

We loved the obsidian stone in the old building and wanted rock work both inside and out on the new building. Jerry Miller was a rock mason who had done some stone work for me called dry chinking (where you cannot see any mortar), we contracted him to lay the stone. We chose the Oakley stone, which you can see today, for the beautiful interior and exterior. For the interior woodwork, I asked if we could have cedar—and it is beautiful. We got to choose the wall covering, tile for the bathrooms, paint, carpet colors, etc.

We are very grateful for our unique and beautiful building. Because of our input, there never has been and probably never will be another building quite like this one. It is truly unique. The groundbreaking ceremony for the present chapel was in August 1979, and the building was completed June 15, 1980, at a cost of $875,000. Twenty years later, in July 2000, it was remodeled and expanded. The cost of the remodel, over $1 million, was more than the cost to build the original building. **22**

Dedication Services

Church of Jesus Christ
of Latter-day Saints
West Yellowstone Branch
Ashton Idaho Stake
West Yellowstone, Montana

Sunday, May 24, 1981 — 6:00 p.m.

LDS Chapel in West Yellowstone, dedicated in 1981

See **22** on the West Yellowstone Map Pages 142-143

Two years after we moved into the new building I was released as branch president and called to be one of twelve Ashton Idaho stake high councilors. West Yellowstone was now a part of the Ashton Idaho Stake. The duty of the high council was to advise and counsel with the stake presidency. This required many evening meetings in Ashton. On a monthly basis, we traveled to different wards and branches to speak at their meetings. Also during this time, it was my responsibility to organize and oversee the Sunday meetings in Yellowstone at Old Faithful, Lake, Canyon, and Grant Village. After having served for nearly four years, I was called on August 25, 1985, to be a counselor to President Ed Clark in the Ashton Idaho stake presidency. This required weekly meetings and supervisory responsibilities over all seven of the wards and branches in the stake. After four years, I was released from that responsibility.

During the time I served in these stake callings, my wife, Linda, was also involved in leadership positions. She served as president of the Relief Society in West Yellowstone and later was called as president of the Ashton Idaho Stake Relief Society. We could ride together to some of the meetings that she and I attended. However, they were mostly different meetings at different times. After all the trips to Ashton and back over those years, we could almost put the car on autopilot and one hour later arrive at our destination.

The Church has a lay leadership. In other words, it does not pay those who are in leadership positions. I have never served in a position but what I have been well paid, not with money but in the feeling that comes from service and from knowing you have made a difference. Serving in some positions require much time and can be taxing to the individual and their spouse. The results, however, are very fulfilling.

One memorable example was when I was in the stake presidency. On a particular Sunday, I got up at 5:00 a.m. and left at 6:00 a.m. for the 57 mile drive to Ashton for a 7:00 a.m. meeting. I attended our first meeting, and then visited and spoke at two different wards. It was a long and draining day spiritually and emotionally, and I felt exhausted. I had been fasting this particular Sunday and returned home tired and hungry. I can still remember what happened and the feelings that followed as I came home to my family. Linda was standing in the kitchen. I didn't say anything, just went over to her and gave her a big hug. As I squeezed her tightly, I could feel her strength come into my body. Finally, I started to let go and she kept holding on and said, "Wait a minute, I'm not through with you yet."

By this time, our three little boys began trying to break us up. They were pushing between our legs and saying, "Break it up, break it up." I chased them all up to our bed, threw them on it, and began wrestling with them. They were all laughing and I was saying, "I'll teach you guys to try and break us up." Mike started calling out "dog pile, dog pile," and sure enough our little schnauzer dog jumped in the middle of us all, barking like crazy. For some reason, I was no longer tired and felt like I could do it all again. There were many rewarding experiences like that.

The Church is very service oriented. When people are in need personally or spiritually, there is always a support group. For over 40 years the local guys have provided wood for those who are in need. Everyone likes to participate, as it is fun to work alongside each other. The Church also has an amazing welfare program that reaches the needs of individuals locally and throughout the world.

It is my belief that behind God and family come country, community, and occupation. I am grateful for all of these blessings in my life. These organizations and the people in them have dropped many pebbles in my little pool of life. I have tried to reciprocate by dropping some of my own pebbles along the way in each of these institutions. Sometimes day-to-day happenings slip by unnoticed and we think they will not be remembered, but looking back over the years, there are things and people that rise to the surface of our remembrance that have had a big impact on our lives.

Pebble 26: From Snowmobile Races to Snowmobile Expo to Bicycle Tours

Guard well your spare moments. They are like uncut diamonds. Discard them, and their value will never be known. Improve them, and they become the brightest gems in a useful life.

~Ralph Waldo Emerson

As I mentioned earlier, when we had the fire on January 2, 1970, we were closed for the winter. However, we had to be open for the March snowmobile races. At that time, we were holding races in December and again in March. Like most West Yellowstone hotels, we closed up at the end of the summer season, not long after Labor Day. We drained the water, put antifreeze in the toilets and turned off all the heat until it was time to reverse the process and open up again.

Reopening was no small matter. We had water wells and holding tanks, individual water heaters, and, of course, water piping that for mysterious reasons would freeze and break in strange places. For several days in advance, I would turn the heat up to warm up the walls and rooms. Then the water was turned on one section at a time. I would hold my breath, hoping there were no dreaded spraying sounds. Finally, I could start to breathe easy again when the water transmission noises ceased, all the toilets were full, and there were no more leaks.

Most of the motels in town were not winterized. Who would have known when they were built that one day there would be a need to keep them open in -40 degree temperatures? Some chose not to stay open at all in the winter. Many were not insulated and their water pipes and sewer lines were too shallow for the cold winter temperatures.

In March 1969, I had taken Linda to her mother's house in St. Anthony so she could be close to the hospital for the delivery of our second child. On March 8th, I was about to give Linda a hug and a goodbye kiss so I could go back to West Yellowstone and open for the March races when she said "You better wait a minute." It was more than minute as I rushed her to the hospital and there Stephanie was born. Opening the motel had to wait as I had more important things do.

In the late 60s and early 70s, the Snowmobile Roundup races were the biggest event of our West Yellowstone winters. As I recall, the first ones were held at the old airport. One of the exciting events was "distance jumping." This consisted of a jump made out of plywood about 4 feet tall. The person would hit the jump going as fast as he dared on his snowmobile and whoever jumped the farthest was the winner. I remember Jack Tremain jumping one year with broken ribs. The suspension on the snowmobiles was minimal then, and it was like sitting on a board when landing. I believe, one time, the winner jumped 68 feet. Compare that with what happens now, forty-plus years later, and that distance seems modest.

The races became a big event for our town, and at that time, speed ovals were becoming the big thing. In conjunction with the Forest Service, a dirt speed oval track was built, complete with banked corners. There was a lot of preparation for the race. The track needed to be in excellent shape. It had to be smoothed, and makeshift water trucks had to wet the track down so a layer of ice would form. Then we would hope the sun wouldn't come out and cause dirt to show through the ice. At that time, it was all about speed.

The oval race track was built about half a mile west of town. This required a tremendous amount of plowing through deep snow for auto traffic to get there, plus pit areas, etc. The expense of plowing the areas and icing down the track made the financial success of the race efforts questionable.

Ultimately, the race events were moved back to the old airport. The Snow Cross race was becoming more popular and didn't require a smooth track. In fact, jumps and erratic corners were built into the track. Operating costs were cut considerably and the town businesses and lodging were much more accessible for the attendees.

West Yellowstone's World Snowmobile Expo

The Expo was first held in tents at the old airport. Then when we built our new West Yellowstone Conference Hotel (Holiday Inn), and it became the Expo headquarters.

It was under the tutelage of Glen Loomis that the Snowmobile Roundup races turned into the West Yellowstone World Snowmobile Expo and the December race was discontinued. I remember those formative meetings in which Glen said "What if we were to have a snowmobile race in conjunction with a snowmobile exposition (expo) in which manufacturers could unveil their next year's product line and other purveyors could rent booth space?" Marge Wanner was hired to manage and handle the details and was charged with the success of the expo. Except for the first few years, she has been at the helm since then. Also, Steve Janes has helped share the vision of the expo through *SnoWest* magazine.

We also formed an expo (now Snow Events) Committee. Most of its original members (including myself) are still serving. Some hair has turned grey, but some new blood has also come on board. My particular assignment is to organize, coordinate, and carry out a volunteer shuttle system of vans that help to move people from the activity venues to the lodging and eating facilities.

Through much hard work and perseverance, the expo has become very successful and has pulled thousands of people to West Yellowstone. We recently completed the 25th annual World Snowmobile Expo, and I marvel at how much the event has expanded. It now includes such things as the kid's (normally between 8 and 12 years of age) 120 Western Grand Championship races, and vintage snowmobile races dating back to machines like the ones I started riding many years ago. In addition to the regular Snow Cross races, they have drag races and bike stunt riding on Canyon Street, and they have the popular casino night.

The biggest draw of the last few years has been the Snowmobile Freestyle competition. This event featured riders who would not only jump, but also do back flips on their snowmobiles 50–100 feet through the air. They would approach the snowmobile ramp at a certain speed, rev up the engine while airborne, and jerk back to cause the track to spin freely in the air. This causes the snowmobile and rider to flip over backwards, and then, hopefully, land upright on a snow hill with a downward slope about 100 feet away. Compared to the sixty-eight-foot distance jump at the Snowmobile Roundup over 40 years ago, today's jumping has literally gone to new heights with these Snowmobile Freestyle events.

This whole concept of daredevil snowmobile jumping was started by the Hungerford brothers from West Yellowstone. The first metal and plywood launching ramp with a high trajectory was designed and built in the West Yellowstone High School shop when Jeff Hungerford was the shop teacher. Kourtney and Whitney Hungerford, Jeff's sons, and a friend named Tyler Nelson started jumping their snowmobiles and improving the ramps. Kourtney first began jumping professionally in 1998. This was the beginning of the concept of free-air jumping. As they took their ramp from place to place, it began to catch on. These aerial shows have since been performed at the X Games and in several countries throughout the world. The Holiday Inn is still the expo headquarters and provides the exhibition hall and a 15,000 square foot tent, which houses purveyor booths. The four manufacturers have much larger areas to display next year's products. In addition to the race and exhibition, we continue to expand expo activities.

The Origination of Bicycle Tours

Another little pebble, which we dropped in the pool of our family, has spread ripples throughout the community. The results have helped to open up another source of enjoyment for thousands and have provided a source of great revenue for the town.

For years, every spring our family was eager to get out the bicycles and go for our evening rides during that perfect time when the temperature was just right. We would take Buzz, our collie, and kids and bikes of varying sizes, and go for rides around town or out to the South Fork, a creek about 2 miles from town.

In the fall, we would load up the kids and their bikes in the truck and go to Old Faithful. We rode down the path, seeing and smelling the geysers, while they did their thing at the Upper Geyser Basin. Among our favorite stops were Castle, Grotto, Riverside, and Morning Glory Pool. Even our toddlers loved it. The pathways are paved; although sometimes we had to share the experience with buffalo, and we often commented on how blessed we were to live in such a phenomenal area. When I was a boy, this pathway was the road on which we drove our cars. That has changed, and this area can now only be accessed on foot or on a bike.

Later, in a chamber of commerce meeting, we discussed how we could increase business in the shoulder seasons. I related our family experiences and suggested that the chamber sponsor a spring and fall cycle tour during those shoulder seasons. Moab, Utah, had become known as a mecca for mountain biking. West Yellowstone had been flourishing with the snowmobile winter business, yet that was now being threatened. Why couldn't we expand the season and become known for our bicycling in the spring and fall as well?

Since it was my idea, I was put in as chairman of the newly formed bicycle committee. From there, we decided to sponsor a spring and a fall bicycle tour. We contacted various businesses to be sponsors and advertised in the local media as well as in *Cycling Utah* magazine.

The roads into the park from West Yellowstone are normally plowed after March 15th; the only vehicles allowed in the park until April 20th either belong to administrators or contractors.

Even though our spring ride followed the earthquake loop outside the park, we decided to get a double whammy out of our advertising campaign. We also encouraged people to come and cycle Yellowstone free without any public cars. The spring warm weather begs for people to pull out their bikes and go for a ride, so why not in Yellowstone? They could either come before our spring tour event or later in conjunction with the ride for a minimal park fee.

Up until this point, the public was unaware that this method to explore the park was an option. This idea was a hit, and we also began to see bikes show up at other times. Now there are days when over a hundred bike riders come to West Yellowstone to go into the park.

Our spring cycle tour passed by the 1959 earthquake area and three lakes. It also went through two states, Idaho and Montana. We arranged for volunteers to man five different feed stations along the sixty-mile trip. We provided sag wagons to pick up tired or broken-down bikes and had mechanics in each vehicle. We also provided a port-a-potty on wheels. Marge Wanner was dubbed the potty queen and was a strange, but welcome sight to those who needed a facility at the appropriate time.

The first tour was a whopping success. At the conclusion of the ride, we put on a discounted spaghetti dinner at our Holiday Inn. I believe the entrance fee for the event was $35.00, which included a West Yellowstone Spring Cycle Tour t-shirt, five refreshment stops, dinner, and a support team of sag wagons, all by a volunteer crew. Normally, we ran this event after the park opened, the Saturday before Mother's Day; however due to too many spring squalls, the official spring cycle tour was eventually discontinued. Still the number of spring park bike riders has continued to increase.

For the first Old Faithful fall cycle tour, in early October 1997, we received permission from Yellowstone Park to do an organized tour to and from Old Faithful with a cap of 300 riders. We provided a light lunch, sag wagons, and a spaghetti feast. I had my camera and took pictures of most people along the way. The one-hour photo place developed the photos, and we laid them out on the table during dinner. Almost everyone could find themselves and take home a picture of them with Yellowstone as a backdrop. People loved it.

Some people flew in from Atlanta, Georgia, multiple times to attend this event. These people had been coming to snowmobile with us in the winter and wanted to come again in the fall. Since each year the Old Faithful Cycle tour increased in popularity, Yellowstone Park agreed to increase the cap to 350 riders. It is still going strong, so if you want to come, you must call the chamber of commerce and register early, as it fills up very quickly.

I was chairman of our bicycle committee for seven years, and then my son Mike was chairman until he moved back to Utah. Melissa Buller, the owner of Free Heel and Wheel bike shop, carried the torch from there. It eventually became too much for a volunteer committee to do all the leg work so a part-time coordinator was hired.

As with all the volunteer-community-sponsored events, it takes a lot of dedicated people to pull it off. Very few people beyond the committee have any idea how many hours of planning and organizational meetings it takes. Few realize how many people were involved in obtaining food and staffing for five different feeding stations, donating vehicles, providing fuel and drivers, finding mechanics to show up at the right time to help out, and so on. All of this effort brings people together to work as a team. It is fun to enable other people to have fun. It makes it worth it when participants come up and cannot thank you enough. After our first event, several people came up and said, "I ride in a lot of these events, but this was the most organized one I have been to."

This event is now beyond its 17th year. These events have truly extended our seasons, and thousands of people have come with bikes on their cars or rent them locally to enjoy the experience of Yellowstone by bicycle. Our original goal has been accomplished, and I believe bike touring will continue to grow in the Yellowstone area just like the Winter in Yellowstone experience did. Everybody likes to come, which is just one more reason why I love to live on the doorstep of this wonderful place called Yellowstone. The cycle tours have not only been successful in and of themselves, they have also created an awareness of this unique way to view Yellowstone— there are few cars on the roads since it's before the park officially opens, and there is no entrance fee.

Part Four: A Time for Rebirth

Pebble 27: The Yellowstone Fires of 1988, a West Yellowstone Perspective

The Yellowstone fires of 1988 were becoming a real threat to the town. Few who lived here will soon forget the anxious feelings when it seemed imminent that our little town and homes were threatened. At the encouragement of others, I have written and included here a description of the role I played and memories of those days when we watched the fire come ever closer until the town was in imminent danger of the fire.

~ Clyde Seely

It's been many years since the Yellowstone fires of '88. Massive fires threatened this national park treasure, resulting in the greatest firefighting effort in the history of the United States. While memories of that horrific event are still clear in our minds, it became apparent many visitors had no knowledge of what actually happened. I have found over the years that many other people have been interested in learning from our perspective what it was really like to live here during those devastating fires. I have related what actually happened numerous times to many different people who have admonished, "You need to write this down or it will be lost forever." I take this time to write down my recollections due to a sense of preserving this snippet of West Yellowstone history, the happenings, and emotions of the Yellowstone fire. This is not only for our grandchildren, but also for those who weren't there or as involved as I was. Many of these memories are as vivid now as if they had happened yesterday.

On July 23, 1988, I was with the boys of our West Yellowstone branch along with 3,000 other youth and leaders at a weeklong jamboree in Island Park. I saw a large plume of smoke just east of us and knew there was a big forest fire. Later, I found out that it was caused by a woodcutter who dropped a cigarette a few hundred yards from the park line. The fire quickly grew and spread into Yellowstone. A logger friend of mine had driven his big "Caterpillar" bulldozer across the park line and was going to put the fire out. A park ranger came and told him to get his equipment out of the park as motorized equipment was not allowed, adding that he would be cited if he didn't. The fire could have been quickly put out at that time had he been allowed in.

The fire was traveling with the prevailing winds northeast, and for a time it looked like it would miss West Yellowstone. The original park policy was to let it burn since the fire was in a mature growth of trees and initially appeared beneficial to that area. Later, when the fire was out of control, the policy was changed to suppress all fires" and bulldozers cut a fire line to protect West Yellowstone later. This was a futile effort since the flames were so high; they jumped the fire line and continued on toward West Yellowstone. The fire was named the North Fork fire and it was destined to become one of the greatest fires in national park history.

With the fire growing quickly, the town's people were concerned that the fire might move north and threaten the town. The park service, along with the fire commander began to hold regular informational meetings for the people in West Yellowstone. We were told the fire could be put out now for approximately $4 million, whereas if it were to be monitored until late August when the normal rains were expected, they believed it could be put out for $1 million. The rains didn't come. No one could have known that this would be the driest summer in the park's 116-year history.

Helicopter flyovers to assess the fire became routine. I was asked if I wanted to go on one of these. It was an awesome sight as the fire was spreading across canyons, mountains, and rough terrain. It became apparent to me that this was no ordinary fire that could be put out on a whim of puny mankind. August 20, 1988, was called "Black Saturday," when 70-mile-an-hour winds helped quickly spread the fire, burning a quarter million acres in just three days. Interior Secretary Donald Hodel said that because of the vastness of the fire and with the impending loss of buildings and life, they had changed to a full-out containment policy.

By now, the townspeople became more nervous as the fire continued to approach West Yellowstone. However, if the normal wind patterns did not change, the fires were predicted to miss the town. I had given our local church authorities a cursory overview of the fire situation. Then, one night at a town council meeting held in the school, the Greater Yellowstone Incident Commander, Denny Bungarz, came and gave a progress report.

Apparently, weather patterns were changing, and he said to the council, "Unless the wind patterns change, we could well be defending West Yellowstone from the fires by tomorrow night." What unnerving news.

I raised my hand and said, "If we could have a sprinkler system set up between the river and town, volunteered by the farmers in Idaho, would you be interested?"

He said, "Yes, let's go out in the hall and talk about it."

And so we did. This was on September first. The time was about 8:30 p.m.

I explained to the commander that our Church (The Church of Jesus Christ of Latter-day Saints) has an emergency preparedness program set up to deal with situations such as this. If he wanted me to, I would go through that procedure and felt certain that we could gather the resources together, bring sprinkler pipes from the farmers in Idaho, and have it set up by tomorrow night. His response was, "Yes, let's do it."

I explained that the use of most of the pipe and labor would be donated but we would have to rent missing components that the NPS would have to pay for. I also explained that I would need the authority to take a backhoe and dig a hole in the Madison River. That would be necessary to create a reservoir in the shallow river deep enough to have a sufficient volume of water to supply the big intake suction hoses.

He agreed to all of this.

Now, this was all rather bold and certainly took a leap of faith, but I grew up on a farm and knew about sprinkler systems and what they could do. My brother Sylvan was also in the sprinkler irrigation business. Still, I went home wondering just what I had committed myself and the Church to do. Yet, as Linda and I stood on the back porch of our house, the horizon of the night sky was lit up with orange fire just about three quarters of a mile away. I knew I had done the right thing. It had to work.

The Church has a line of authority that is automatically followed whenever there is an emergency. Here is how it worked. I was a counselor in the stake presidency in Ashton, Idaho, and made the call for help to my stake president, Ed Clark. He made a call to his superior, Claytor Forsgren, the regional representative over the St. Anthony Idaho Region, who called the authority over North America, Northwest America Area in Salt Lake who gave us authorization to proceed. Elder Forsgren also called two other regional representatives. The area covered in these three regions stretches from West Yellowstone through most of South Eastern Idaho as far south as Blackfoot. Now four calls had been made going up the line of authority.

Once the go sign was given, each of these three regional representatives called the stake presidents (totaling about twenty) under them. Each president called the bishops in their stake (approximately nine each), who called the priesthood leaders in their wards, who in turn called the farmers who had sprinkler pipes and/or volunteers available.

The process reversed itself again as the farmers' inventory was reported back up the line of authority to the bishops, then the stake presidents, then the regional representatives, and back to President Clark who in turn called me and said, "We can do it," so the process worked. A similar process is automatically implemented whenever there is an emergency anywhere in the world. It was shortly after 9:00 p.m. when I called and explained what our predicament was. In just two hours, between 9:00 p.m. and 11:00 p.m., hundreds of phone calls had been made, and I received the call telling me it would happen. I had made one call and received one back, and I knew the pipe would start arriving about 9:00 a.m. the following morning.

Implementation

With fires lighting up the sky, we wondered if tomorrow morning would be too late. It was a short night for me as well as the farmers who, on September 2nd, began pulling their sprinkler pipe out of their fields at 5:00 a.m. and loading them onto their pipe trailers. By about 8:00 a.m. they started to arrive in West Yellowstone. For those locals and tourists who didn't know what was happening, it was a strange sight; farmers' pickups and pipe trailers loaded with sprinkler pipe began pulling into our little tourist town along with the other components necessary to effectively protect West Yellowstone.

This was before the current commercial developments such as McDonalds, the IMAX, and other hotels were built. There was quite a bit of open land behind the Museum and it was here that we created a staging area and the command base. My plan was to cover the east side of West Yellowstone the first day and the north side the second day.

Meanwhile, I was instructed to meet a park ranger at 7:00 a.m. to decide where we could put the pumps in the Madison River. We drove to the place he chose for us to put the pumps in, where the water was deep enough. I told him it was too far away, and we could not make it work from there. I then took him to the site I wanted to use, which was straight east of the town and the shortest distance away. This is where I wanted the backhoe to dig the hole in the river bottom for the reservoir. To my dismay, I was told I couldn't use a backhoe because it would leave pod marks on the banks of the river. I cannot convey adequately my frustration. I had made it clear we needed a hole dug by a backhoe. The farmers were already arriving. Huge pumps and semi truckloads of ten-inch mainline pipe would soon be arriving to carry the water from this spot to the town.

I said to the ranger, "Would you rather have two backhoe pod marks on the river bank or let the town burn?"

He replied, "You cannot use a backhoe."

Then, a thought hit me—one that I thought would be totally out of the question. "What if we blasted a hole in the river?" I asked.

He quickly said, "Oh that would be okay."

It was now about 8:30 a.m. The pipes and equipment were arriving, and we had no place to pump the water from. I got in touch with the firefighting people and asked if they had any dynamite we could use. They were using coiled up dynamite rope that they would roll out like garden hose through the grass and timber to blast fire lines to prevent fire from crossing.

I found the chief of explosives and explained our predicament. I asked if he thought he could blast a hole in the Madison River. From the way he reacted, you would have thought that I had just turned a kid loose in a candy store. He said, "Oh, I would love to," and we met at the river.

I explained to him that we needed a hole in the bottom of the shallow river so we could create a reservoir. He said, "No problem."

By now some of my other helpers and farmers were standing around when he said, "You better get your people to back away." We did, and there was a big boom.

I ran back over expecting there to be a hole as I had requested. I couldn't see that the blast had done anything. Now, what were we going to do? What were the farmers thinking? Did we come all the way up here for nothing? I sought out the chief of explosives, obviously disappointed, and asked, "Can't it be done?"

He responded, "Oh that was just softening it up." Then he said, "How big did you say you wanted the hole?"

I responded, "We need it 4 feet deep and 8 feet across."

They worked for a while, and then he said, "Now, you better get your people back—way back."

By now, there were other pickups and 15 or 20 people there. I gave the word, and they started running or driving their pickups on the grass (to the dismay of the park) to get about a quarter of a mile away. We stayed in or under the pickups for protection. There was a big blast. Water and rock exploded into the air and started to rain around us. I hurried back over to the site and there, right next to the bank, was a dry crater. It was about 4 feet deep and 8 feet across. We thanked the explosive guys profusely, and they went on their way.

We had two huge diesel generator pumps standing by. We backed them to the appropriate place, put their intake suction hoses in the bottom of the hole, shoveled away the up and down stream sides of the crater, and the water flowed freely into it. It was a perfect reservoir. Now we could get to work assembling two ten-inch mainlines to carry the water to the town with valves along the way so we could take off lateral lines that would run north and south, parallel with the town. We made it possible to take sixteen of those lines off the mainline so we could have sixteen lines of sprinklers running to create a vast wet zone between the river and the town. Farmers with their portable welders and well-honed ingenuity made adapter fittings to mesh together about six types of sprinkler systems. Now the problem was to figure out how to carry sprinkler pipe through a dense forest. Normally, a pipe changer carries the pipe perpendicular to his body over the top of grain or potatoes. It wasn't possible to carry the pipe over the top of the trees. So I got permission from the Park Service to cut pathways through the trees so the pipe could be laid there.

Meanwhile, the pipe trailers and sprinkler installers were accumulating in the holding area just north of the Union Pacific property. As was stated, this area was still fairly vacant prior to the building of Grizzly Park. There were over 100 people there waiting for instructions. They were local town folks—both members of the Church and others. Loads of people in cars and pickups began arriving to help. Now the question was how to organize them. I remembered Brigham Young and the pioneers who were divided up under captains over ten and captains over 50; I decided to do the same thing here.

I had broadcast an appeal through the local radio station asking people to come and help and to bring their chainsaws. I assigned a saw man with the captain over ten volunteers. I believe we ended up with about eight captains and crews. I sent for an old sheet from our Three Bear Lodge and a can of spray paint. Two guys held up the bed sheet and with the spray paint in hand, I drew out how they should bring the pipe off the mainline and go north.

Clyde Seely, center, explains plans to volunteers.

Mormons respond to plea for pipe

Mapping out a plan for 100 volunteers to lay sprinkler pipe

I remember asking local woodsmen Big John, Mike Bryers, and others with saws to lead the way. They cut down any trees that were in the way of the pipe. The captains with their crews cleared away the trees and carried the pipe. The saw man would head in a straight line north, felling trees so these could be moved out of the way by those in his group. Two men would lift up the ends of two pieces of pipe (one pipe on each shoulder), carry the pipe to the end of the pipeline, hook it up end to end, and then walk back through the trees and get two more pieces. The captains over 10 concept worked very well.

The captains over 50 concept was a little fuzzier. I just explained to them what we wanted to have happen and they took it from there. This group installed the mainline and, with portable welders, made fittings to meld together various kinds of pipe. They were also in charge of getting the pumps running.

By now, people were coming in quickly to help. If they couldn't find me or anybody else for directions, they just found somebody who looked like he knew what he was doing and asked, "What can I do to help?" There was no set organization with this group. They were the farmers who knew how to make things work. Some people were cutting pathways through the trees, carrying pipe, and unloading semi-loads of big mainline, while others were getting the two big pumps hooked up to the pipe and preparing for pumping. The process began to smooth out and was becoming more like a well-oiled machine.

Volunteers unloading miles of sprinkler pipe to fight fires

We were finally finished on the east side of town by about 2:00 p.m. There were sixteen lateral lines running the length of the town between the Madison River and Boundary Street in West Yellowstone. If we could get the pumps working and the water pushing through the network of pipes, we were certain the fire could never penetrate through to the town.

Meanwhile, the fires were burning across the river from the pumps where we were working. I began to wonder, "what if the winds changed and the fire jumped the river?" My mind began to envision the pumps and pipe being damaged and the helpers being forced to evacuate. However, I didn't have time to worry much about that, as there were many things and people to coordinate.

I remember there was a side hill from the river, and I would run back and forth, up and down, to the pumps and the lines above to tell somebody this or that. The park ranger stopped me and said, "Clyde, you have to stop running, it excites people." So, I conscientiously tried to slow down and appear calm. Running was just in my nature. From running after the sheep when I was herding them as a boy on the farm to running across the parking lot at the lodge to get something, I enjoyed running and it seemed to speed things up. I have often wondered if perhaps others could get more done if they would hurry a little instead of just ambling. However, I suppose the ranger was right, as it could have appeared that I was panicking when that was not the case at all. I just was trying to cause a mammoth undertaking to come together quickly.

During the day, people and their cars were parked along Boundary Street of West Yellowstone to watch what we were doing. Some were just curious onlookers. Others were what I thought of as naysayers, who first wondered what we were doing and then thought it was foolish and that it would never work. I circulated among this group and explained what we were doing, but there were still those who did not believe it would happen.

I must admit there were times when I began to wonder if we could mesh all these different kinds of pipe together, correlate the efforts of 150 volunteers, and make it all happen before we ran out of daylight. Finally, we were ready and the first pump was started. The ten-inch mainline began to sag with the weight of the water gushing through it as it rapidly climbed the hill and sent the water on its way. We would open one valve and wait for that line to pressurize, and then the next, and the next, and by 3:00 p.m., the last line along Boundary Street began to spurt out water through each of the nozzles. It smelled like rain as the water wet down the grasses and the trees. Those on Boundary Street watched in amazement and then gradually began to disperse.

The first day was a success, but everyone was worn out. The Relief Society ladies brought food; however, we still ended up with more volunteers than provisions. We released everyone for the day except the pipe-tenders who were assigned to watch the pipe and turn valves off and on, alternating the lines that were pressurized. Day one was a success, but day two still loomed ahead when this whole process would need to be repeated in order to protect the south side of town.

***

There were two times I became very emotional during this whole event. After the pumps were all running and everyone had gone home to rest, I went down to the river. I sat alone on the big mainline, feeling its vibration under me and listening to the big diesel engine that was pushing hundreds of gallons of water per minute through all of those farmers' pipes into the forest surrounding West Yellowstone, Montana. It was replacing a tinder box with a wet area, making West Yellowstone—the town we loved—impervious to the flames that had been threatening us just 24 hours ago.

It was just getting dark. I sat there for a long time, tired and yet filled with gratitude. While the water rushed to wet down and protect the town from a potential disaster, a big lump came into my throat as I sat there. I could not have talked if I had wanted to. Tears began to run down my cheeks as I thought about how blessed we were to have so many people from the town and from all over Southeastern Idaho, come to our aid in this time of need. I had always been able to be on the giving end when times of need came. I had never known what it felt like to be on the receiving end. Now, I knew. I looked back over the last 24 hours and could scarcely believe what had happened with just one call for help. I remembered the statement made by the fire commander that, "Unless the wind patterns change, we could well be defending West Yellowstone from the fires by tomorrow night." Tomorrow night was here, and water was wetting down the forest.

Second Day – South Side of Town

After another short night, we began implementing the plan for the second day. Fires were coming from the east, just across the river. If the fire jumped the river, we were ready. They were also coming from the south plateau, about a mile and a half away. If a good wind came up it would be a matter of hours before the fire would be upon us.

It was September 3rd, and the second pump and mainline was in place. We now had to get it across the highway to the park entrance. I didn't know how we would accomplish that. Hundreds of cars were going into the park daily; I suppose some even to see the fires. I asked the park if they would consider allowing us to lay mainline across the blacktop and covering it with a bridge of gravel. They agreed to the plan.

The town was undergoing the installation of a public water system that included curbs and gutters and paving the streets. H-K Contractors had heavy equipment for the job. I asked the foreman if they could bring some loads of gravel and cover the mainline across the entrance road. They graciously did so at no charge. We laid the mainline across the highway; they dumped and smoothed enough gravel over the pipe to prevent any damage. Within fifteen minutes the traffic was driving over the pipe.

We used the open area that later contained the Grizzly Park (including the IMAX and current hotels) to lay six pipe laterals, each running the length of the town. We did not have to cut many trees in order to get the pipe in a straight line, and the second day efforts were going fairly well. In addition to the local people and farmers' help, busloads of students came up from Ricks College (now Brigham Young University–Idaho) to help.

The fires were now coming down the hill from the south plateau. From there, it was a straight shot to where we were laying pipe on the south of town, about a mile away. I was no longer worried about the east side of town; now I wondered if the fires would keep coming closer to where we were. By now I became fairly certain that the sprinkler system would protect the town but didn't want to see the forest burned in our very backyard.

The pipe was now being laid methodically as over a hundred people were stretching out the long lines. I suddenly found myself tired and somewhat discouraged with the oncoming fires. It was at this time that I got in my pickup and slowly began driving to nowhere. Emotions mounted as I looked around and saw what was happening. I suppose this was partly because the stress of the previous day was over, partly out of gratitude for the many people who were laying pipe after pipe, almost automatically, and partly because the final outcome of the fires was still unknown. These mixed feelings resulted in that lump coming back into my throat, and I again had to fight back the tears.

Around 2:00 p.m. the lines were finished, the second big diesel pump was started in the Madison River, and the water gushed to fill all six sprinkler lines on the south of town. The familiar spurt, spurt, spurt of the sprinklers began to wet the grass and timber just 50 feet from the back porch of our house. We were finished.

The park people were now having local daily public briefings on the status of the fires. I was asked to report on the progress of the sprinkler system. Eventually, the fires mostly passed us by. I asked if we should shut the system off, but was told to leave the east side running for a time.

Old Faithful

It was September 6th, about 11:00 p.m. when I received a call from the fire commander at Old Faithful. She said the fire was now converging on Old Faithful and asked if I could have a sprinkler system set up by 8:00 a.m. the next morning. She stated that if the fire reached the power line, there would be no power in the Old Faithful area, resulting in closing it down for the winter. I replied that I could not do it by 8:00 a.m., but I would check and see if we had the materials and manpower to do it by tomorrow night.

By 8:00 a.m. the next morning, we had loaded the pipe and were able to take one of the pumps into Old Faithful and start setting up the system. There was a creek on the west side of the buildings. The power line crossed the creek, ran straight east to the big sub-station, and on to feed other buildings, including the Old Faithful complex. About eighteen of the locals and Idaho farmers, wearing yellow fire hard-hats, placed the big pump in the creek and began to lay the pipe on the uphill side of the power line. When we got to the substation, the main cause of concern, we placed a water cannon that put out a stream of water about an inch in diameter. We trained the huge nozzle that shot a stream of water 200 feet, so that it would go back and forth over the electrical substation and structures. We continued laying the pipes we had with us, but were one pipe short from being able to cover the total length of the power line.

By now we felt like old hands at this as we got the pump started and heard the familiar sound of the spurting water began to wet down the area. However, this brought great frustration to one of fire fighters who was trying to get a fire started to create a back burn. All of a sudden, he got wet from the sprinkler, which also put out his fire. Apparently, no one had told him about the sprinkler plan. He began swearing profusely and wanted to know what we were doing. I explained we were doing just what we had been asked to do by his fire commander. He must have thought we were raining on his parade. He took his equipment and left.

The system began working without a hitch. The fire, as it turned out, would not come for another day or so. I asked three friends from Idaho, Layle Cherry, Dale Clark, and Leon Martindale, if they would stay and act as the pipe-tenders. The rest of us went back home to West Yellowstone, about 30 miles away.

The fires finally came on September 7th. The big fireballs, about 150 feet high, began to boil over the hillside. The winds of the firestorm carried firebrands across the Old Faithful complex and the fire started burning on the other side. It was certainly going to come over the whole area. There was an evacuation order given. A video of the firefighting efforts is now available and shows the hot, reddish thick smoke that made visibility almost impossible, and you can hear firefighters yelling, "We are going to lose it! We are going to lose it!" Our pipe-tenders were radioed and told they had to leave and come to the Old Faithful Inn area. It was just in time. They left the sprinkler system running and retreated to the Old Faithful meeting area. When they were driving out, the heat from a big rolling fireball came hot through the back window of their pickup.

Our assignment was to wet down the timber on the uphill side of the power line so the fire would jump over the wet and humid area. Our plan was about to be tested. Sparks and firebrands leap-frogged over the area. The roof of the Old Faithful Inn was wetted down with a water deluge system, and even with the sparse but dry timber in the immediate area, the Inn was not burned. The fire fighters waited as the fire went over the complex, and continued on. Eventually, when the flames had passed and it was deemed safe, the three pipe tenders went back to the sprinkler line. Upon approaching the line, they noticed the sprinklers were not running. Could the fire have burned the diesel motor and pump? To their relief, when they got to the pump, the motor was still running. The pump had worked until the fire had passed, and the debris floating down the creek had plugged the intake screen.

Had it done its job? The whole hillside was black, charred, and still smoking, except for a green band of vegetation and trees that ran the full length of the power line. The substation was still unharmed and power was never lost. The fire had jumped over the wetted down area and pipe. For a few feet at least it was like there was no fire. A few days later, I received a nice letter from Montana Power thanking "this joint volunteer endeavor of The Church of Jesus Christ of Latter-day Saints and the Friends of Yellowstone." Without the sprinkler system they would have lost the whole power system, like they had at Grant Village and Madison. There would have been no winter season, and it would have costs hundreds of thousands of dollars to replace.

In a letter dated September 9, 1988, Ann Gibson, Manager of Montana Power Company said. "As it was, we lost one pole and two cross arms when the fire storm jumped over the irrigated water belt where our substation and line was located." We were one pipe short from covering the entire line. The pole mentioned was where we ran out of pipe. In total, the Old Faithful area only lost a few cabins and a truck that were located beyond the scope of our assignment. The Old Faithful fire was the climax of the most dramatic fires in the history of the park.

A video titled *Yellowstone Aflame: The Yellowstone Fires of 1988!* was made at the twentieth year anniversary of the fires and is worth watching and even purchasing, since it captures a major piece of Yellowstone history. During this time, Yellowstone resembled a battleground. Smoke columns from the fires climbed to 60,000 feet. The fires were so hot they created their own winds. There were over 400,000 acres of watershed that were burned. The White House authorized military forces to help with the firefighting effort. Campsites were set up near the West Yellowstone airport. Government personnel filled vacant lodging rooms and restaurants that normally supplied tourist needs. Huge military planes brought in heavy equipment and personnel. This was the greatest firefighting effort in the history of the United States. To my knowledge, there was no loss of human life and only 250 large mammals died—mostly from smoke inhalation. The August rains never came, but the fire was finally put out in November by the rain and snow. The total cost was in excess of $98 million.

Duck Creek

When the danger passed, we loaded up our sprinkler system with its pipe and hauled it back to West Yellowstone. By this time, the active fire had passed West Yellowstone but was still burning 8 miles north and was approaching the Duck Creek housing area. Fire engines and firefighters were working in the area trying to keep the fire from getting to the houses. I contacted the North Fork Fire commander again and took him for a ride in my pickup. We rode from Fur Ridge down to Duck Creek along the park line. I suggested that, if he wanted us to, we could bring the sprinkler system we had used at Old Faithful and set it up to protect this area. He could take his people and go north, farther than what our system could reach. In anticipation of the commander making this request, we had the complete system on trailers waiting at Junction 287, less than half a mile away. The fire commander said he agreed with our plan and asked us to go ahead. Within thirty minutes we were setting the pump in Duck Creek and stretching out the line as far as it would reach. We then attached to the end of that line small hand lines similar to what firemen use. We could now cover Duck Creek up to the Fur Ridge Cemetery.

Many of us worried that if the fire came, it could jump the highway and destroy the many houses on the west side of the highway including our Parade Rest Guest Ranch. The fires were approaching our line. Firefighters and fire engines were deeper into the woods; however, they were being driven back. Then, all of a sudden, here they came with some of the fire engines dragging their hoses behind them. The fire was too hot, and they soon realized they were fighting a losing battle. The pressure was on us once again. With the fires approaching, the sprinkler was in place and we got the diesel engine running, but we could not get the pump primed to energize the line. We worked frantically as we saw the fire getting closer. Finally, the pump groaned as it started pushing the water up the hill. The water started spurting out the nozzles, wetting down the fire's fuel source. About thirty minutes later, the fire with its orange flames and black smoke burned to the pipe. When it arrived, the orange fire turned to white steam as it came to the wet foliage. The fire sputtered and died. It had worked.

The Aftermath

We were now faced with getting the entire 16 miles of pipe, two pumps, and thousands of feet of mainline back out of the woods. We had to separate it into the different kinds of pipe in order to give the pipe back to the original owners. I had asked David Rightenour to keep an inventory of the pipe and equipment as it arrived from each farmer. Now we needed to be able to return that same inventory. As is always the case, it was easier to get people to respond and help on the leading edge of an impending emergency than to clean up after it had passed. Sixteen miles of pipe had to be carried back out of the woods piece by piece. The mainline had to be disassembled and loaded by hand onto semi trucks. The farmers came to pick up their pipe, and any damaged pipe was accounted for and the farmer compensated.

Eventually the farmer's pipe trailers began making their exit from West Yellowstone and all the pipe was returned to the original owners. An innovative and huge undertaking had just taken place and was very successful. Sprinkler systems were later used by the park and Forest Service in other areas. I am not sure if our success played any part in those decisions or not. I only know that the farmers and others who rallied around our little town showed once again the giving nature of people to help others in time of need. It would have been easy for some farmers to have said to themselves, "Someone else can go. It is not convenient for me right now." But those who came did not regret coming and still remember being a part of helping to defend West Yellowstone from the fires. It is more blessed to give than to receive. Out of fear of leaving someone out, I have refrained from mentioning many names of people who were a great help to me. The two Bills, Bill Schaap and Bill Howell, however, I must mention as they were always there when they were needed. I would put my life in the hands of men like that.

I have related these events many times as people have asked what it was like to live here during the Yellowstone fires. I have told snippets of the story but have never sat down and put it all together. People often ask, "What drove you to take on such a huge undertaking?" In answer to that, I often refer to my favorite definition of hell. Applying this definition has been a driving force in my life. It has led me to take on some far out projects and stick with them until they were done. The definition is this: "When the man that I am, comes face to face with the man that I could have been, that is hell."

It's all about avoiding the regrets that come from not doing something that my gut tells me that I should do. How would I have felt, if I did not follow up on that prompting to initiate this huge undertaking? How would I have felt if the fires were about to invade the town and I had to say, "If only I had done what I was prompted to do." How would I have felt if the Old Faithful power plant had been destroyed? How would I have felt if the fire had burned houses at Duck Creek? How many times would I say to myself, "If I had only done what I knew I should have done, this would not have happened?" Even though confronting the fires was similar to being in the jaws of hell itself, I escaped the regret of my definition of hell, as I felt I had done all I could do.

LETTERS OF APPRECIATION:

ANN M. GIBSON
MANAGER

P.O. BOX 490, BOZEMAN, MONTANA 59715 • TELEPHONE 406 / 586-1331

September 9, 1988

Mr. Clyde Seely
West Yellowstone, Mt.
59758

Dear Mr. Seely,

Our Yellowstone Park engineer, Mike Cech, called me
this morning and informed me of your group's massive effort
in installing the sprinkler system at Old Faithful last
Wednesday. In Mike's opinion, we would have lost our substation and transmission line without this joint volunteer
endeavor of the Church of Jesus Christ of Latter Day Saints
and the Friends of Yellowstone.

It is my understanding that your group was asked by
the National Park Service to install the system at Old
Faithful after your successful West Yellowstone stand of
the previous weekend when 15 miles of sprinklers were installed at that town's perimeter.

As it was, we lost one pole and two cross arms when
the fire storm jumped over the irrigated water belt where
our substation and line were located. Our previous losses
at Grant Village and Madison were very substantial due to
a lack of protection but the sprinkler system concept has
been a life saver where ever we were fortunate enough to
have it installed.

The fires have been so devastating for so many, but
for a group of Idaho farmers to pack up their own irrigating
systems and head to West Yellowstone and Old Faithful strictly
on a volunteer basis is a bright spot in an otherwise so de-
pressing saga and we at Montana Power thank you all.

Sincerely,

Ann M. Gibson
Bozeman-Livingston
Division Manager

AMG/jc
cc: John Quinn
       Randy Sullivan
       Mike Cech

Letter thanking Idaho farmers for bringing sprinkler pipe and
saving the Old Faithful substation and power line

United States Department of the Interior

NATIONAL PARK SERVICE
P.O. BOX 37127
WASHINGTON, D.C. 20013-7127

IN REPLY REFER TO:

SEP 23 1988

Mr. Clyde Seeley
West Yellowstone City, WY 59758

Dear Mr. Seeley:

While I was in the Salt Lake City Airport recently, I read a Church News article in the Desert News paper concerning the splendid work and help you and your fellow LDS farmers gave to the successful fire fighting efforts to save the Old Faithful Inn and West Yellowstone. Superintendent Bob Barbee has also mentioned your efforts to me. Your support renews my faith in people. I was brought up as a Quaker but I have always admired the LDS Church for its caring.

The National Park Service is also a caring organization. We care for the visitors, each other and the resources that have been entrusted to us to preserve and protect forever. We have done everything possible to put out the fires but the very unusual weather conditions have worked against us. We do know that in time nature will restore the area and Yellowstone National Park will emerge environmentally better, more productive and more beautiful.

My most sincere thanks and warmest appreciation to you and your fellow members of the LDS Church, for your help, support, and caring. I not only thank you personally but, also, for the thousands and thousands of people who enjoy and appreciate the National Park System.

Sincerely,

William Penn Mott, Jr.
Director

cc: Secretary Hodel

Letter of appreciation from the Department of Interior

Pebble 28: Three Bear Lodge Fire, 2008

We ask for strength and God gives us difficulties, which makes us strong. We pray for wisdom and God sends us problems, the solutions of which develop wisdom. We plead for prosperity and God gives us brain and brawn to work. We plead for courage and God gives us dangers to overcome. We ask for favors and God give us opportunities. This is the answer.

~Jule Johnson, as quoted in *Ensign,* May 1973

Fire has played an important part in the history of West Yellowstone and of the park itself. In some cases it causes a renewal, such as with Yellowstone's fires of 1988 and the Three Bear Lodge fire of 1970. In other cases, it brought about a literal rebirth where it seemed that out of the ashes came life anew. Such was the case with the Three Bear Lodge fire on February 15, 2008.

It was about 8:00 a.m. when I was informed that there was a strong propane smell in the housekeeping office at the lodge. It was so strong that I called my son-in-law Merrick to assist. I was afraid the pilot light on the main water heater could cause an explosion. We turned off all the electrical breakers to the circulating system to avoid causing the water heater to reignite and we also shut off the main gas valve coming into the building. Then we called the propane company to come and fix the obvious leak.

The technician arrived and said he would fix the problem. Linda and I were leaving for Idaho Falls, so I arranged to have a couple of our guys shovel away any snow that needed to be removed so the leak could be fixed. We then left and at about 3:00 p.m., I received a call from the technician saying he had found the leak and fixed it. He added that the smell would continue for some time because of the residual odor that was in the snow surrounding the building.

At 7:00 p.m. we were gassing up the car in Idaho Falls, just ready to return, when I received a call from our office saying there had been an explosion and the back part of the lodge was burning. It was a long drive home with our daughter Stephanie calling to update us every few minutes. She told us the trees by the back of the lodge had also started to burn. The fire engines finally arrived and began trying to put the fire out, but the flames were apparently more than they could contain.

As we finally came over Targhee Pass we could see the orange sky light up 7 miles away. We had assumed by the time we arrived the fire would be about out. We found quite the contrary. All of the local fire trucks were there, as well as some neighboring ones, trying to put out the flames. I felt helpless and like I had been hit in the stomach. Thirty-eight years of our lives had been devoted to remodeling, upgrading and, in 1990, mostly rebuilding the Three Bear Lodge and Restaurant. Linda and I were at the stage in life where we felt we could begin to slow down a little. We felt we had Three Bear Lodge in pretty good shape. We had been through one fire and, with all that I knew would be involved, I was not sure I was up to dealing with another. It was about 11:00 p.m. when we realized we had to go home and try and get to sleep. The flames were still burning.

The next morning we were greeted with the sickening sight of the fire aftermath. The back corner of the U-shaped main section of the lodge was burned, with the roof almost touching the ground. Two customers' automobiles had been burned. Icicles were hanging from the charred wood, the exposed wires, and burned-out vehicles. From all outward appearances, the front parts of both ends of the building, including the lobby and the conference rooms, were still intact. The second story exterior hallway, however, had acted as a conduit for the smoke from the fire, which had blackened the entire hallway and the interior of the upper rooms. It was difficult to walk through the rooms without emerging blackened by the soot.

Fortunately, even though the lodge was almost full that night, the explosion happened when most people had gone out to dinner. However, some guests were still in their rooms. One man, whose room was located near the source of the explosion, was blown across the room and injured his shoulder. He had the presence of mind to go around knocking on all of the other doors, telling people that the building was burning and they needed to get out. We felt very fortunate that nobody was hurt more seriously.

Our immediate desire was to tear down the back part of the burned building, rebuild that section, clean up the smoke damage, and get the lodge back open for business as we had done after the 1970 fire. However, we were in for a long, drawn out waiting game before we could do anything. The entire burned part was blockaded off, and we could not even go in until a thorough investigation was completed. That took about two weeks. Since Fall River Propane was determined to be at fault, we now had two insurance companies to deal with. I happened to be president of Fall River Electric at the time, the parent company of the propane division. That was a little awkward, but I let the insurance companies and the legal entities work out the details.

Finally, we were given permission to begin demolition of the building, and I was able to line up a contractor to do the rebuilding. Until that time, I was optimistic that we would not have to demolish the entire building. However, since we had to remove all of the smoke affected sheet rock and insulation in the unburned portion, it was determined by the local building official that more than 50% of the original building had been removed. Because of that we would have to tear down the entire building in order to bring it up to code. This was another blow because it was now going to be a much bigger job than I was interested in taking on, and the cost to demolish and rebuild was staggering.

As I will discuss further later, I do not sleep well at the best of times. Now, with all the planning and figuring and worrying, my problem was exacerbated. It was during these sleepless middle-of-the-night sessions that I decided I could not just tear down all of the good wood, material, and, in some cases, artifacts of the old Three Bear Lodge and haul them to the dump. A track hoe and a lineup of side-dump trucks were used to tear down and haul away all of the burned section of the lodge. The original bid was to tear down and haul away the rest of the building in like manner. However, when they started pulling down the good section of the building I just couldn't take it. I was raised not to waste anything and decided to cease the planned demolition and tear the rest of the building down ourselves, using the helpers at Three Bear Lodge. I didn't know what we were going to do with all the material at that time, or even where we would put all of it. I just knew I couldn't throw it away.

Then the idea came to me to use some of the wood to build a few themed rooms at Three Bear Lodge. I began to think, why not use the theme "Goldilocks and the Three Bears?" I wanted to reuse the wood and build the furniture to tell the story of the Three Bears in at least four rooms. Outside each room I would route a sign saying "The Three Bears" and a plaque saying, "Once upon a time, there were three bears that lived in their own house in the woods," etc. Inside these rooms other little story plaques would continue the story. I wanted to make a papa bear bed, a mamma bear bed, and a baby bear bed. I wanted to build a big shelf with oversized porridge bowls, have paintings done of the Three Bears coming home and finding Goldilocks in the baby bear's bed, with another showing Goldilocks jumping out of the window and running down the path, and "they never saw her again." There would be some birds and other interesting decorations to reinforce the storybook theme.

In the meantime, as we were tearing down some of the 1990 building, I decided to salvage a portion of that area in big chunks. We began to cut the roof and walls into big sections. We hauled these sections on our trailers and put them back together like a puzzle at Parade Rest Guest Ranch. This created a 30' x 90' building for a future conference room. Its immediate use, however, was a wood shop where we stored and built the furniture for the new lodge.

The experiment of making our own furniture for the themed Goldilocks rooms worked so well, and we had so much wood that could be recycled, that I decided to build all of the furniture for the new lodge with our crew. Clark Frontin and a crew of four other helpers worked all winter in the new workshop relocated at Parade Rest Ranch. We built distinctive new furniture for all the rooms including massive headboards made from the 4" x 8" beams, night stands, desks, mirror and picture frames, as well as unique towel shelves and holders. The wood was recycled and was also used in all of the common areas of the lodge.

It was really interesting to tear down the old 1940s and 1950s buildings. We meticulously removed some of the more historic items while other large sections were removed with big equipment. We finished the demolition on schedule, and the first wall of the new lodge went up in late fall 2008. RMR (Rocky Mountain Rustics) was the general contractor.

When I was a boy on the farm near St. Anthony, I spent a lot of time on the rocks that had been blasted with dynamite in 1935 to dig a canal. I would climb over mountains of these rocks of all sizes; sometimes my friends and I played cowboys and Indians on them. I always wondered if there was some way to use these for a good purpose. I now had the perfect idea and asked the architect to design these rocks into the new lodge.

My helpers, mainly Angel Vega, his brothers, and other employees, and I hauled many big trailer loads of these rocks during summer 2008. These were huge rocks; some of them handpicked for specific places in the building, loaded with my backhoe and hauled to West Yellowstone. The rock construction both on the outside and inside add a distinctive massive feel that, to my knowledge, cannot be found in any other building.

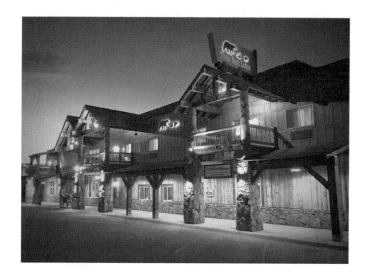

Rock from the farm incorporated with reclaimed wood becomes a thing of beauty

Because of my feelings for Three Bear Lodge and Restaurant and those who had gone before, I wanted to preserve the history as much as possible. I wrote up historical information that I knew about and had Scott Bevan, my son Doug's father-in-law, create pictorial displays and signage for the interior. The charm and rustic elegance of the past has been captured for generations to come. Three Bear Lodge and Restaurant was reopened in July 2009 and received the EcoStar award for its recycling efforts.

For the open house, we served breakfast all day long from the original breakfast menu of the Three Bear Restaurant when it opened in 1955 (except for Postum, a coffee substitute which is no longer made). There was only one item on the menu that was over $1. It was fun to listen as people kidded back and forth about who got to pick up the tab. Oh, let me get the tip on this one, was also a common comment.

During the open house, we took people on guided tours
through the new lodge and showed the historical exhibits we had
created. The theme of one of the main displays was the legacy of
the white shirt. As a result of the frugality of my parents I felt the
urge to write this story about Dad's white shirt and follow it from
the time it was new through the many uses Mother made of it until
its ashes were used to make homemade soap so that she could wash
Dad's new white shirt.

Next to the display is Mother's old treadle Singer sewing
machine, complete with her used buttons in the center drawer and
the nose rags in the left drawer. A white shirt hangs along the side of
a picture of my folks in a large bubble glass frame. Also on display
are pictures of our recycling efforts of the wood from the torn-down
lodge. The story reads:

The Legacy of the White Shirt

Long before recycling was the in thing, I thought it
was something people just did in order to survive.
Take for instance, my dad's white shirt. Farm life
was hard, and there was not much money for store-
bought things. Dad wore his white shirt to church
every Sunday. When the collar began to get frayed,
my mother would unstitch it from the shirt, turn
it over, and sew it back on. It looked pretty good,
but Mother washed it with her homemade laundry
soap so often the shirt was no longer quite as white.
After the collar was worn out again, Dad used it as a
work shirt. No one cared if the collar looked worn.
When the white shirt got stained or there were too
many holes to be patched, Mother would cut off the
buttons to reuse and cut the shirt into cleaning rags
and smaller pieces for nose rags. When we needed
to blow our nose, we would go to the top left hand
drawer of her old Singer sewing machine and get

a white rag. After a good blow, it was taken to the cook stove where it contributed to the fuel supply. The final use of the white shirt became part of the ashes, a substitute for lye. My mom would then stir the ashes along with other ingredients in a big copper kettle over an open fire as she made her laundry soap so she could—you guessed it—wash Dad's white shirt!

Here is the inscription on the bottom of the legacy of the white shirt:

> When it came time to demolish Three Bear Lodge after the fire, the principle of the white shirt that I grew up with protected the historical and sentimental materials from being crushed and hauled to the landfill. Even though it was not known at the time what some of the items would be used for, because of the legacy of the white shirt, they were saved. It is interesting to see, touch, and feel the homemade room furniture throughout the lodge and in the décor of the common areas. The result of this recycling effort has now become part of the history of Three Bear Lodge.

Ferry and Oneta Seely and the legacy they passed on

From our grand opening until today, people continually comment about the passion they feel as they look at and touch the recycled wood and enjoy the huge fireplace made from the massive rocks we gathered from my old farm.

The new Three Bear Lodge is truly unique in many ways and can never be duplicated. It quite literally rose out of the ashes and will remain for years to come. Like a pebble in a pool, the rippling effect of Three Bear Lodge will continue to be felt long after I am gone.

Part Five: Conclusion

Pebble 29: The Seely Wiggles

"He ain't heavy; he's my brother."

~The Hollies

I have had a condition all my life that, other than my family, few people knew about. I was 51 years old before I finally found out the real name of what had plagued me up, until that time I only knew this condition as the "wiggles." My first recollection of having the wiggles was when I was about 5 or 6 years old. I was sitting still on the kitchen stool with a cloth pinned around my neck, as my dad cut my hair. Dad was not fast and, after a little while, a sensation ran up and down my body. It caused me to wiggle around and I could not sit still. This body response went against my wishes, as I knew if I wiggled at the wrong time a nick with the clippers could leave a noticeable mark in my hair. Dad was sympathetic, and I was allowed to interrupt the hair-cutting process long enough to get down and walk around for a few minutes. From there, the wiggles became a condition that I learned to live with.

I specifically remember another time when I was taking a math test in the eighth grade. Once the test was completed and turned in, I could leave. But the pressure to finish was mounting, especially as other kids began to leave, and I began to struggle with my wiggles. I could not sit still or concentrate on my test. I remember the awful experience, but I don't remember the outcome of the test. My frequent attempts to control my problem were normally in vain, and the harder I tried to sit still and concentrate, the more severe the agitation became.

I got the wiggles many times during a movie or while watching TV. I would also get them when confined in a tight space, traveling in a car (especially if I wasn't driving), or sitting in meetings. These were all times and places I learned to avoid. Once I got the wiggles, the only way I knew to relieve the situation was to get up and move around. Thinking back now, I wonder if Linda knew what she was getting herself into when she married me. If she had, perhaps she would have had second thoughts.

My condition was also a huge contributing factor to my poor sleeping habits. If I couldn't go to sleep right away, I got the wiggles, with my body feeling like electrical shocks were running through it. When that happened, I would have to get up and walk around.

In order to avoid the wiggles, I had to get involved with something that diverted my mind or engaged me in something that overrode my physiological reactions. Sometimes I got up from bed and wandered around for part of the night. As a result, my body wouldn't get enough sleep. Instead, I would become more tired, and my condition would become worse. My wiggles contributed to my insomnia, or my insomnia contributed to my wiggles. Both caused me to keep long, active days so that my nights wouldn't drag on. On the one hand, I would have paid dearly to find a cure, but on the other hand, my condition made me want to keep busy and probably helped me to accomplish much more. Because of this, I have always tried to keep a log of things to do and things to accomplish in order to avoid boredom and these wiggles.

***

Over the years I went from doctor to doctor. But describing to them my problem was difficult. I soon learned that saying "I have the wiggles" didn't quite cut it. I explained that it was like an electrical current going up and down my body. Then to divert the misery,

I stretched my legs or dug my fingernails into my hands. In my late thirties, I went to the University of Utah where a doctor did a muscle biopsy to see if it would be revelatory. It wasn't. Unfortunately, all of my doctor visits, and all of my own feeble explanations, were to no avail. The only thing doctors did was give me sleeping aids in hopes of masking the problem before the bad wiggles set in.

I once ran across a poem entitled "Pain," which I want to include here. But I have searched for it in vain, so asking for the indulgence of the reader, I will try to personalize and replicate it in my own words. It gives some substance to the intangibleness of pain and distress as well as the unforeseen benefits that have come as I've dealt with the "wiggles" all these years.

Pain

Pain, you have been my companion too long;
Now why don't you leave me alone and be gone?
Even when I was a little guy and so small;
I would put up with you by trying to feel you, not at all.

As I grew older various things hurt so bad;
Everyone said to be brave, but I was just a lad.
As I grew older you bothered me
every day with those "wiggles,"
Creepy crawly pains caused my legs to do the jiggles.

As I've grown older, you've even introduced me to your twin brother, Aches.
Aches and Pains, teaming up together makes
me want to pull on your reins.

Pain, like darkness, you lurk around every corner too,
And I dread to meet you for what you'll do.
Why don't you leave me alone and to another, go bother?
I wish so badly that you will soon be a goner.

Then one day, Pain turned and said back to me:
There are many lessons of life I have caused you to see.

I, who you thought to be your enemy, was really your friend.
Hang in there with me and you will be a better man in the end.

Remember those times when you would
have taken the easy way;
Instead you suffered and struggled and pulled
yourself up to stay.
It was I who made you strong, when you would
have taken the lower road.
If I'd not been there to try you, you'd be too
weak to carry your load.

If I had not been there for you,
I'll bet you would have just given up too.

Because of the "wiggles," how many
times have you said, "Be gone!"
I who have been your friend have tested
and tried you to the end.
Am I wrong?

Look at you now after all you have suffered;
Recollect what I have done for you as others wondered.
I have caused you to be tender hearted,
For others in pain that has just started.

Patience you learned from me while keeping so busy,
Look at all you have done because I kept you in a tizzy.
Are you sure you want me to be gone,
or shall I linger a while longer,
So that you can still become a little stronger?

As it turns out, I am not the only one in our family who has had this condition. Apparently, it runs in the family. The condition seems to get worse the older we get. My dad had it, and my brothers and sisters have it to varying degrees. We thought it was something unique to our family so we dubbed it the Seely wiggles.

I suppose Dad knew what I was going through when it first manifested itself while he was cutting my hair. In fact, it was he who first referred to it as the wiggles.

When Dad would start fidgeting, Mother would ask, "What's the matter?"

And he would reply, "I've just got the wiggles."

He never made a big deal of it, and I never did with my kids either until later in life when the die was already cast. It was only when our kids became adults that Linda and I told them about my wiggles. We masked it from them all those years while we watched for tell-tale signs in each one of them. A couple of our kids have some symptoms, but to a much lesser degree than I have.

***

In spring 1989, Linda had a carotid artery body tumor removed at the Mayo Clinic in Rochester, Minnesota. While there, we were both impressed with the clinic's depth of knowledge and professionalism as well as the expertise found in the many different teams of specialists. I began to wonder if they could find out anything about my insomnia and wiggles.

On August 26, 1991, when I was 51 years old, I checked in to the Mayo Clinic. Initially, I told Dr. Lin I was going to introduce him to a new term, a unique condition called the Seely wiggles. I teased him that finding a cure would make him famous. In response, he sent me to do a sleep study at the Sleep Disorders Center at the Mayo Clinic, which amounted to a very long night. There, they hooked me up to a million electrical wires and expected me to go to sleep. This, of course, only brought on the wiggles.

I laid there twisting and turning, hoping the answer would show up on their monitoring screens. It didn't. They were only testing for sleep responses. After getting up several times with what seemed to be my regalia of Christmas tree lights, I finally got sleepy enough and would just start to doze off when a voice would come over the speaker system, "Mr. Seely, you're going to sleep." I thought that was what I was supposed to do.

Finally though, the voice ceased, and I got a couple hours of sleep. Although my hopes were dashed when nothing showed up on the screens explaining my wiggles.

However, the next day I was told what I had been waiting 51 years to hear. Dr. Lin told me that I had Restless Legs Syndrome (RLS), although I had never heard of it before, there it was, the real name for the Seely wiggles.

I told Dr. Lin that the sensations I had were more than just in my legs. I explained that my problem was in the entire trunk of my body, and that I only moved and stretched my legs to divert the sensation from my body. He was not deterred, and I was relieved, at last I found a doctor that seemed to know what my problem was, and he even had a name for it.

Dr. Lin talked about my insomnia, which RLS contributed to, and gave me a hint that has turned out to be very helpful. He said that if I could not sleep I should take a hot shower or bath for about twenty minutes to raise my body core temperature, then not put many covers on for a while and let my body cool down quickly, because this cooling process triggers a sleep mechanism. I had already been using a hot tub for a long time and had found this to be true and was, in fact, already using this as a safety net. Many times when I couldn't sleep because of the wiggles, I would go to the hot tub. So I had stumbled on to a partial solution myself. With this new information and the medication Dr. Lin prescribed, I had new high hopes of being wiggle free.

Dr. Lin prescribed Sinemet to help with the RLS and told me I needed to get off Xanax, the sleeping aid I was using, because it was habit forming and was not a good drug. I was to taper off slowly and not stop cold turkey. However, that night I was so anxious to see if it worked, I took only the Sinemet. I lay there in the motel bed looking wide-eyed at the ceiling. I could not go to sleep, but I loved every minute of it. For the first time in my life I dared the wiggles to come, and they did not.

Later, Dr. Lin called and said he wanted me to try something new. He suggested another drug that was normally used to treat Parkinson's disease, and he wanted me to stop taking Sinemet due to the possibility of negative side effects. The new drug was Mirapex, and it worked great. While this was the first time that I could take medication and be reasonably certain I would not have the restless legs, it did not always work as planned. Sometimes if I forgot to take it, or took it too late, it felt like old times returning.

Overall, while Mirapex has been a great help in containing my RLS, it is by no means a cure. There may not be such a thing. I still use the word wiggles instead of RLS. The wiggles have almost become personified in my mind, like an old friend. It is a more endearing word to me because of our long life and companionship together.

My friend, Wiggles, has been a blessing because it has compelled me to continually have a project to work on. I watch very little TV to avoid getting the wiggles; instead I spend my time working on things like this memoir. This project has given me many, many hours of enjoyment typing out and writing down some of the memories of my life. Whether others find satisfaction in reading this or not, the fact remains I have had something to do while avoiding the wiggles.

Over the years, while sitting in the hot tub trying to avoid both friends, Wiggles and his partner, Insomnia, I came up with the Buffalo Roam project, the West Yellowstone historical walking tour, and the spring and fall bicycle tours.

Also, I used the time to go to the wood shop and build something or work with wood to avoid these friends. The big routed Three Bear logoed dividers in the restaurant, the homemade furniture for

Parade Rest Ranches' Aspen cabin, and other items were planned and made at home during those after-normal hours.

Wiggles was a blessing during the sleepless nights after the Three Bear fire in 2008 (See Pebble 28). I conceived and laid out in detail the concept of The Goldilocks and the Three Bears lodge rooms. The legacy of the white shirt hanging in the lobby, and the concept of recycling and making all of our homemade furniture for the entire new lodge were all by-products of avoiding these unwanted visits.

Also, I have tried to give back to the community by serving on committees and boards. Many of those commitments required nighttime meetings and were challenges for me, but they also helped to occupy long evenings. For instance, I remember those early years when serving on the Fall River Electric Board in Ashton, the meetings were held in the evening. Sometimes Wiggles would visit, causing me to wince and stretch out my legs under the table. Then I would often have to stand up and lean against the wall, which seemed to help. But no one ever knew what I was going through.

However, Wiggles was a curse to me in Washington DC when I learned the hard way never to leave my Mirapex at home when going on a trip. Bill Howell, Glen Loomis, and I went to Washington DC to lobby for keeping snowmobiles in Yellowstone. While on the plane, I realized I did not have my medication. That night I stayed up as long as I could, then I tried to go to bed, all to no avail.

Finally I got up, got dressed, and went for a walk at 2:00 a.m. It was raining. I walked up to the Capitol building, climbed to the top of the steps, and went into a door opening for shelter. There I encountered two policemen. They of course wanted to know what I was doing at the Capitol at that time of the night in a rain storm. Then once I had walked off my problem, I fell asleep around 6:00 a.m. We had to meet with our legislators at 8:00 a.m. I am afraid the snowmobile effort suffered a little that day.

***

I have always tried to keep my wiggles under cover. With this document, however, my cover is blown. I am relating my story of these experiences so that perhaps some readers, like me, who are suffering from RLS without knowing what it is, may be able to relate to and benefit from reading my wiggles-turned-Restless-Legs story. They may be uncomfortable talking about it for fear of not being understood or fear of being seen as a complainer. Such was my case.

Today, RLS is a hot topic. There are volumes of studies published, and the media is often referring to it. Even though little was said or known about RLS when I was growing up, the symptoms had been described before the 1800s, although there still was not much known at that time, much less any helpful medication.

Now that RLS is becoming well known, it is believed that over 10% of the US population suffers from the condition. Soon after the 1990 edition was published, I purchased the *Mayo Clinic Family Health Book*. It is about three inches thick and describes every malady and treatment imaginable. Ironically, on page 1031 under "RESTLESS LEGS, the Signs and Symptoms," they confine their explanation to the legs. "Unpleasant creeping sensations deep inside the calves and occasionally in the feet, thighs, or arms while awake, especially while lying down." It goes on with only two more paragraphs describing the symptoms that poorly describe my condition. Today Mayo Clinic has published the fourth edition of its book. It would be interesting to compare what is written today compared to what was written over 25 years ago.

While being treated for the wiggles, and in the years to follow, I thanked Dr. Lin profusely and let him know how much he had helped me. I wanted to pay him back for his efforts, so I invited him to come to Yellowstone many times to reciprocate in some way the help he has given me.

He always said, "No, it was fate that brought us together" and wouldn't accept any gifts to repay him. After almost 10 years, he never charged me a dime.

I am convinced that because of Dr. Lin, Mirapex became an accepted drug for RLS and after all these years, it is still being used today. Thank you, Dr. Lin!

> While Mirapex has helped me tremendously, the wiggles are still a great problem. Traveling long distances is a challenge—I get sleepy, and I let Linda drive so I can catch a quick nap. Most of the time, when I start to nip off, BAM, my old friend Wiggles returns. He pesters me so I can't relax, bringing on the twisting and turning, sometimes I have to stop and walk around. I long to be able to just sit and relax in the car or an airplane, take a nap, watch TV, or just read for pleasure.

***

I would love to find a cure. I think of the little poem my mother used to recite to me about the rocks. It is now prominently displayed in the lodge lobby on the rocks that came from the farm.

I wish I was a little rock, a sit'n on a hill
A do'n nothin' all day long but just a sittin' still.
I wouldn't eat, I wouldn't sleep, I wouldn't even wash.
I'd sit and sit a thousand years, and rest myself, by gosh.

Actually, the thought of sitting still for long periods of time gives me the wiggles just thinking about it, but it would be nice for a little while anyway.

I am often asked, "When are you going to retire?" According to the numbers attached to my age, I suppose I should be considering it. Linda certainly deserves it.

However, my response is normally, "Never."

And Linda retorts, "There is no such word in his vocabulary."

Incidentally, there is no such word as retirement in the scriptures. If retirement was not in their vocabulary, then perhaps it shouldn't be in mine.

Pebble 30: The Final Outcome: Winter Use Controversy—The End or Just the Beginning?

What lies behind us and what lies before us are tiny matters compared to what lies within us.

~Ralph Waldo Emerson

According to National Park Service statistics, during winter 2001–02 there were 64,063 snowmobile passengers and 6,302 snowcoach passengers that visited the park. In contrast, statistics show that during winter 2012–13 there were 13,946 snowmobile passengers and 15,706 snowcoach passengers. The reduced number of snowmobile visitors and the increase of snowcoach passengers are a result of the restrictions placed on snowmobile access in the park and the outcome of ongoing lawsuits.

Since the beginning of this controversy, we have been involved with the National Park Service and top people in the Department of the Interior in Washington DC. Originally they met with us in West Yellowstone. Then we continued to meet with them in Washington.

Over the years, we have seen the power that Congress, the Department of Interior, and the Department of Agriculture yields. Like the swing of a pendulum, we saw attitudes change from one administration to another. With the change to the Bush administration, the cordiality of these Departments changed in our favor. There were champions in Congress that fought for our cause to keep Yellowstone open to snowmobiles. However, there were other times when members of Congress fought to ban snowmobiles.

The Yellowstone fires of '88 resulted in the largest firefighting efforts in the history of the United States and lasted five months at a cost over $98 million. (See Pebble 27). A similar firestorm of words over snowmobile and snowcoach use in the park has lasted for over 15 years and has cost even more. The fires of Yellowstone were eventually put out by the snows in November. The winter use controversy was eventually put to rest by a more balanced approach instigated by multiple public meetings and orchestrated by our new Superintendent of Yellowstone, Dan Wenk and Wade Vagias.

In February of 2013 the Final Winter Use Plan/SEIS was released. It proposed to manage oversnow vehicles (OSV) based on "transportation events" rather than the number of snowmobiles and snowcoaches allowed in the park each day. The Final rule was released in October authorizing OSV use based on Transportation Events.

The results were implemented in 2014–15 and have appeared to work—not perfectly, but reasonably well. Our goal of having the public able to choose to tour the park in the winter by snowmobile, snowcoach, or cross-country skiing has been achieved.

After all of the controversy for the last 15 years over winter use in the park, I am happy to see there is a solution close at hand. Therefore, I will return to this subject with a condensed version of the outcome: the issuing of the NPS's request for proposal (RFP), and the issuing of the new ten-year snowmobile and snow-coach contracts.

The RFP was issued in January 2013. Those operators wishing to apply were required to submit a prospectus. These are very time-consuming and expensive proposals that are ultimately compared against others who have also submitted proposals.

Writing the prospectus and applying for contracts was an interesting process. There were eleven contracts that would be awarded at the west gate. Each contract would consist of four transportation events. All four events could be used for four snowcoaches or two of those events could be used for up to two groups of ten snowmobiles with an average of seven per day per season. In other words, you had to operate two snowcoaches in order to operate twenty snowmobiles. If the successful contractor did not want to operate both, he could name a sub-concessioner to operate snowmobiles or snowcoaches but not both.

I won't go into all of the details of writing the prospectus other than to say it was a very intense time for the applicants. In order to operate snowmobiles or snowcoaches in the park, you must become a concessioner of the NPS. If the operator did not win a contract, he or she would no longer be able to operate in the park.

Some of the components of the prospectus deal with cleaner and quieter over-snow vehicles, protection of the natural environment, and the ability to educate the public. Other components are quality of the visitor experience, visitor and employee safety, the overall business organization, and financial capability. The last refers to the franchise fee the concessioner is willing to pay to the park. The franchise fee is only supposed to be considered as a tie-breaker with those things being considered between two competitors. These fees amount to a lot of money in the coffers of the NPS.

We felt that our prospectus was very well written. We felt that we exceeded the minimum requirements in all categories. All things considered, we felt we had done the best we could and because of our experience, track record, and the complete services we offered, we felt we had a good chance of receiving a contract.

On April 15, 2014, I was sitting at my computer watching a television recording of "Face the State," a Sunday morning program that KBZK had sent to me on a thumb drive. Over the past 15 years, I have been on a number of TV programs and debate forums. On this particular one, there were three of us featured on the show. I had been asked to represent the local snowmobile and snowcoach operators. Superintendent Dan Wenk from the National Park Service was also there, as well as Jon Catton, a professional environmental representative. As I was about halfway through listening to the recording, an email popped up. It was from the NPS announcing the contractors that were chosen for the upcoming contracts. I was not one of them.

Obviously, I was very disappointed. After being the first to put together complete "Winter in Yellowstone" snowmobile packages, after all the years of developing the winter program and helping to turn the town into a winter destination, and after fighting to keep snowmobiles in the park, I would no longer be able to take people into the park. I was out. Of course I was disappointed. However, Linda said, "All your life you have been known for making lemonade out of lemons, and you can do it again." So now the impending question is, how?

Many winters have passed since I purchased that old Johnson Skee Horse snowmobile. Little did I know the impact snowmobiles would have on my life and on the life of our little town. Now, after 43 years of taking people in to see the beauties of Yellowstone on a snowmobile, I am at the end of an era. By not receiving the ten-year contract to continue operating snowmobiles in the park, my world had changed.

I have written at length regarding my desire and efforts to provide snowmobile and snowcoach transportation for those who wish to come and have an experience of a lifetime in Yellowstone. This has been a motivation, a passion, and a driving force in my life. Of course we have benefitted economically from this venture. However, it is more than just the economic opportunity. It is also the thrill of showing and making it possible for others to enjoy the Yellowstone country that my family and I love so much.

Over these past many years we have built facilities to take care of the needs of thousands of people. This began with the first groups I contacted in Minnesota and the Scout packages we provided. We have built our operation around packaging the complete experience in West Yellowstone. These packages include lodging for multiple days, dining, guided snowmobile and snowcoach trips, snowmobile clothing, guides, and even transportation from airports. As my wife's very colorful uncle used to say in the days of the silver dollar, "Them dollars are made round to roll." In contrast to day-trippers who come in the morning and leave in the evening, by bringing people who will stay multiple days, "them dollars" roll all around the community.

As mentioned, the last winter use study was completed in February 2013, and the rule was published in the federal register on October 23, 2013, which makes it law. It looks like there is finally a Yellowstone winter use plan that will be sustainable. For the last 10 years, we had been operating snowcoaches under "See Yellowstone Tours" as an authorized Yellowstone Park Concessioner. Those contracts expired in 2013. We had been operating snowmobiles as Three Bear Rentals under a conditional use authorization (CUA) with continual extensions of one or two years. All of this is now at an end and will become part of my history.

***

I don't know why our prospectus was not chosen. Knowing what was in it and our background, I felt we should have been successful. However, the fact remains we were not. At this point, I can only congratulate the winners and move on. The question now for us is how can we deal with this change? We have made some major mid-course adjustments in our life. We have done it before and we will again. I know that in the end, it will work out all right.

About 10 years ago, I was asked to speak to a group of Fidelity Investments managers who had come to the Holiday Inn for a training seminar. I was asked to speak about my life and also how we were coping with the changes happening in Yellowstone. For part of my talk, I spoke about the book entitled, *Who Moved My*

Cheese? by Spencer Johnson. Perhaps there is an application of this little book in my life.

Who Moved My Cheese is a lighthearted way for the reader to step back and analyze the effects of change in life. The four characters in this parable are two mice named Sniff and Scurry (who wore tennis shoes for running) and two little people named Hem and Haw. All of them live in a maze and spend their days in the eternal pursuit of cheese. One day the four stumble onto a piece of cheese so large that Hem and Haw declare that they shall never again need to search for cheese. The two mice, however, never stop exploring their surroundings for new cheese. Eventually the cheese began to dwindle and finally it was gone.

By this time Sniff and Scurry had already found new cheese while Hem and Haw were incapable of coping with such an abrupt life-altering change and instead had to sit down and then take stock of their new state of affairs. Like most of us, they did not cope well with change.

The moral of the story is that each of us will experience change at some point in our lives, and how we deal with it makes all the difference. Some will never be satisfied with the status quo and will move on looking for new opportunities that even may instigate change. Others remain steeped in their traditional way of thinking and remain behind missing a potential for a new source of happiness and security.

When I first read this little book, I wondered which of these characters I am most like. When I was younger I was like Sniff and Scurry. I always liked to run and hurry and scurry about, thinking I could make up for my inefficiency by covering more ground. However, I must say I also liked to think outside the box to find new opportunities, or sometimes, they would find me. My brother Dean used to say, "Always keep options in front of you." I have tried to do that.

The fact remains I have had to cope with some life changing experiences: the death of my daughter Rochelle, two fires at Three Bear Lodge, the Yellowstone fires of 1988, and others. With the help of others, we survived those challenges and we can survive this. Instead of this causing negativism and pessimism, we will use it as a springboard into the future. Struggles are the best part of life because they are what make us grow to become who we are. We can and will come through this trial and will be just fine in the end.

Linda and I have thought about selling out on occasion, but what we have worked all our lives to create, as an asset to the community, would be broken up and sold off. We fear that what we have worked so hard to accomplish and what the town of West Yellowstone means to us would be fragmented and soon forgotten.

We have always been grateful that Mike and Frances did not seek to sell to the one who was able to make the highest offer. Quite the contrary, they wanted to give a couple of kids, just 32 years old, an opportunity to pick up where they left off and forge ahead into the future. They put their trust in us, and we are pleased to say we did not abuse that trust.

Far better it seems to keep the operation going and follow the advice I have heeded through the years: to hire people who are better than me and then get out of their way and let them do their job. That is our intention at this time. We have formed a board of directors consisting of our three sons and ourselves. Several years ago we hired Travis Watt as the general manager of operations of our properties. He came to work in West Yellowstone not long after he graduated from high school and has worked in almost every position in our organization since that time. While working for us, and after he was married, he also needed to finish up school and graduate from college. Travis is one who has earned our respect by having an impeccable character, a cheery personality, and the ability to always go the extra mile. We feel comfortable having Travis take over the reins and to give him and those younger than ourselves the opportunity Linda and I had.

We have surrounded ourselves with and will continue to hire other very capable people. They will carry the legacy of Three Bear Lodge and the vision we shared onward into the future. Linda and I will not be the last to drop a pebble in the pool of West Yellowstone.

***

This book is written regarding memories and things that have happened in the past, not the future. However through the process of completing this book, our situation continues to change (as indicated in Pebble 22).

As mentioned, we did not receive a ten-year contract with the park. However, as one door closes another usually opens. In 2014, we were able to purchase Yellowstone Alpen Guides' property and their fleet of eight Bombardier Snowcoaches and cross-country ski business (See Pebble 21). Also included in the purchase were ten-year contracts to operate snowcoaches and forty snowmobiles. Since 1971, as evidenced by this book, my passion has always been taking people into the park on snowmobiles and later in snowcoaches. We now have that opportunity again.

Suffice it to say, Three Bear Lodge and its sister entities will be able to continue providing services for people who come from all over the world to see what I consider to be the world's greatest collection of natural phenomena. I am excited about the future. People love the Yellowstone country and love to come here. We are anxious to continue doing what we have done for the last forty-plus years, which is showing off Yellowstone.

***

As I begin to wind down this typing marathon, I would like to leave a few words of wisdom that would live on for my posterity to remember. However, when I think about it, I realize that if my life hasn't said what I want it to say, mere words would be just superficial, meaningless expressions.

I have been contemplating how many pebbles have been dropped in the lives of countless individuals over the last 380 years since the arrival of Robert Seely in the new world. Robert came with the Winthrop Society to America in 1630. He came to the new world in search of a better way of life, new opportunities, and religious freedom. Over 200 years later, Justus Azel Seely came with the Mormon pioneers to another wilderness, also in search of religious freedom and a better way of life. The ripples caused by the pebbles dropped in the pool by Robert and Justus Azel have spread immeasurably and affected not only my life but also many thousands of others.

Linda and I moved to West Yellowstone, also in search of a better way of life. Like our forefathers before us, we found that better life and new opportunities in what was for us a new world. What more can one ask than to live in West Yellowstone and raise our family on the doorstep of Yellowstone Park? I believe I have lived the American Dream. It has now been nearly 56 years since I first came to work in West Yellowstone as a laundry boy. If we consider West Yellowstone's official beginning to be when the train arrived in 1908, I have lived here more than half of its life.

I am grateful for those who first came here to what has become West Yellowstone and for those pioneers who had the vision and the fortitude to lay the foundation for those of us who became the benefactors of their efforts. As I look back on my life, I feel a debt of gratitude to all the people who have dropped pebbles of influence in my little pool. I hope the pebbles I've dropped along the way have also helped others and that the ripples caused will be felt for many more generations to come.

Printed in Canada